Saltwater Slavery

Saltwater Slavery

*A Middle Passage from Africa
to American Diaspora*

STEPHANIE E. SMALLWOOD

Harvard University Press
Cambridge, Massachusetts
London, England
2007

Figures 3.1, 3.2, 5.1, and 6.1 are reproduced courtesy of the
National Archives of England, Wales, and the United Kingdom.

Library of Congress Cataloging-in-Publication Data

Smallwood, Stephanie E.
Saltwater slavery : a middle passage from Africa to American
diaspora / Stephanie E. Smallwood.
p. cm.
Includes bibliograpical references and index.
ISBN-13: 978-0-674-02349-9 (alk. paper)
ISBN-10: 0-674-02349-8 (alk. paper)
1. Slavery—United States—History—17th century.
2. Slavery—United States—History—18th century.
3. Slaves—United States—Social conditions—17th century.
4. Slaves—United States—Social conditions—18th century.
5. Slave trade—United States—History—17th century.
6. Slave trade—United States—History—18th century.
7. Slave trade—Africa—History—17th century.
8. Slave trade—Africa—History—18th century.
9. African diaspora. 10. Africans—Migration—
History. I. Title.

E441.S65 2007
306.3'62097309034—dc22   2006043511

For John W. Blassingame
1940–2000
with gratitude for his great generosity of mind and heart

Contents

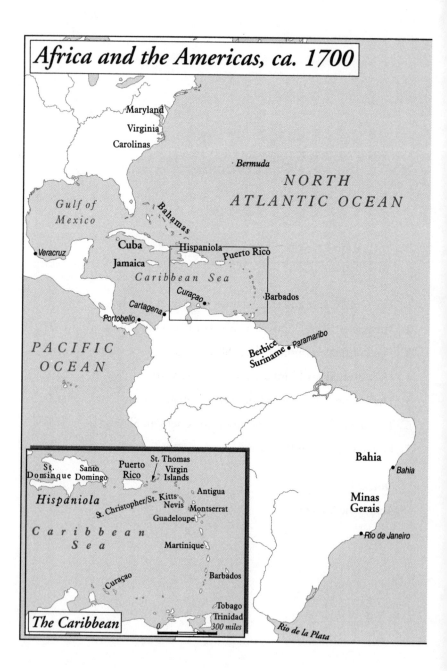

Africa and the Americas, ca. 1700

Maryland
Virginia
Carolinas

Bermuda

NORTH
ATLANTIC OCEAN

Gulf of
Mexico

Bahamas

• Veracruz

Cuba

Hispaniola

Puerto Rico

Jamaica

Caribbean Sea

Curaçao •

Barbados

Cartagena •

Portobello •

PACIFIC
OCEAN

Berbice
Suriname • Paramaribo

Bahia

• Bahia

Minas
Gerais

• Rio de Janeiro

Rio de la Plata

The Caribbean

St.
Dominque
Santo
Domingo

Puerto
Rico

St. Thomas
Virgin
Islands

Hispaniola

St. Christopher/St. Kitts
Nevis

Antigua

Montserrat

Guadeloupe

Caribbean
Sea

Martinique

Curaçao

Barbados

Tobago
Trinidad

0   300 miles

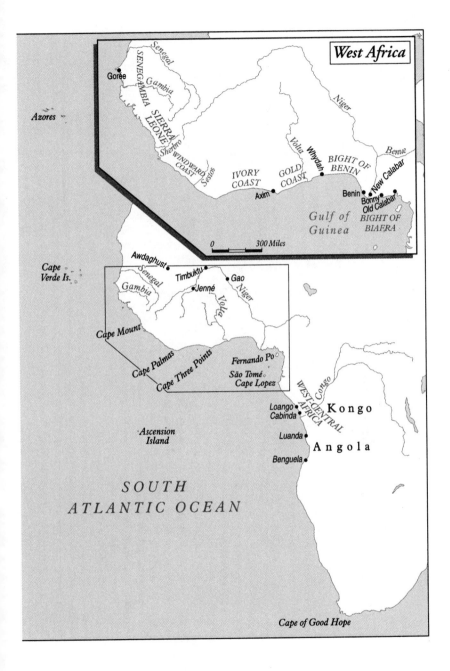

West Africa

Azores

Gorée

SENEGAMBIA

Senegal

Gambia

SIERRA LEONE

Sherbro

WINDWARD COAST

Sestos

IVORY COAST

GOLD COAST

Axim

Volta

Whydah

BIGHT OF BENIN

Niger

Benue

New Calabar

Benin

Bonny

Old Calabar

BIGHT OF BIAFRA

Gulf of Guinea

0   300 Miles

Cape Verde Is.

Awdaghust

Timbuktu

Gao

Jenné

Senegal

Gambia

Niger

Volta

Cape Mount

Cape Palmas

Cape Three Points

Fernando Po

São Tomé

Cape Lopez

Loango

Cabinda

WEST-CENTRAL AFRICA

Congo

Kongo

Luanda

Angola

Benguela

Ascension Island

SOUTH ATLANTIC OCEAN

Cape of Good Hope

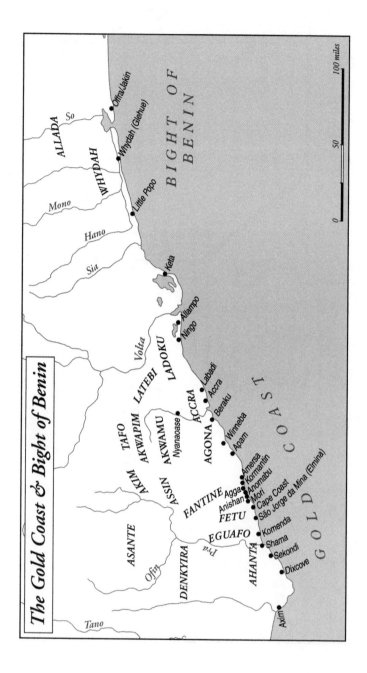

The Gold Coast & Bight of Benin

ALLADA
So
WHYDAH
Mono
Hano
Sia
Volta

Offra/Jakin
Whydah (Glehue)
Little Popo

BIGHT OF BENIN

Keta
Allampo
Ningo
LADOKU
LATEBI
AKWAPIM
TAFO
AKWAMU
Nyanaoase
ACCRA
Labadi
Accra
Beraku
AGONA
Winneba
Apam

AKIM
ASSIN
FANTINE
Agga
Anishan
FETU
EGUAFO
DENKYIRA
ASANTE
Ofin
Pra
AHANTA
Komenda
Shama
Sekondi
Dixcove
Axim

Amersa
Kormantin
Anomabu
Mori
Cape Coast
São Jorge da Mina (Elmina)

GOLD COAST

Tano

100 miles
50
0

Saltwater Slavery

Introduction

York River, Virginia. Spring and summer were the prime season for the arrival of slaves in tidewater Virginia in the eighteenth century. Beginning as early as April or May, ships filled with slaves for purchase were a familiar sight. In 1721, the season of arrivals on the York River began on 6 April, when the *Greyhound* appeared. Two and a half weeks later, on the twenty-fourth, the *Margaret* arrived, followed by the *Swift* and the *Gascoigne* on 9 and 15 May, respectively. The peak period was generally June, July, and August, and the greatest concentration of arrivals that year took place in June, when five slave ships entered the river in the space of one week. The *Prince Eugene* appeared on the twenty-first, followed by the *Rebecca* and the *Sarah* on the twenty-sixth, and then two more, the *Henrietta* and the *Commerce,* came in on the twenty-seventh. Thereafter, three more ships entered the river with slave cargoes: the *Otter* in mid-August, the *Baylor* on 17 October, and finally the *Mayflower,* bringing the year's slave trading season to a close, on 30 October. Hundreds of ships would reach the York River in the ensuing months, but none carrying slaves until the following summer, when the *Greyhound,* having returned to Africa for another cargo of captives, would appear on 5 June 1722, to begin the season of slave arrivals anew.

It is from their place in the commodity chains set up by English

1

merchants that we can most readily learn something about the people who came to the York River aboard slave ships in 1721. Recording the names of ships and the masters that commanded them, the ports from which they departed and the African places they visited for trading, the dates the ships reached their American destinations, the number of slaves each delivered, and on whose behalf, colonial authorities in Virginia did their part by preparing the report that aided members of the Board of Trade in London in their work. In reporting "what number of Negroes the said Colony is yearly supplied with and at what rates and how paid for," the "Accot. of Negroes imported into the District of York River" supplied the kind of quantitative evidence the Board of Trade needed to monitor overseas commerce and ensure that its wheels turned efficiently in the service of the English nation.[1]

"Mathematical Reasoning" was, in the words of one seventeenth-century commentator, "the best means of Judging in all concerns of human Life." It was through systematic collection and evaluation of quantitative data that councils, boards, and other bodies charged with oversight of the nation's commerce fulfilled their task, that being "to consider of some way that a most exact account be kept of all commodities imported and exported through the land, to the end that a perfect balance of trade may be taken."[2] On the basis of data such as these, authoritative bodies like the Board of Trade measured the nation's economic and political health. The people aboard the twelve ships that arrived at York River, Virginia, in the summer of 1721, who were represented merely as ciphers in the political arithmetic, thus feature in the documentary record not as subjects of a social history but as objects or quantities.

Embedded in the data chronicling the course and conduct of merchant shipping, however, are the elements of another narrative, comprising the stories of 1,735 people whose lives, having eventuated in voyages of captivity from Senegambia, the Gold Coast, Calabar, and Madagascar, converged in Virginia, where they were funneled into the burgeoning institution of chattel slavery. *Saltwater Slavery* brings the people aboard slave ships to life as subjects in American social history.

Like the Africans' forced migrations, the story begins in a specific place and moves outward with the widening circles of the diaspora in the Americas. I will follow the tributary representing the forced dispersal of some 300,000 captives who departed from the Gold Coast (present-day Ghana) between 1675 and 1725 aboard ships bound for the English American colonies. Quantitatively speaking, the people sent into Atlantic captivity from the Gold Coast do not occupy the place of greatest prominence in the slave trade in the late seventeenth and early eighteenth centuries. Captives from the Gold Coast boarded English ships at only half the rate of those from the neighboring Bight of Benin in the second half of the seventeenth century, for example; and among the half-dozen migrant streams leaving the African coast, that from the Gold Coast ranked third in volume.[3] But the comparative weight of numbers should by no means be seen to establish a hierarchy of relevance. The enormous size of the migration from other regions, such as the Bight of Benin and West-Central Africa (Kongo and Angola), certainly determined key aspects of the slave experience, but the sheer number of slaves exported from those regions of Africa does not make those migrants either more or less appropriate subjects of inquiry than those from the Gold Coast, or even than migrants like those from Madagascar, who were shipped far more sporadically into the Atlantic slave system. Even though the Gold Coast was not the biggest slave exporter, we can obtain just as true an understanding of the slave experience by examining that modest tributary in the Atlantic slave trade as by looking at the countries that sent the most slaves to the New World.

The half century 1675–1725 marked the most active years of England's Royal African Company, the chartered firm that from the time of its inception in 1672 until the close of the century held a monopoly on all English trade to Africa and that continued to play an active role in the first several decades of the eighteenth century, an era of "free trade."[4] The company employed a network of colonists as agents responsible for receiving slave cargoes in Anglo-American ports. As the Gold Coast was a region whose Atlantic exports moved through the bevy of coastal trading forts initially established to manage gold exports, most of the area's human traffic flowed through those settlements in the seventeenth century; and any that did not pass through these holding centers was closely monitored by the fort administrators.

From this English slaving system emerged a unique documentary record of slave trading on both African and American sides of the ocean. Working out of African and American ports, the agents of the Royal African Company generated a voluminous record of the system's inner workings. Moreover, it is a record that, unlike the papers of most of the private individuals and independent firms that had come to dominate the English slave trade by the middle of the eighteenth century, has survived in relatively comprehensive form. The corpus of records produced by agents stationed in both West Africa and the English American colonies is uniquely transatlantic in scope, affording a kind of detail regarding the various stages of African migration in the Atlantic arena that is rarely available elsewhere.

The business of slave trading produced two interrelated but distinct bodies of archival material—one quantitative, and the other largely textual. The former comprised the ledgers, bills of lading, and other instruments of accounting by which traders monitored and measured their investments. The latter comprised internal correspondence between and among officials in London and agents stationed in Africa and the Americas. It was the quantitative content of the archives that entered most directly into the public domain, in the form of commercial vital statistics published for British consumption. Circulating alongside the formal accounting of economic exchange, the correspondence formed a more private transcript that was largely hidden from public view. It is from the rich content of the company's internal correspondence—between the trading factories along the Gold Coast and the company's main fort, Cape Coast Castle; between the agents at Cape Coast Castle and their superiors in London; and finally between London and the company's agents in the American colonies—that we gain a remarkably detailed picture, a window opening out onto the day-to-day conduct of the commerce in human beings.

In this less visible transcript both traders and those traded appear as actors on the transatlantic stage. Distinct from the public transcript that produced the winners' version of the story (how many units of merchandise sold, how many pounds sterling earned, how much profit, how much loss), the more hidden, internal transcript tells a fuller story—the human story of the Atlantic slave trade. At every point along the passage from African to New World markets, we find a stark contest between slave traders and slaves, between the traders' will to commodify people and the captives' will to remain fully recognizable as human subjects.

The correspondence, voyage journals, and other texts that slave traders produced show us the inner workings of the system and its constitutive practices. They serve as a kind of mirror in which we can see reflected aspects of the human experience of captivity and migration. The documents detail the activities of the Europeans who traded for slaves in Africa and transported them to markets in America, the merchants from whom slaves were purchased on the African coast, and the planters to whom they were sold in American colonies. In documenting their roles as buyers and sellers of humans, the slave traders in their records also unwittingly reveal part of the slaves' own stories. From the interplay of these stories, we can excavate something of the slaves' own experience of the traffic in human beings and of life aboard the slave ship.

Following the trace of African life within the commodity circuits of the Atlantic economy brings an essential element of the African diaspora into focus—the inexorable one-way trajectory of African dispersal via the transatlantic slave trade and its implications for African life in the Americas. Always doubling back on return voyages, ships made loops and spirals as they carried the commodities that sustained transatlantic markets: gold and silver, sugar and tobacco, rice and coffee, woolens and silks, cottons and linens, wine, brandy, and rum, muskets and gunpowder . . . and captive people. Unlike the ships, which plied back and forth, though, the human commodities followed a relentlessly linear course: the direction of their transatlantic movement never reversed. Ships traced circles. Commodities traveled in a straight line.

For people who traveled not as emigrants seeking new lives in new places but as commodities, transatlantic exile admitted none of the return journeys, correspondence, and other means of contact by which migrants shaped networks of social and information exchange between their origins and destinations, the Old and New Worlds. Atlantic slaves in diaspora did not lack connections to the "Old World." But the ties that bound New World slave communities to their places of origin ran only in one direction. After one slave ship departed from African shores, another always followed in its wake, carrying new groups of captives. This diaspora was nourished, then, only by the perennial flow of captives on the slave ship's one-way route of terror. In the seventeenth and eighteenth centuries, it featured none of the regular correspondence and return journeys that figured so significantly in the dispersals of voluntary emigrants into the Atlantic system.

Both planters and slaves developed a keen awareness of the ways the continual churning of the Atlantic trade in captives from Africa gave specific shape to the slave diaspora in the Americas, particularly in the significance they accorded to an American, as distinct from African, place of birth. Writing of Barbados in the first decade of the eighteenth century, John Oldmixon observed that there was "a great deal of Difference" between persons who came to Barbados from Africa and their descendants born in the Americas. "Those that are born in Barbadoes are much more useful Men," he explained, "than those that are brought from Guinea."

It was a view shared by American-born slaves. Not only did slaveowners favor "the Creolian Negroes"; so too did slaves born in the New World "value themselves much on being born in Barbadoes," and "despise" African "New Comers," whom they disparagingly referred to as "*Salt-Water* Negroes." Edward Long noted the same in eighteenth-century Jamaica. Native-born slaves, he observed, held "the Africans in the utmost contempt, stiling them, 'salt-water Negroes,' and 'Guiney birds.'"[5]

The "saltwater" defined the relentless rhythm of the slave ships. But its pejorative connotation also hinted at what was problematic about the perennial appearance of newcomers in immigrant communities seeking stability and coherence. One could never completely escape the saltwater, for even once an African captive's own middle passage had ended, the communities where that slave's life played out in the colonial Americas continued to be molded by the rhythm of ships returning to deposit still more bodies. Through their own terminology, the descendants of saltwater slaves articulated their awareness of the problem of enforced emigration. In speaking of "saltwater" origins, they gave a name to the interchange between the slave ship and the slave community, between the new African migrants continually arriving to take their place alongside the survivors and the American-born children who were putting down tentative roots in the new communities, between the ongoing experience of forced migration and its collective memory.[6] In place of the networks that link origins and departures, and transform the emigrant into an immigrant, for African captives in the Atlantic system reverberated the traumatic echo of commodification: the return of the slave ship, the arrival of new exiles into American slavery, the renewed imprint of the saltwater on the African diaspora.

"Saltwater": this fragment of the slaves' language put a name to the crooked lines (social, cultural, epistemological) that shaped their Atlantic world. It affords an analytical and conceptual category that defines the Atlantic in historical time and place in a fresh way. It places the emphasis not on the African "background" of American slavery, on migration (focusing on captive Africans as "migrants" instead of "slaves"), or on the "middle passage" as a metaphor for all that was wrong with New World slavery. Instead, the concept of saltwater slavery illuminates what *forced* migration entailed.

The social geography of black life in the Atlantic arena was demarcated by the blurred and bloodied boundaries between captivity, commodification, and diaspora. Slaves did not so much leave one behind and enter another as proceed involuntarily, propelled always by agendas and agents other than themselves. With no itinerary and no directional control over their movement, captives had no clear cognitive map to guide them through the transition from land to water, the shift from smaller to larger ships, or the passage from coastal waters to open sea. The migration of the black captives was an unforgiving journey into the Atlantic market that never drew to full closure.

Considering the "saltwater" dimension of slaves' lives allows us to piece together a picture of a place, a time, and an experience that does not otherwise figure in the archival record. Such an analysis of what happened to captive Africans in the Atlantic offers something we cannot get at simply by including Africa in our histories of African America or by singling out African captives as involuntary migrants or by naming the Atlantic crossing the middle passage. Here is a history of American slavery that begins in Africa and the Atlantic, in the saltwater slavery of peoples in motion, a diaspora shaped by violence encompassing the African, Atlantic, and American arenas of captivity, commodification, and enslavement.

1

The Gold Coast and the Atlantic Market in People

When the captives boarded the *Sarah* in the winter months of 1721, at least some of those consigned to the ship had an idea where they were headed.[1] After several centuries of commercial and cultural exchange with Europeans, people from the coastal polities of the Gold Coast possessed an understanding of the wider Atlantic world unmatched in other African regions. Whereas many other Africans feared that their captors had cannibalistic intentions, most residents of the Gold Coast understood that Europeans planned not to eat them but rather to put them to work in distant homelands. No less than for Europeans, the "world" had become, for coastal Africans at least, Atlantic in scope.[2]

Even "sensible" captives from the Gold Coast, however, would find their geography of the Atlantic world woefully inadequate when it came to following its slave routes. By the eighteenth century, the practices of forced Atlantic migration and chattel slavery had grown to such proportions, that departure from the Gold Coast aboard a slave ship in 1721 could lead a captive to no fewer than fourteen American destinations. Topping the list was Jamaica: a third of ships sailing from the Gold Coast in the period between 1721 and 1725 delivered their human cargoes to work in the cane fields of England's premier sugar-producing colony. Next in the line of likely destinations were the mainland Dutch Guiana colonies

(Suriname and Berbice), where nearly 20 percent of the people exported from the Gold Coast in this period ended their journeys. At least a thousand (10 percent) went to Barbados, and another thousand to each of the Dutch Caribbean island colonies, Curaçao and Saint Eustatius, while the remainder went in varying numbers to the Danish Virgin Islands, Virginia, Antigua, Cuba, Rio de la Plata, Saint Christopher, mainland Spanish America, or Montserrat.[3]

Moreover, if English traders had their way, captives from the Gold Coast were soon to be en route to Brazil. The scheme was to persuade Brazilian slavers to bring gold from that colony's newly developed mines at Minas Gerais and exchange it for slaves at English forts on the Gold Coast.[4] Through this alchemy, proceeds would return to English hands in the form of the gold that African labor had extracted from Brazilian mines, and that gold would in turn be converted back into (embodied in) commodified labor, now available to begin the process anew. In this way, England's Royal African Company would enjoy the greatest possible gain (in hard currency) while avoiding the great expense and risk associated with transporting human commodities to American markets.

Neither Brazil, Barbados, nor Virginia was represented on the captives' own mental maps of the Atlantic world. But that is not to say that the African concept of space was static and unchanging. On the contrary, the geographical context of those who inhabited the Gold Coast had changed dramatically in the two and a half centuries since strangers displaying excitement at the sight of gold and overzealous interest in it had first appeared in those parts. So much so that through the alchemy of the transatlantic commerce in people captives from the Gold Coast were intricately bound to a geography of American places whose coordinates they could not know.

The Gold Coast in the Atlantic World

When they rounded the promontory they would call Cabo das Tres Pontas (Cape Three Points) early in the year 1471, Martim

Fernandes and Alvaro Esteves encountered villagers whose lives centered on extraction of fish and salt from the sea—and something else: men whose personal adornment signaled their possession of, and perhaps willingness to trade in, gold. A half century of eager exploration had passed since Afonso Gonçalves Baldaia found an inlet some three hundred miles south of Cape Bojador and declared it to be the mouth of the legendary "River of Gold," known since the thirteenth century to both Christian and Arab geographers as the gateway to "fabled lands where spices and precious metals were as common as salt was in Portugal."[5]

In 1442, a decade after Baldaia turned geographic myth into cartographic reality, Antão Gonçalves had become the first Portuguese mariner to lead an exploratory expedition that actually yielded gold. When captives who had been seized the previous year in the vicinity of Baldaia's Rio do Ouro (the southern coastal boundary of the present-day territory of Western Sahara) had revealed some familiarity with Sudanese and Saharan trade routes, their possession of such priceless knowledge earned them their release from European slavery. Returning with those lucky few from this first group of people exported from Africa aboard European ships, Gonçalves ransomed two of the captives in exchange for "a buckler, several ostrich eggs, and a small quantity of gold dust."[6]

Three decades later, the expedition led by Fernandes and Esteves in 1471 proved the merit of Portugal's long exploratory enterprise in Africa. For these two mariners had come upon a place where "huge quantities of the purest gold could be exchanged for cheap trade-goods of cloth and metal." The site entered into European cartography accordingly, as *a mina do ouro* (the gold mine), or simply El Mina (the Mine).[7]

Extending from the western side of Cabo das Tres Pontas to the promontory the Portuguese designated as Cabo das Redes, "because of the many nets that were found here when this land was discovered," the so-called mine occupied more than a hundred miles of coastline when mariner Duarte Pacheco Pereira surveyed the region before the close of its first decade of European contact.[8] By the end of the sixteenth century, the Afro-European gold trade reached as far east as Accra, and the whole region from Axim (just west of Cape Three Points) to the Volta River, encompassing 230 miles, was known as the Gold Coast.[9]

More than two thousand miles distant from the coastal Saharan site that first received a Portuguese name associated with gold, this forested region between the Tano and Volta Rivers that was drawing Portuguese attention held one of the world's richest deposits of gold ore. For this reason, the territory that entered the European geographic imagination as the "Mine of Gold" in the second half of the fifteenth century also occupied an important place among the major trading centers of the western Sudan.

In the main, West Africa's impenetrable southern forest belt did not attract long-distance traders from the ancient urban centers of the western Sudan. Such sophisticated commercial and cultural hubs as Awdaghust, Timbuktu, Jenne, and Gao thus marked the southern termini of the great trans-Saharan trade routes. Forest peoples brought kola nuts and dried fish to market in Timbuktu and the other trading centers situated at this point where the northern reach of the forest met the southern edge of the savanna, and they carried away textiles and other goods received in exchange. Sudanese trade goods thus traveled south beyond the savanna deep into the forest belt, but for a long time Sudanese traders on foot did not.[10] Gold, however, had made the area that would draw Portuguese interest the exception to that broader pattern, giving Sudanese traders reason to venture deep into the forest pocket that became known as the Gold Coast. Far less is known about this period than about the centuries following European arrival, but by using archaeological evidence and traditional histories, together with contemporary European sources, it is possible to sketch, at least in broad outline, some key elements of the region's social and political landscape.

On the basis of archaeological evidence indicating a marked shift in pottery style, it is thought that Akan-speaking peoples entered the forested region between the Ofin and Pra Rivers beginning around the turn of the eleventh century. They absorbed or displaced Guan-speaking groups already there and developed a social order dedicated to meeting the Sudanese demand for gold.[11] From the eleventh century to the time of Portuguese arrival, commercial and cultural ties to the Sudan brought material resources from outside the forest zone (Saharan textiles and other luxurious imports, salt, and slaves). Those ties encouraged development of a settled social order and a sedentary agricultural society in the forest, along with the accompanying sociopolitical institutions.[12] That this had taken place by the time Europeans came to the region is evidenced not only by the Portuguese mariners' encounter with men (probably merchants) who wore gold ornaments, but also by a system of gold weights and measures derived from those in use at Jenne, Timbuktu, and other Sudanese commercial centers.[13]

The historical shift from more nomadic hunter-gatherer communities to permanent agricultural settlements that was under way at this time received a powerful impetus from commercial and cultural interaction with the Euro-Atlantic system in the fifteenth century. The beginning of Afro-Portuguese exchange opened a period characterized by an intensified pace of migration and settlement, following the adoption of maize (the American cultigen introduced by the Portuguese), and by the southerly pull of Atlantic commerce. It was this mixture of dynamic forces that tipped the historical balance, so to speak, in favor of sustained settlement, formation of towns, and ultimately transition to the landscape of centralized polities represented on European maps of the African landscape.

The two centuries that passed after the arrival of the Portuguese were a time of dramatic change in nearly every facet of life in the region: much of the political, economic, social, and cultural terrain of African life in the seventeenth century would have been unfamiliar to the people who greeted the first Portuguese ships in the fifteenth century. At the outset of the Afro-Portuguese encounter, the locus of urban settlement and state formation was the northern fringe of the forest—at such places as Begho and Bono Manso, some two hundred miles distant from the coast.[14] When the Dutchman Pieter de Marees visited the area at the turn of the sixteenth century, the tiny coastal fishing and salt-making villages Pereira described had been replaced by proliferating dense urban port towns. Where Pereira had identified only a handful of villages and towns beyond Cape Three Points, no fewer than seventeen settlements now stood along the coast from Axim as far as Chinka, just short of the Volta River. Many port towns, such as Shama, Elmina, Cabo Corso, Mori, Kormantin, Accra, and Chinka, were outlets for gold; others were marketplaces for agricultural produce, fish, or cattle.[15]

The maize Portuguese mariners brought from the Americas quickly attained a prominent place among the agricultural staples in the Gold Coast. It could be seen growing "in abundance" all along the coast, together with other New World plants such as pineapples and sweet potatoes.[16] Its high yield and protein content made maize a food staple far superior to the sorghums and yams that were indigenous to West Africa. By the substantial boost it gave to average caloric intake, the New World import fueled dramatic population growth throughout the southern forest region. No longer the periphery to a Sudanese center, the region's Atlantic littoral now was a center in its own right: a magnet that drew people and trade from all sides to its burgeoning "central places," it was the leading edge of a social order characterized by the population density, ethnic plurality, and economic diversity typical of urban centers.[17] Thus, in addition to the fishermen, salt makers, and common peasants who dominated the coastal towns, it was not uncommon to find intermingled with them "interpreters," "toll-takers," and representatives *(batafo)* of upland traders.[18]

The Place of People in the Atlantic Market

From the beginning, slavery and slave trading played crucial roles in the Afro-European commerce that developed in the Gold Coast. Indeed, from 1475 to 1540, more than 12,000 people passed through its coastal ports as human commodities.[19] These, however, were not slave exports from the region. Rather, people were among the goods that African merchants wanted to buy from their new Portuguese trading partners.

Within the first decade of establishing commercial relations with the Portuguese, the Gold Coast had become an importer of people enslaved elsewhere in Africa. Gold-bearing African merchants traveling to the coast from upland forest territories required large retinues of porters to transport the bulky European goods they purchased. To meet this need, it was a simple matter for Portuguese traders to supply slaves alongside the textiles and metals they sold to African buyers.

Making their way to "the Mine" in 1479, for example, an interloping Spanish fleet stopped on the Windward Coast, where local traders presented items they hoped would draw European trade, offering "women and children for sale." Eustache de la Fosse, a Flemish adventurer traveling with the fleet, reported that the Spanish ships purchased the slaves and subsequently "resold" them "without difficulty" when they reached the Gold Coast.[20] Indeed, an established routine for bringing slaves into the region had already taken shape by the end of the first decade of Afro-European trade here. During the time that de la Fosse was at São Jorge da Mina Castle, he witnessed the arrival of two Portuguese vessels returning from voyages eastward to Calabar (the Bight of Biafra), "with some 400 slaves to be sold on the Gold Coast."[21]

The Gold Coast fell well behind Europe and the Atlantic islands among destinations for the more than 150,000 slaves (mostly from the Bight of Benin and the Kongo), exported aboard Portuguese ships from the mid-fifteenth century through the first two decades of the following century.[22] Thereafter, the steady flow of slaves entering the area through the maritime market slowed considerably. A maverick mariner's search for a western route to Asia having brought the New World into the European universe; the Atlantic arena was shifting, imperceptibly at first, into a new alignment. The first stirrings of American impact on the Gold Coast were felt in the second half of the sixteenth century, when demand in the Americas grew sufficient to divert slaves purchased in Africa into transatlantic routes that terminated in the major Spanish-American markets at Veracruz, Cartagena, and Lima.[23]

More than 700,000 Africans boarded ships bound for the New World in the first half century (1580–1640) of slave trading along the transatlantic routes that brought the Americas into the orbit of European and African worlds. Few of these ships, however, departed from the Gold Coast.[24] Indeed, with the decline of slave imports in the Gold Coast came the virtual disappearance of slave ships there. The immediate impact of the American market was not to reverse the direction of the slave traffic but rather to eliminate the region's maritime market for slaves altogether.[25]

American developments began to reverberate in the Gold Coast, however, around the turn of the seventeenth century. The interest of Portugal in developing the nation's sole colonial possession in the Americas turned Brazil into the first New World sugar producer and gave the Portuguese crown its own American market for slave labor. The establishment of sugar plantations in Brazil, and the decision to exploit African rather than indigenous Indian labor to run them, had already put some 50,000 Africans from Senegambia, the Bight of Benin, the Bight of Biafra, and especially the Kongo, en route to the Americas before 1600.[26] Soon that demand was felt in the Gold Coast.

The impact of the American demand for slave labor in the Gold

Coast entailed more than a simple directional reversal in the flow of people through local maritime markets. Merchant elites that had once purchased people reduced to captivity elsewhere were now asked to produce exportable captives and sell them alongside the gold brought to the coastal markets. To assuage concerns registered by local leaders, the Portuguese imposed geographic restrictions on the developing export trade in slaves, in order to protect the territories of central Gold Coast polities with which the Portuguese could not afford strained relations. Accordingly, "after about 1590" the Portuguese made proposals that the king should "set aside a strip of coast ten leagues on either side of São Jorge and exempt that area from slaving activities." This solution was not put into practice, however, until 1616. By that date, "the pressure was great to permit open slaving operations all along the Mina coast," and "the Brazilian demand for African labor was so strong that the Portuguese crown permitted slaving operations to be conducted within Mina itself."[27]

When it arrived on the Gold Coast in 1619, the Portuguese ship *San Francisco* signaled not only the return of slave ships after at least half a century of negligible human traffic in coastal markets there, but also a new role for slave ships. Laden with goods suitable for buying people from the region's merchant elite, the *San Francisco* was there not to deliver a human cargo from elsewhere, but rather to obtain people enslaved there in the Gold Coast: "a premium price of about 20,000 *réis*" could be had for "a prime Mina slave" in Pernambuco or Bahia.[28] When the *San Francisco* departed, eighty-odd members of local Gold Coast communities had been offered as commodities in exchange for the goods the ship delivered, and had now become cargo themselves, en route toward the slave market at Cartagena.[29]

Over the course of the seventeenth century, what had been an exclusively Portuguese arena became a site of close competition among European colonizing nations, as French, Dutch, and English incursions challenged the Portuguese claim to a monopoly on European trade in Africa. Dutch traders led the effort to undermine Portuguese rule at the beginning of the seventeenth century and initiated an assault on São Jorge da Mina Castle that ousted the Iberians in 1637. By the middle of the century a different configuration was firmly in place.[30] The Dutch and the English became the key European players; and for the African sellers of gold, competition between these and other European traders became enormously profitable.[31] Moreover, for African merchants with insufficient access to gold, ships like the *San Francisco* represented an expansion of opportunity—a fresh avenue to wealth and power. But the new dynamics marked the beginning of a century of change on the Gold Coast that would have more ambiguous consequences for other Africans there.

Dutch and English slave ships began to appear with regularity after the middle of the seventeenth century. But it was England in particular that envisioned a role for the Gold Coast in its Atlantic system, one as open to trade in slaves as in the trade for gold. When Charles II chartered a company to oversee England's trade in Africa in 1672, people were considered a standard component of exports from the Gold Coast. Describing the Royal African Company's trade settlements on the Gold Coast, an "Account of the Limits and Trade of the Royal African Company" explained that the agent-general stationed at Cape Coast Castle "furnishes thence all their under-factories with goods, and receives from them gold, elephants' teeth and slaves."[32]

To be sure, gold remained the primary focus of all Afro-European trade on the Gold Coast until the beginning of the eighteenth century.[33] But a rapidly growing demand for labor in Barbados, the Leeward Islands, newly acquired Jamaica, and even the tobacco-producing Chesapeake colonies meant that English traders would look to the region to serve as a dual market for the purchase of gold and people, and the pull of the Atlantic market for slaves would henceforth be felt on the Gold Coast as it had elsewhere in Africa in the preceding two centuries.

It is impossible to determine the volume of slave exports from the Gold Coast in the first half of the seventeenth century with any accuracy, except to say that it remained quite small by comparison with that from other regions of Atlantic Africa. Of 10,053 slaves purchased by the Dutch in "Guinea" from 1637 to 1645, only a little more than 17 percent (1,721) came from the Gold Coast region—an average of barely 200 slaves per annum. In contrast, during the same period the kingdom of Allada in the Bight of Benin exported an average of just over 500 people per annum through its main port at Jakin, while a yearly average total of close to 400 people departed through Calabar and other ports in the Bight of Biafra aboard Dutch slave ships. Meanwhile, Angola alone supplied more than half (55 percent) of the 26,286 slaves imported to Brazil by the Dutch between 1630 and 1653.[34]

Given the presence of Portuguese, Dutch, and English slave traders on the Gold Coast at various times in the first half of the seventeenth century, it is plausible that at least several thousand enslaved Africans boarded European slave ships there during this period. In the century to come, the stream of departing slaves would increase dramatically. While the Dutch are estimated to have exported 9,263 African slaves from the Gold Coast between 1662 and 1700, their English counterparts (interlopers in violation of the Royal African Company monopoly included) exported an estimated 55,288 slaves from the region during the same period.[35] In short, slave exports from the Gold Coast never fell below an average of 1,300 people per annum in the last four decades of the seventeenth century. By that point, one ship carried away as many captives as had arrived in an average year during the preceding century. Exports in the 1660s were four times what the average annual volume of slave imports had been a century earlier and would grow exponentially in the half century to come (Table 1.1). As the market

Table 1.1 Seventeenth-century Gold Coast slave exports compared with
sixteenth-century slave imports.

Decade	Average annual exports	Ratio of exports to imports[a]
1662–1670[b]	888	4:1
1671–1680	1751	8:1
1681–1690	1267	6:1
1691–1700	1709	8:1
1701–1709[c]	2760	13:1
1710–1719	3518	17:1
1720–1729	4708	23:1

a. Using an estimate of about two hundred average annual slave imports, 1500–
c. 1540, in Ivana Elbl, "The Volume of the Early Atlantic Slave Trade, 1450–
1521," *Journal of African History* 38 (1997): 31–75.

b. Export figures for 1662–1700 from David Eltis, *The Rise of African Slavery
in the Americas* (Cambridge: Cambridge University Press, 2000), Table 7–1.

c. Export figures for 1700–1729 from David Richardson, "Slave Exports from
West and West-Central Africa," *Journal of African History* 30 (1989), Table 5.

for slave labor in the Americas began a period of explosive growth,
it pulled a torrent of captives from the Gold Coast into a very different role in the Atlantic world than had been offered to their ancestors two centuries before.

War, the State, and the Consequences of Captivity

In its eighteenth-century expansion as well as in its seventeenth-century beginnings, the current of men, women, and children leaving
the Gold Coast aboard European slave ships comprised for the
most part people reduced to captivity by war. But as neither warfare
nor its social consequences were unknown phenomena in the seventeenth century, explaining the region's shift to slave exports entails
something more than a simple chronicling of the rise to power of
centralized "states." Understanding of how and why a region that
had been an importer of people from elsewhere became an exporter

of its own people requires analysis of the relation between emergent institutions of political authority and the Atlantic market economy, by then firmly rooted in the Gold Coast. For it was because of the complex interplay of these factors that the consequences of captivity began to take a decidedly unanticipated turn by the end of the seventeenth century.

During his residence on the Gold Coast from 1614 to 1620, Samuel Brun observed that warfare nearly always led to the taking of heads.[36] Not only were men beheaded, but it also was common practice summarily to execute women and children. "The Blacks say it is better to strangle women and children than men," explained Brun, "because then they will not reproduce quickly; and the children, if they came of age, would want to seek revenge."[37] Similarly, when Michael Hemmersam was at Elmina in the 1640s, he observed that in war, "whoever gains the upper hand lets none of the other side live." As he explained, "even if they shoot someone dead, they nevertheless cut off his head."[38]

When Wilhelm Johann Müller began his seven-year residence as chaplain at the Danish fort Frederiksborg (near Cape Coast) in 1662, however, it no longer was customary to neutralize the threat posed by surplus prisoners of war by executing them. By then the sale of such captives on the coast had emerged as a means to achieve the same end—and to purchase European trade goods at the same time. Thus, Müller explained, whereas persons wounded or killed in warfare were beheaded according to custom, a different fate befell prisoners who were taken alive. "But if someone falls into the enemy's hands unharmed and alive, he is tied with cords and taken prisoner, and must remain a bondsman for the rest of his life," Müller wrote. "In order that the masters do not have to worry about bondsmen running away," he continued, "prisoners are sold to far-off places. This," he surmised, "is why so many slaves are sold annually on the Guinea coast and exchanged for goods."[39]

The growing market for human beings gave casualties of war—

captives made vulnerable by war's destabilization—an unaccustomed commercial value. The result in the seventeenth-century Gold Coast was a shift in the potential consequences of captivity, from the give-no-quarter policy observed by Samuel Brun in the early part of the century to the direct link between warfare and enslavement that became apparent at mid-century. When two English ships from Barbados appeared at "Comany" (Komenda) in December 1658, a Dutch report noted that the English vessels sought between them 220 slaves, "of which they had already obtained 80." The English trade "giv[es] us a great reduction in receipts," the Dutch complained, "for what the Blacks can obtain for slaves, they need not give any gold, and through such are the wars so waged."[40]

But the logic of African engagement with the Atlantic market for slaves was more complex and more nuanced than Müller or other European observers could comprehend. The wars Müller observed and the captives who appeared at the littoral in growing numbers reflected larger historical processes accompanying the region's economic integration into the global current of Atlantic commerce.[41] The changing political salience of two institutions—the state *(oman)* and the matriclan *(abusua kɛsɛɛ)*—that were central to the social organization of Akan-speaking communities helps explain the changes Müller witnessed.

In brief, the *oman* derived its claim to authority from the idiom of kingship; its corollary, the *abusua kɛsɛɛ,* articulated authority through the idiom of kinship. The two institutions are thought to have developed contemporaneously in the formative centuries of the settled agricultural social order. By the time Müller wrote, in the second half of the seventeenth century, however, the power vested in kingship, or stools (the ultimate symbol of the power of the state), presented a formidable challenge to the importance of the matriclan and its expression of power and authority based on kinship. The reasons it was not possible to load ships at the Gold Coast before the second half of the seventeenth century were, on the one hand, the enormous local demand for labor and, on the other hand, the absence of states or other institutions with sufficient political power to enslave people on such a massive and sustained scale.[42]

The rise of states in the Gold Coast was accompanied by two economic developments central to their function as institutions of territorial and political aggrandizement. First, the importing of European firearms introduced a new instrument of military might. Second, the exporting of people in the Atlantic slave trade served to broaden access to the Atlantic economy and also provided an expedient means for managing the human by-product of expansionist state building. By adding war captives to the flow of gold exported through Atlantic market channels, states turned surplus people into valuable commodities.

Firearms imported from Europe were in regular use among coastal peoples by the middle of the seventeenth century, and the unprecedented power they afforded to those who acquired them and mastered their use was evident in new missile tactics that appeared on the battlefield and new approaches to statecraft that shaped the region's political geography.[43] To suggest that the introduction of firepower *caused* the rise of centralized states would be to misrepresent the relationship. Political centralization was a process already well under way among the Gold Coast communities at the time of the Portuguese arrival. But the integration of guns was sharply reflected in the kind of influence wielded by the states that appeared fully formed in the second half of the seventeenth century: gun-toting armies mobilized to serve political leaders whose power came from their participation in Atlantic commerce.[44]

The adoption of European guns in the second half of the seventeenth century changed the way wars were fought and dramatically expanded the geographic scope of warfare. In the first half of the century, military power was relatively well balanced between the polities of the coast and those of the forest hinterland. According to historian Ray Kea, "no single state was militarily stronger than its neighbors," and no state was able to use military power to pursue territorial conquest. Warfare was primarily defensive or "was limited to comparatively small-scale offensive operations, embracing tens rather than hundreds of square miles."[45]

While conflicts were frequent among the numerous polities, usually the prearranged battles were over after only a few days. De Marees observed in 1602, for example, "The wars do not last long; they are started with great speed and also quickly ended."[46] Müller noted that there had been instances where "the enemy, having obtained the upper hand, practiced great violence, stealing, plundering, [and] burning the houses," but in general, he wrote, such destruction "happens very seldom, since they are usually content with a hard fight, especially when they notice that one of the parties in dispute is a match for the other." He went on: "This is why a war for which people have prepared for such a long period comes to an end in two or three days."[47]

After midcentury the kind of short-lived military encounters Müller witnessed increasingly gave way to more extensive and destructive wars of territorial expansion and commercial aggrandizement. These conflicts, and the associated trail of vulnerable and displaced persons reflected the growth of states able and willing to wage systemic military campaigns against neighboring territories.[48] Through diplomacy and militarism, such polities became still more powerful, forming alliances with some and pressuring others into relationships of dependency.

In this way, the states that took root along the coast and in the forest hinterland vied for place and power in the region's rapidly evolving Atlantic market—Denkyira, Akwamu, and Asante chief among them. Denkyira was the first of these states to show up on European maps of the region, as it emerged as a major force controlling gold supply routes leading to the western ports of the Gold Coast in the second half of the seventeenth century.[49] In the closing decades of that century, Akwamu made its presence felt near the littoral in the eastern Gold Coast and became the engine of the region's emerging export market for slaves.[50] Asante rose to prominence in the central forest hinterland and staked a claim to regional dominance by its decisive defeat of Denkyira at the turn of the eighteenth century.[51]

Akwamu had its roots in the early sixteenth-century migration of a northern Akan-speaking group—the Abrade—into southern forest territory thirty miles inland from Elmina, where they founded a town in the vicinity of present-day Twifo-Heman.[52] The Abrade were primarily traders, who facilitated and capitalized on the late fifteenth- and sixteenth-century development of commercial routes directing the flow of gold toward new markets on the coast. A splinter group of the Abrade continued to move eastward until the end of the century, when they settled in the Nyanaoase district, on the northern edge of the Ga-speaking polities around Accra.

The Abrade settlement was at first welcomed by the Accra rulers, whose growing power as middlemen in Afro-European trade centered on their ability to control access to the seaboard. As clients of the Accra rulers, the Abrade traders helped consolidate control of the northern Accra frontier and the trade routes down to the coast. As a result, a large gold market established at Abonse, near Nyanaoase, "by the third decade of the seventeenth century" formed a boundary beyond which upland merchants transporting gold were not permitted to travel. The Abrade merchants consolidated their control over the main routes into Accra and then extended their reach to other north-south routes to such a degree that by the middle of the century nearly all trade in the vicinity of the kingdom flowed into and out of Abonse. "By this period," Ivor Wilks has suggested, "it becomes possible to speak of the Akwamu kingdom of Nyanaoase, which, although still technically under Accra, was rapidly becoming more powerful than its patron."[53]

The Accra region had been a major outlet for gold brought to the coast by traders from Akyem and other upland gold-producing states. Akwamu's initial aim had been to control the trade in gold in the region. But when it became clear that dominance over Akyem was an untenable aim, Akwamu turned to the other type of commerce in the region's Atlantic market: the trade in people. With its production of captives, the area now became a more reliable outlet for slaves than for the precious metal.[54]

Under the direction of the Akwamu ruler Ansa Sasraku, a relatively benign pattern of growth gave way to a decidedly militaristic policy of imperial expansion during the last quarter of the century. First, rising tensions between client and patron were resolved when Akwamu seized control of Great Accra, the kingdom's capital city, in 1677; then the kingdom's three main seaboard towns fell in 1680–1681, thereby completing the subjugation of Accra and securing Ansa Sasraku's status in the region as the head of a powerful expansionist state.[55]

During the brief lull between the two principal campaigns against Accra, the neighboring Ladoku kingdom also was brought under Akwamu jurisdiction. Campaigns against polities in the Akwapim hills to the east and Agona to the west followed, bringing rapid conquest of the former and defeat of the latter polity by the end of the decade. The fall of Agona, formally acknowledged in 1688–1689, ended a twenty-year alliance between the two states. For two decades, friendly relations with Agona had been an essential aid to Akwamu's defense of its western border with Akyem and an important strategic means to "prevent Akyem and other inland traders from bypassing Accra and Akwamu control by trading to the coast through Agona." Then, however, Akwamu turned to a strategy of repeated assaults against Agona in the 1680s, to avert "an Akyem alliance with Agona which would have provided Akyem access to such coastal settlements as Winneba and Apam."[56]

In the meantime, Akwamu regularly skirmished with neighboring states throughout the period—Tafo to the northeast, Akyem to the northwest, Assin to the southwest, and Allampo, a coastal town near the mouth of the Volta River that was a major supplier of slaves for the Atlantic market. When Ansa Sasraku died shortly after the Agona conquest, the Akwamu state claimed jurisdiction over an eighty-mile stretch of coast from Winneba to the Volta River, and a vast hinterland that reached as many miles inland. The drive for territorial conquest continued under new rulers, so by the turn of the eighteenth century Akwamu's military presence was felt as far east as Whydah.[57]

Many of the captives produced by Akwamu's military campaigns were marched to the state's capital district at Nyanaoase, where their labor as slave cultivators supported the fledgling military power by feeding it.[58] Among the likely outcomes for captives of elite status were ransom and prisoner exchange, while ritual murder remained the fate of some (if no longer most) nonelite combatants. War captives, particularly men, who were not absorbed into the slave population of Akwamu were taken along the forest paths that led down to the coast and eventually found themselves in the holds of European slave ships.

For women, war captivity generally meant further subjection to the processes of circulation and exchange that had already shaped their gendered roles in their communities. Female captives were often made to leave their homes to join the conquering group. In this way, victors acquired both the productive and the reproductive labor of defeated communities. The human spoils of war produced two forms of wealth: if assimilated as slave laborers and wives, war captives supplied productive and reproductive labor; alternatively, if disposed of through sale, war captives could be made into profitable commodities and exchanged for European goods on the Atlantic coast.

As long as local demand remained high (through the second half of the seventeenth century), more captives became slaves in the Gold Coast than were put aboard European ships for export. But when it was convenient or expedient to do so, African elites with access to captive people could find a seller's market at the region's waterside towns in the closing decades of the seventeenth century. Indeed, by this time gold could be purchased from Europeans in exchange for captives, making the sale of people in the Atlantic market a means of obtaining hard currency. Accordingly, in 1686, Royal African Company officials ordered agents to end a practice that had evolved in the increasingly competitive market for human beings in the Gold Coast: "Wee find it necessary [to] absolutely forbid you to use any Longer that Custome of buying Negroes with Gold if ye People will not take Goods for their Negro Slaves lett them keep them."[59]

The opportunity to substitute people for all or part of the gold generally required to buy imported textiles transformed both the political and the social economy of the region. On the one side of this new channel of economic exchange, a substantially wider spectrum of would-be entrepreneurs was able to participate in the accumulation of wealth afforded by Afro-European trade. On the other side of those transactions stood people from within the communities of the Gold Coast who now had value on the Atlantic market. The vulnerability of life lived at the far periphery of social networks suddenly portended a new category of terrible consequences. In the closing decades of the seventeenth century a pattern was establishing itself, as wars involving Akwamu, Tafo, Assin, Akyem, Agona, Fantine, Akwapim, Ladoku, and doubtless other polities, began to send some among their captives to the waterside.[60]

Gold being the most prized commodity the region had to offer to the Atlantic market, that "subterraneous treasure" blunted the full force of the market's fast-growing demand for captives through the end of the seventeenth century. But by the turn of the eighteenth century, the region's gold fields were reaching the point of exhaustion at the same time that American gold deposits in Brazil, coming into production, provided an alternate source of supply in the global market. The movement into new arenas of colonial enterprise—centered on gold and other mineral resources (diamonds) in Brazil, on rice in South Carolina, and on continually expanding sugar production in Portuguese, English, and French-American colonies—brought about an enormous expansion in the American demand for slave labor.

In this context, Asante, like Akwamu in the preceding century, was positioned to respond creatively, turning into opportunity the very circumstances that might have appeared to portend a declining role for the Gold Coast in the larger Atlantic economy.[61] When Akwamu began to assert its power in the eastern Gold Coast in the last quarter of the seventeenth century, the Asante polity was a tributary of Denkyira. But by the turn of the following century, a member of the Asante ruling family—who had once resided at the Denkyira capital as an apprentice in warfare and statecraft but had returned to the Asante capital at Kumasi and led successful campaigns against neighboring polities—was looking to lead an attack against the ruler of Denkyira Ntim Gyakari.[62]

Osei Tutu's decisive victory over the Denkyira king in a series of battles that concluded in 1701 elevated the power and authority associated with the title Asantehene to new heights. His success marshaling supernatural forces to aid the Asante army in its battle against the mighty Denkyira state and his introduction of innovative forms of military and political organization formed the backdrop for the creation of the Golden Stool (sika dwa). The ultimate symbol of statecraft and kingship, the Golden Stool reflected the idea that the Asante state and its leader, the Asantehene, embodied secular authority possessing the highest spiritual sanction.

The simultaneous rise of an Atlantic market for slave exports and of states whose power derived from engagement with the Atlantic economy brought about social upheavals in the central and southern forest communities of the Gold Coast. Imperial expansion, warfare, and competition for preeminence in the Atlantic commercial sector sent thousands of people into captivity and growing numbers into saltwater slavery. Arguably, none saw more of the disruptive side of the region's involvement in the Atlantic system than those who occupied the lower rungs of society. The Atlantic market for slaves changed what it meant to be a socially, politically, or economically marginalized person. Though full "belonging" remained an unattainable goal for the most marginalized, such as slave women, it was nonetheless true that even those at the bottom of the social hierarchy were bound in a mutually obligatory relationship to some corporate group.[63] Captives "acquired through war, kidnapping, or purchase" joined a community as a "trade" or "bought" slave, and were vulnerable to further involuntary displacement through resale until they were well along the path of assimilation. But assimilation was the operative process that governed the exchange of people.[64]

At this juncture, however, in place of the dreaded experience of incorporation into a new African community—an experience nonetheless familiar from hearsay—some captives found themselves sent to the waterside markets. Captivity for these unfortunates was not a temporary status while they were en route to the less vulnerable position of the slave (one who, though debased, "belonged" to a community). Rather, theirs was a "social death," a form of exile to which no end was foreseeable.[65] They inhabited a new category of marginalization, one not of extreme alienation *within* the community, but rather of absolute exclusion from *any* community. In this sense, the commercial opportunities that accrued to traders who exchanged people for goods soon rendered the Atlantic market for slaves something more than a means for dealing with war prisoners who could not be assimilated. Any and all who were vested with political power over subordinates—husbands over wives, elites over peasants and slaves, as well as the victorious over the vanquished—could and did find incentives to send people down to the waterside.

The flourishing of trade in captive people so soon after initial Afro-European contact, and in nearly every coastal area where Portuguese mariners alighted, suggests that slavery and slave trading were already well established throughout much of precolonial West Africa before the arrival of the Portuguese. But the development by the turn of the sixteenth century of a Portuguese trade network putting thousands into circulation annually as commodities in coastal Africa indicates also a shift of enormous proportions. It is a change to which the Dutch mariner Pieter de Marees alluded when he explained the absence of an export market in slaves on the Gold Coast at the turn of the seventeenth century. "They also enslave one another," De Marees observed of the Gold Coast, "but not in the same manner as in Angola or Conge [Kongo], for it would not be possible to load ships here with blacks." De Marees explained, "They do not have at their disposal a multitude of Captives," and so on the Gold Coast "they cannot be purchased in large numbers."[66]

The Portuguese had not introduced slave trading in African regions where no such commerce had existed prior to their arrival. But through the commerce they did introduce, they helped initiate a dramatic and abrupt shift in the scale of slave trading. The multiple channels of trade through which people flowed as commodities in the new Atlantic arena reflected a profound transformation—one that institutionalized markets for people and practices for treating people as commodities that had been tenuous at best, and in certain places nonexistent, before Portuguese intervention. Purchasing "in large numbers" and dealing in "multitudes" of captives transformed the very nature of captivity.

From the place Portuguese mariners named El Mina in Africa in the fifteenth century to the American place they came to call Minas Gerais in the seventeenth century, the Gold Coast was a player in the production of local and global wealth in the Atlantic economy, but the nature of the African region's role and the consequences had changed dramatically. In this sense, the Royal African Company's Brazilian scheme was the ultimate farce, for it meant that a part of Africa named by the Portuguese for its export of gold now was being tapped instead as a supplier of human commodities for export to the gold mines developed by Portuguese colonizers in America. In the end, the Brazilian scheme faced too many obstacles to pick up much momentum. For one thing, as the company's chief agent at Cape Coast Castle explained the limitations of the plan in June 1721, the Portuguese would "barter only with Gold for Young Men (from 18 to 20) and Women Boys & Girls they buy with Tobacco" (the latter being the more valued commodity by far at nearby Whydah).[67] Also pressing was Brazilian anxiety about violating of crown policy. A contract that had been reached with Brazilian ship owners willing to exchange gold for slaves at the English fort at Whydah "broke off" in 1723 for this reason, "there being so strict a prohibition against bringing Gold from Brazil to Africa," the agent at Whydah explained, "that they could not comply with it."[68]

For the most part then, Brazilian gold mines received relatively few captives from the Gold Coast. But the Gold Coast became one of the leading suppliers of African slaves to other Atlantic markets in the first half of the eighteenth century, as captives outstripped gold after 1700 to become the region's prime export commodity.[69] The Gold Coast was in actuality becoming a slave coast.

2

Turning African Captives into Atlantic Commodities

The sloop *Cape Coast* was carrying gold, corn, and slaves obtained on a trading voyage to Winneba on 6 September 1721, when its human cargo seized an opportunity to overpower its captors. "The Captain being a'shore, the Slaves rose, kill'd one man and a Boy, and run the Sloop ashore and escaped." Several weeks later, officials at the castle reported what news they had gathered about the event. "Severall Goods" had been on board the vessel that were "the remains of her trading Cargo at Annamaboe," but what was not already "stole by the Natives" had "received damage by the Salt Water." The same was true of the ninety-two chests of corn that had been put aboard by the company agent at Anomabu.

As for the vessel's human cargo, it was reported, "ten of the Slaves have been taken up by the Towns people which we are afraid will be all that is to be expected of the Seventeen; the others missing have had time enough to make their escape to some distant part, if not otherwise mett with by those who think it their Interest to conceal them." Finally, giving their summary assessment of what had transpired, the officials called attention to implications greater than the sum of the economic losses incurred. "It would be a very unaccountable history," they observed, "that Thirteen men & four boys Slaves should attempt to rise upon Seven White Men was it not that it seems they were all out of Irons by ye Master's orders."[1]

By pointing to the captain's foolhardy departure from standard procedure, the officials shielded themselves from the disturbing image of slaves overpowering their captors and relieved themselves of the uncomfortable obligation to explain how and why the events had deviated from the prescribed pattern. But assigning blame to the captain for his carelessness afforded only partial comfort, for by seizing their opportunity, the Africans aboard the *Cape Coast* had done more than liberate themselves (temporarily at least) from the slave ship.

Their action reminded any European who heard news of the event of what all preferred not to contemplate too closely: that their "accountable" history was only as real as the violence and racial fiction at its foundation. Only by ceaseless replication of the system's violence did African sellers and European buyers render captives in the distorted guise of human commodities to market. Only by imagining that whiteness could render seven men more powerful than a group of twice their number did European investors produce an account naturalizing social relations that had as their starting point an act of violence.

Successful African uprisings against European captors were of course moments at which the undeniable free agency of the captives most disturbed Europeans—for it was in these moments that African captives invalidated the vision of the history being written in this corner of their Atlantic world and articulated their own version of a history that was "accountable." Other moments in which the agency and irrepressible humanity of the captives manifested themselves were more tragic than heroic: instances of illness and death, thwarted efforts to escape from the various settings of saltwater slavery, removal of slaves from the market by reason of "madness." In negotiating the narrow isthmus between illness and recovery, death and survival, mental coherence and insanity, captives provided the answers the slave traders needed: the Africans revealed the boundaries of the middle ground between life and death where human commodification was possible.

Turning people into slaves entailed more than the completion of a market transaction. In addition, the economic exchange had to transform independent beings into human commodities whose most "socially relevant feature" was their "exchangeability."[2] The process began at the littoral, the border where the African landscape disappeared into the sea. It was here that captives came face to face with the market in human beings. Captives who may have been sold one or more times previously now stood at the center of transactions that put them finally, irreversibly, en route to saltwater slavery. The shore was the stage for a range of activities and practices designed to promote the pretense that human beings could convincingly play the part of their antithesis—bodies animated only by others' calculated investment in their physical capacities.[3]

The methods by which traders turned people into property that could move easily, smoothly through the channels of saltwater slavery took the form of both physical and social violence.[4] Along the coast, captives felt the enclosure of prison walls and the weight of iron shackles holding them incarcerated in shore-based trade forts or aboard ships that functioned as floating warehouses as captives were accumulated. The practices that underwrote African commodification also reflected a rationalized science of human deprivation. Through the trial and error of experiment and observation, European traders determined what constituted a prison that was "too crowded," or shackles that caused too much discomfort, as was determined to be the case at Cape Coast Castle in the first decade of the eighteenth century, when the chief agent there shared the observation: "Double Irons are too painful for ye Slaves."[5]

The littoral, therefore, was more than a site of economic exchange and incarceration. The violence exercised in the service of human commodification relied on a scientific empiricism always seeking to find the limits of human capacity for suffering, that point where material and social poverty threatened to consume entirely the lives it was meant to garner for sale in the Americas. In this regard, the economic enterprise of human trafficking marked a watershed in what would become an enduring project in the modern Western world: probing the limits up to which it is possible to discipline the body without extinguishing the life within.

The aim in this case being economic efficiency rather than punishment, this was a regime whose intent was not to torture but rather to manage the depletion of life that resulted from the conditions of saltwater slavery. But for the Africans who were starved, sorted, and warped to make them into saltwater slaves, torture was the result.[6] It takes no great insight to point to the role of violence in the Atlantic slave trade. But to understand what happened to Africans in this system of human trafficking requires us to ask precisely what kind of violence it required to achieve its end, the transformation of African captives into Atlantic commodities.

"Slaves in Chaines"

Everywhere that the slave trade evolved into a significant commercial enterprise, it relied on a variety of institutions geared toward the accumulation of captives: coastal settlements where African brokers collected captives for sale to Europeans; and the shore-based and floating factories (trade forts and coasting slave ships) where Europeans assembled purchased captives into human cargoes. Various sites of incarceration, therefore, became a regular feature of the African coastal landscape from the second half of the seventeenth century on.

In the earliest days of English slave trading on the Gold Coast, African captives were probably housed in the same ground-floor rooms used to store trade goods in the coastal forts and trading factories.[7] As the volume of Africans incarcerated within the walls of these settlements increased, however, their presence convinced European officials that the threat of escape or insurrection called for strategies specifically geared to the traffic in human beings. Thus, varying types of prison facilities were designed at the Royal African Company's more important posts.

Each of the English trade settlements at Cape Coast, Accra, and Anomabu included a space for housing captives purchased for export. A dungeonlike underground prison was built into the rock foundation at Cape Coast Castle by at least 1682, when Frenchman Jean Barbot described the facility. At the smaller, satellite posts, English factors devised facilities of varying types to house the men and women they purchased. Captives resided at the different coastal settlements for as little as a few days or as long as several months. Those purchased at the smaller settlements might be sent to the castle almost immediately, provisions often being in especially low supply at these sites. Alternatively, they might reside at these outposts for some length of time, where their labor might often be exploited in the routine maintenance and repair of buildings at the settlements.

The Royal African Company officials used an unabashedly precise lexicon to refer to the captives they purchased for shipment to American slave markets, to distinguish these "shipping slaves," or, still less subtly, "slaves in chaines," from the enslaved people who lived and worked at the company's fort at Cape Coast, called castle slaves, or Arda slaves (in reference to the place from which most of them came).[8]

Viewed from the water, Cape Coast Castle was an especially imposing sight. Rising abruptly above the shoreline, the fortress was rendered "almost inaccessible" by the large rocks that guarded its perimeter.[9] Coming ashore at the landing place just past the eastern end of the castle, captives entered through the nearby side gate, before being led to the prison where "slaves-in-irons" were housed until ships arrived to carry them away. Barbot considered this "slave house" to be the castle's "most noteworthy item" when he described the site in 1682. "Cut into the rock, beneath the parade-ground" that formed part of the castle's large, open courtyard, the facility "consist[ed] of large vaulted cellars, divided into several apartments which [could] easily hold a thousand slaves."[10] Barbot observed, "The keeping of the slaves thus under ground is a good security to the garrison against any insurrection."[11] Once inside this dungeonlike space, slaves could hear the loud violent surf that crashed against the rocks on the other side of the prison walls.[12] A drawing of the castle rendered in 1682 illustrates vents built into the ceiling, though they did little, as will be seen, to relieve the suffocating closeness of the dark space below.[13]

The location of James Fort, seventy miles to the east at Accra—nearest to the wars that plagued the eastern Gold Coast and downwind of Cape Coast Castle—meant both crowded conditions and lengthy stays in the slave prison. Warfare waged by Akwamu produced a steady supply of captives, but the long windward voyage to the castle made it difficult to dispatch the captives there in a timely fashion. Thus, captives generally accumulated at the fort for weeks before either a coasting vessel arrived to transport them to the castle or a slave ship appeared to take them directly aboard.

The officials who operated the fort at Accra fashioned a space to hold slaves by fitting the hollow core of the fort's defensive bastions, or "flankers," with ventilation shafts, transforming these dank chambers into spaces deemed suitable for imprisoning captives awaiting shipment.[14] Built of bricks made on-site by African laborers, the fort's northwest bastion served as "lodging for our women slaves," while the southwest bastion made a "prison for men."[15]

The physical security of such enclosures was dubious. Unusually heavy rains (so strong "that since the memory of man the like has not been known") in May 1694 "washed down" the northwest flanker and damaged other parts of the fort at Accra, leaving the facility with "no lodging for our women slaves," as the factor explained. The damage was no surprise, for the structures were "built of nothing but stone and red earth," the latter substance making a mortar that "cements no more than the sand on the sea shore." These conditions the factor promised to remedy in rebuilding and repairing the facilities. In August, the northwest structure used to house women had been "secured," and repairs completed by November made three of the fort's four bastions "sufficiently strong." There remained only the southwest flanker, "under which is our prison for men," which "wee now designe to strengthen," the factor wrote, "by joyning a substantiall wall of 4 or 5 foot thick." This wall, he hoped, would "be a great security to the mens prison which is under itt." He noted, "The Old Flankers were built without any foundation and itt is a very easie thing for the slaves to breake their Prison."[16]

At Anomabu's Charles Fort and other smaller trading factories at Anishan, Agga, Komenda, and Sekondi, the company agents housed captives in whatever makeshift spaces were available, particularly in the last quarter of the seventeenth century, when the volume of slave exports from the Gold Coast remained modest. Charles Fort, at Anomabu, for example, was a structure of mud-and-thatch "turf" when Barbot viewed it in 1679, and when he visited again three years later, efforts to rebuild had resulted in only a new "compact main building" and four bastions built of slave-made bricks. The fort's outer wall "consist[ed] merely of a turf circle, 7–8 feet high," Barbot reported, while "various lodgings . . . for the paid blacks and the slaves" were "built of the same material."[17] As the traffic in slaves grew rapidly at the turn of the following century, prison facilities like the ones at Cape Coast, Anomabu, and Accra began to appear in greater number.[18]

A burden of iron around the limbs being an obvious and effective impediment to escape, shackles were an important element in the arsenal of tools used to physically disable captives during their incarceration in coastal factories. "Please advice me," the agent at a new factory at Komenda asked: "What I am to do concerning the purchasing of slaves which daily come hither to be sold, I have not irons to put any in so desire you to send up some by the canoe that brings up the [trade] goods."[19] A variety of implements served different aspects of the task: "short irons" binding captives' wrists ensured that slaves could neither raise a hand to strike their tormentors nor seize a weapon, open a door, or scale a wall without great difficulty; "long irons" around the ankles likewise held captives fast.

Though shackles were always in demand by factors and ship captains procuring slave cargoes, the inefficiency of English operations on the coast made irons a luxury that none could rely on. "Pray send some short irons," requested Arthur Richards, the factor at Anishan, writing in February 1681, only weeks after the establishment of a new factory there.[20] Eight months later Ralph Hassell, the factor at Accra, requested both long and short irons, "for wee have none here," he complained. "I bought three men and three women yesterday & am afraid of their running away for wont of irons to put them in."[21] When Peter Blake, captain of the *James,* tried to retrieve "30 paires of shackells" on loan to the factory at Anomabu in January 1676, he was told that the factor "had slaves in them, and could not let them out lest they should run away."[22]

Although factors relied heavily on shackles to manage captives, it does not appear that slaves wore irons at all times while incarcerated at the coast. For one thing, the numerous requests for irons indicate that shackles were often in short supply.[23] In July 1697 one hundred Africans and "considerable more" were expected in the slave prisons at Accra, for example, when the factor sent word of his dire need for irons. "Not having a pair in the [fort] but what is in use," he would be forced, he wrote, to "keep what men I buy out of irons till return of the canoe" that would transport them up to Cape Coast Castle.[24]

Even when irons were on hand, they did not stand up well to the corrosive effects of humidity, and they were often found to be in a useless state of disrepair. Forty captives ("most of them men and boys") aboard the *Cape Coast* in March 1682 watched as some of the irons intended for their limbs fell apart in the captain's hands: "I wish I had a few more irons," the captain wrote, "for believe I shall have occasion for them having but 25 pair aboard and some of them the rust has eaten quite out for when I go to make use of them they break in the eye of the shackle."[25] In October 1691, almost all the irons at Accra were in need of repair. They "are out of order for want of bolts which I desire may be fixed and sent by the sloop," the factor reported. "If we should meet with slaves," he warned further, "we should want them, the good ones we have are but few."[26]

Escape from onshore settlements and coasting slave ships was a course of action that nearly every person sold to Europeans on the coast envisaged and many attempted. For some, opportunity, together with personal strength and luck, brought success, and they were able to liberate themselves from exile into slavery across the Atlantic. In practice, irons and prison walls often failed to hold the captives. Lapses in security at the settlements presented numerous opportunities for Africans to attempt to free themselves, and where slave irons were not in regular use, the poorly constructed walls already described often figured in escape plots.

James Fort at Accra was crowded with more than fifty captives, and corn was in short supply in July 1682, when a group of thirteen men and one woman "undermined the prison walls and got out." Despite the presence of a guard stationed at the prison door, they escaped in the middle of the night.[27] Similar conditions prevailed when some of the sixty captives in the fort in March 1687 managed, "in one night's time," to dig through three and a half feet of a six-foot wall and, after being discovered, tried to attack the garrison. Having lost this opportunity to escape, some of the rebels found themselves among a group of forty-five men and women sent up to Cape Coast Castle that month.[28]

Other opportunities to escape appeared whenever captives were taken out of the prisons and put to work at such tasks as cutting wood, gathering stones, or making "swish," the mud clay used in the construction and repair of the European settlements.[29] Though these tasks generally were reserved for the Arda castle slaves, their counterparts in irons were sometimes put to similar work—particularly at the satellite posts, where castle slaves were often in short supply.[30] When such labor was performed away from the immediate confines of the settlements, captives sometimes found their best, and perhaps only, chance to run away.

On one occasion, the need for lime to repair the buildings at Accra created an opportunity for ten men to make their escape. Sent out "in long irons to go and cut wood for burning of the same," the two "bumboys" (slave foremen) assigned to supervise the work crew were no match for them, "10 of the lustiest men in said irons."[31] When the group arrived at the work site and the men in irons "found their advantage," they "seized the said bumboys and wounded one of them in the back." Only two of the men in irons returned to the fort, one of them wounded.[32] Similarly, two who were employed making swish for a newly established factory at Winneba found their window of opportunity when the bumboy sent along to supervise them "went away and left them to themselves," which "carelessness" enabled the two to break out of their leg irons and run away.[33]

Though slaves once onboard ship faced far more difficult obstacles, the two to three miles of rough coastal waters that separated the vessel from the shore did not deter captives determined to seize this last opportunity to prevent expulsion into an alien Atlantic world. On occasion, individuals managed to escape from slaving vessels while still on the coast; the only means for captives to regain land was to swim ashore, unless they were assisted by the canoemen responsible for bringing them out to the ships.[34] In January 1683, for example, one male slave was taken out of the slave prison at the castle to go aboard the *John & Thomas*, "in lieu of a man slave that ranaway from on board" the ship.[35]

At other times, slaves actually organized themselves to revolt against the white crew and seize control of a ship. In January 1686, the slaves aboard the sloop *Charlton* killed the entire crew while the vessel stood off Little Popo in the Bight of Benin. Once the crewmen had been removed as a threat, the slaves proceeded to cut the cable that held the ship's anchor, after which the vessel ran aground. No doubt some slaves were killed or at least seriously injured by the violent smashing of the hull, but presumably some survived the wreck and succeeded in making their escape.[36] The captives aboard another vessel, an English interloper procuring slaves not far from Accra, found their opportunity to revolt when many of the crewmen went onshore to fill the ship's water barrels. Though the captives managed to kill the ship's doctor, boatswain, and two other crewmen, a hundred slaves also were killed in the fighting that ensued, and the surviving rebels were eventually subdued.[37]

"The Reason of the Slaves Dying So Fast"

Turning captives into commodities was a thoroughly scientific enterprise. It turned on perfecting the practices required to commodify people and determining where those practices reached their outer limits (that is, the point at which they extinguished the lives they were meant to sustain in commodified form). Traders reduced people to the sum of their biological parts, thereby scaling life down to an arithmetical equation and finding the lowest common denominator.

This was especially, painfully, evident with regard to captives' need for food. European accounts describe a wide variety of plant and animal foods supported by the landscape of the Gold Coast littoral, including maize, millet, yams, bananas, pineapples, peas and legumes, goat, fowls, chickens, oxen, buffalo, pork, fish, and shellfish. Commodification removed captives from that landscape of abundance and put them into a situation of unmitigated poverty.

Having lost the ability to oversee their own nourishment, captives were forced to subsist instead on rations—meals whose content and size reflected a calculation balancing the cost of the slaves' maintenance against their purchase price. The task before factors on the African coast was to ensure that the "cheapness in the price" paid to obtain captives would "sufficiently make amends for the charge of keeping them."[38] Dalby Thomas warned when he wrote to his superiors as the chief factor at Cape Coast Castle in 1704, "You are not like other traders, for if we have goods here we are buying Negroes and they eat and dye as too many have done of late."[39]

Meant not to support health but rather simply to ensure subsistence, the diet on which captives tried to survive provided, at best, a consistent intake of nutritionally empty calories. At Cape Coast Castle and the other English factories, slaves generally received a daily allotment of corn dressed with malagetta pepper and palm oil. African women prepared the grain following local custom. First, it was ground into a coarse meal, by means of a millstone known locally as a cankey stone; then it was mixed with water, shaped into "large round cakes, the size of two or three fists," and boiled to a dense consistency. The resulting breadlike porridge was also called cankey.[40] In March 1686, for example, the factor at Accra notified the castle, "We shall want corn and a kettle to boyle Canky in for the slaves."[41]

Though we do not have evidence regarding the treatment of captives under the control and in the possession of African traders, Africans who brought slaves to the waterside for sale made the same kinds of economic choices as their European counterparts, by determining the least possible expenditure that could be made on food and water to sustain the captives for the time the traders anticipated having them in their possession.

All things being equal, the general practice at the Royal African Company trading factories was to provide rations in the amount of roughly one- to two-tenths of a bushel of corn per person per day. In June 1682, for example, the factor at Accra reported that his imprisoned population of more than fifty slaves "eats a chest of corn everyday," a chest generally containing a thousand stalks, which amounted to "about five Bushels" of grain.[42] At Cape Coast Castle, authorities listed nine chests of corn allotted "for castle's use" in January 1682. Assuming that this corn was used to feed the eight "chain slaves" in the prison, these captives also consumed nearly one-fifth of a bushel of grain per day.[43]

Often, however, things were not equal, for the supply of corn in the local markets regularly fell short of European demand, and the price frequently exceeded what the company's factors were permitted to spend. When the number of captives rose, officials at Cape Coast Castle, for example, usually held expenditures on food constant. While incarcerated on the African coast, captives therefore suffered under a calculation according to which economic considerations weighed more heavily in the balance than human need.

Captives held at Accra's James Fort frequently faced shortages of food, when there were too many captives for the quantity of provisions stored. When corn became scarce, efforts at the local markets to purchase a supply for the captives often failed. And when the factor at this most isolated of the company's Gold Coast settlements sent frantic requests for additional supplies, or for a vessel to dispatch the captives, authorities at the castle were not quick to respond. With no more than six chests of corn in the fort, and "none to be had for money at any rates" in the local markets, the captives held at the fort in June 1683 were suffering. "Beg a supply within this week," the factor wrote; "else must send what slaves I have to Cabo Corso in the 5-hand canoe for they will be starved else."[44]

The preferred practice was to send captives up to Cape Coast from Accra when the number at James Fort approached fifty. But in the frequent instances when the castle officials failed to send a vessel to retrieve the captives, it was not uncommon for groups as much as twice that size to be crowded into the slave prison at Accra, and slaves purchased at Allampo often added to the already crowded conditions there.[45] In June 1687, the captain of the sloop

Adventure was forced to deposit fifty captives at the fort when poor sailing conditions made it impossible for him to reach the castle before running out of food and water. "Do not know when I will be up at Cape Coast Castle," he reported on June 29, "the breeze continuing much out and leeward currants so that I cannot get off, I have been 10 days from Allampo and have not got three leagues of ground, and corn wood and water spends apace." The captain had sent men out in his canoe to purchase more corn, "and by chance with much ado and some cost have got some water here, else I should not have had a drop to drink." He continued, "My wood is almost gone and of that I can get none."

New orders having already been sent directing the captain to deposit his cargo at Accra and return to Allampo for more, this contingent of captives was spared further deprivation.[46] Having been succored by four chests of corn sent from the fort, they reached Accra themselves by July 8, the fort now being "plenty with slaves," as the new arrivals brought the number there to "upward of 100 and odd."[47] One week later almost all who were in the fort went aboard the slave ship *Maynard*.[48] If they had continued under such circumstances, the captives aboard the *Adventure* would probably have died of dehydration and starvation before reaching the castle; the captain's new orders to carry them to Accra rather than proceed in all likelihood prolonged their lives, at least for the time being.[49]

Meanwhile, the *Adventure* returned to Accra on 25 July 1687, this time depositing forty-eight new captives (twenty-six men and twenty-two women) procured at Allampo.[50] With this new supplement, the number of people in the fort again approached a hundred, and the factor was forced to cease buying any more, "by reason corne is here so scarce and none to be procured for money." Given that the prisons were full and food was in short supply, the situation was growing dangerous for the ninety-four captives held there.[51] There being "not above 30 chests left" of the fort's supply of corn, the captives were forced to subsist on exceedingly small rations. Now only three chests of corn were expended every two days—a 20 percent drop from the tenth of a bushel generally allotted per day. "I cannot keep them much longer without further provisions," the factor warned, hoping to hasten the return of the sloop.[52]

Though orders did come soon, instructing the sloop captain to bring "what slaves he can conveniently carry" up to the castle, the message also conveyed the unwelcome news that no additional food supplies would be sent to Accra. As a result, most of the small quantity of corn left in the fort would have to accompany those people selected to depart aboard the *Adventure;* as a consequence, the thirty-odd who would remain would be subject to ever more pitiful conditions. The vulnerability of these captives was plainly evident to those responsible for their preservation. "What to do for them I know not," wrote the factor at Accra. He could find "no manner of provisions for their substenance unless," he explained, "wee buy fish and give them half allowance in Canky."

On 7 August, thirty men and thirty women, "with all things convenient for their passage up," boarded the *Adventure,* and they departed for Cape Coast Castle two days later. In the fort there remained "but 14 chests of damaged corn" to feed the captives still held there. In their weakened condition, illness had begun to encroach. "We have lost more slaves of the smallpox" was the report from Accra on the day the *Adventure* departed, and one of the captives aboard the sloop was sent back on shore for "being newly taken with the same."[53]

Most enslaved Africans brought to the waterside for sale probably experienced the range of conditions encountered by three women originally purchased at the English factory at Winneba in April 1695. Sent up to Cape Coast Castle, their ill appearance upon their arrival caused them to be rejected by the officials there. When they returned to the trading outpost at Winneba, the factor claimed that they did not appear as "they were when I bought them" and offered the opinion that "the scarcity and want of corn brought them so low." No doubt the factor spoke in part to protect his own position, and it is impossible to know more precisely the women's condition at the time they were purchased at Winneba, or what they had endured before that.

Rations at the factory in April appear to have been especially scanty, for the recently established settlement apparently received few or no regular supplies from the castle as yet, and corn was available locally only at a higher price than that authorized by the castle officials. Upon the captives' return to Winneba in May, however, conditions seem to have improved. For "now," the factor remarked, "they begin to grow and look very well." Nonetheless, the factor chose to "send three more in room of them having already 2 more by me," which decision perhaps gave these three women further opportunity to regain some measure of vitality before facing the challenges that lay ahead in the Atlantic waters.[54]

Food shortages notwithstanding, the rations provided in the English settlements certainly may have represented an improvement over the food supplied in the preceding days, weeks, or even months that had passed since the slaves' initial capture and arrival at the waterside. For the impoverished among Gold Coast communities in general, and for persons of any rank seized, removed from the protections of kin and community, and given over into the hands of African slave dealers, regular and adequate food surely was not guaranteed. Also, war captives were unlikely to have been well fed during this interim; and even those who may have spent some period of time as slave cultivators before their sale on the coast were among the most materially impoverished members of their communities. It is possible, in fact, that the relatively lengthy time that enslaved Africans might spend incarcerated here at the waterside settlements could, under certain conditions, in fact provide a chance for rest and some minimal restoration of health.

For most, however, the abject conditions of their incarceration made this an exceedingly narrow range within which to subsist: between abject and benign starvation, between the absolute or near absence of food at worst and daily rations even at best too scanty and nutritionally limited to supply nourishment beyond a minimal level. Captives passed this time negotiating an unpredictable course between reliable sustenance and starvation. Some recovered their physical strength, but some also starved to death.

It fell to the agents at the factories, who oversaw the day-to-day work of buying people and packaging them for export aboard English slave ships, to construct the epistemological foundation on which the enterprise of commodification stood. Through trial and error, observation and experiment, the agents assembled a body of lore suited to the exigencies of human trafficking. Their reliance on empirical evidence reflected the broader shift toward a "new" scientific discourse in post-Restoration English society.[55] Accordingly, when a rash of deaths occurred in the slave prison at Accra in February 1694, John Bloom, the factor stationed there, reported the problem to his superiors at Cape Coast Castle along with his laborious musings about the probable cause. "Sundry of our slaves being lately dead and others falling sick dayly makes me get to think that they are to[o] much crowded in their lodging and besides have not the benefitt of the Air."[56]

Upwards of a hundred men and women were being held at Accra when that wave of illness and death swept through. The small openings cut into the prison walls for ventilation did little to counteract the heat and closeness of the air when the rooms grew so crowded.[57] Awareness of these stultifying conditions supplied Bloom with the evidence he needed to solve the puzzle—to "make [him] think" that with more than a hundred bodies within its walls, the prison had surpassed the limit beyond which the human property it held was likely to expire.

In a similar incident, a belated discovery about local culinary technology reveals the contradictions inherent in the practice of human commodification. The backdrop was the Royal African Company fort at Accra, where the company agent Edward Searle learned that the stones used to grind corn had important consequences for the valuable merchandise in his charge. The grinding implements available in the region ranged from those "as hard as marble" to others "as soft as sandstone," and as Searle was to discover, it mattered what type of stone one used to prepare the cankey fed to captives at the fort.[58] The millstones produced locally at Accra were of the "soft" category, and it was these the factor had purchased for the captives' use. "I never heard till now," Searle explained in December 1695, "that the free people here buy their stones from other places," those obtained locally "being only in a manner sand."[59]

Searle was relieved to learn of his mistake because, by his analysis, the discovery solved a mysterious problem he faced. In the preceding month, captives he purchased had been dying without apparent cause and in alarmingly rapid succession. Now the untenable loss of company property could be checked. "I judge the reason of the slaves dying so fast is cheifly the fault of the Cankey stones grinding away amongst the corn," he wrote, "for here is lusty good slaves taken with the gripe one day and dead the next, others fall dead at once and no other reason can I think of them."[60]

We recognize in hindsight that the rate and timing of mortalities at the prison suggests an outbreak of infectious disease among the captives. It is not the cause of death, however, but rather the wretched circumstances of captives' existence that call out for interpretation. For Searle, his discovery offered the explanation for an otherwise implausible outcome: the bewildering disappearance of precisely those men and women to whom the descriptions "lusty" and "good" could be applied.

For the captives themselves, though, when "lusty" slaves died without warning, it merely confirmed something they all knew only too well: what the Europeans empirically determined to be conditions adequate to support life the prisoners recognized as calculated deprivation that did not sustain life but attempted only systematically to control its depletion. Whether they died or not, all of them, even the captives who appeared healthiest, knew that the mouthfuls of stone they were made to ingest were one more indication of the impossibility of existence under such conditions, and of their own utter alienation from the most basic norms of everyday life.[61]

The documentation European buyers produced in their line of work reveals the important role language played in the process of commodification. Commercial records represent the people captured, whether sick or healthy, young or old, injured or strong, as equally suitable for exchange on the Atlantic market. European slavers on the African coast relied on the power of language to make the slave cargo truer to expectations, to present a reality that would reflect the beholder's fantasy. Thus, bodies that visibly ran the gamut in age and physical condition became in the sellers' descriptions a collection of uniformly "likely" or "lusty" workers available for sale.

Consider incidents aboard the *Cape Coast* brigantine, for example. Two days after boarding the vessel at Allampo in 1682, a woman who refused to eat and displayed a "sullen" demeanor died suddenly. According to the captain's report, she was "as likely a slave as any I have on board." Within the week, another slave, "one of the best men that [Towgood] had on board," also died, overtaken by a "violent feavour" just days after coming aboard. The two captives themselves, their testimony having been silenced not only in death, but more fatefully by their enslavement while they were living, now yielded up an explanation in response to the probing of the autopsy knife. Upon opening the dead woman's body to assess the cause of her death, the ship's doctor found her internal organs to appear "verry sound but starv'd for want of eating."[62] The body of the dead man provided few clues to the immediate cause of his death, but it did expose the physical trauma of his captivity. Observing mysterious scorch marks on the man's tongue, Towgood surmised that the unusual wounds were produced "through the Negroes beating of him when hee was panyard [kidnapped]."[63]

As we see in such terms as "slaves in chains," "lusty slaves," or "likely slaves," merchants used a special lexicon to cast their human wares in the mold of the qualities buyers desired in the people they purchased. In a single word, "lusty," purveyors captured the image of the ideal slave, and in their deployment of this hyperbolic term daily disavowed the weakness and exhaustion apparent in nearly all who fell victim to Atlantic captivity. Through this designation traders made a pretense of offering what the market demanded, by depicting the absence of outright illness as evidence that these were bodies brimming with vitality.

The Social Death of the Saltwater Slave

The imperatives of a market that valued people as commodities interposed a nearly impassable gulf between captives and any community that might claim them as new members. Captives learned that when they reached the littoral, their exchangeability on the Atlantic market outweighed any social value they might have. The price put on their persons pushed most captives beyond the possibility of eventual reintegration as members in any community. The crisis of captivity on that coast, in other words, was that only with great difficulty or great luck could the prisoners' "commodity potential" be masked or converted back into social currency.

On occasion, families or communities sufficiently near at hand and powerful to secure the "redemption" of their members were able to effect their return. For example, two were fortunate enough to be released from the chains in February 1712, when agents at Cape Coast Castle credited the "shipping slaves" account "for Redemption of a free man." Likewise, the woman taken out of the slave prison to join the "Castle working slaves" six months later most probably was the beneficiary of intervention on the part of a "cabosheer" or other well-placed member of the local elite.[64]

Besides the rare good fortune of "redemption," resale to other buyers might very occasionally take captives out of the castle and away from the slave ship. When need or lucrative opportunity arose, for example, agents at the castle sometimes sold captives to local Africans or to other European trading interests. Thus, on the same day that agents spent tobacco to buy two men, they also sold four men, seven women, and three boys for a quantity of tobacco valued at three marks, six ounces.[65] But such instances of accommodation in efforts to "redeem" persons known to be held captive aboard a European ship occurred only seldom. Moreover, those redeemed usually won their liberation at the expense of others, sold in their stead.

For most, in contrast to those few whose status made it possible to be "redeemed" from the Atlantic market, the only way out was escape. Those who managed that feat found that, here again, the most powerful force opposing their desperate efforts to return to a place of social belonging was not the physical constraint of prison walls and iron shackles, but rather the market itself. Whether they burrowed their way under prison walls, broke out of the irons on their legs, or swam away from coasting vessels, the captives who managed to work free of European ships and settlements were easily recognized as "slaves in chaines" on the run and were extremely vulnerable to recapture and resale. Exhausted, emaciated, or injured from the traumas experienced thus far, escapees could not easily disguise their condition; nor was it easy to hide from those whose commercial interests had led to the fugitives' sale into slavery in the first place.

Not long after the eight men in irons made their escape from a work detail at Accra in December 1687, the English factor knew "where they [were] sheltered" and hoped to have the men back in his possession soon, "Ahenisha having promised to see them returned."[66] Similarly, one of the two men who escaped from Anomabu in June 1687 was back in chains and aboard a canoe bound for Cape Coast Castle one month later. Isolated and vulnerable once beyond the walls of the castle, he was unable to travel very far before falling into the hands of local cabosheers, who chose to return him to the English fort for the price of "3 peize."[67] Transactions such as this one, whereby Europeans paid for the same captive twice, were frequent, reflecting the power the market held to ensure that captives bore the indelible mark of commodification.[68]

"Please tell me," Arthur Richards asked, "what price I am to pay to Africans who return runaway slaves?" Richards was the factor stationed at Anishan in July 1681 when local elites offered to retrieve several captives who had escaped from English settlements—for a price. Having given money to one official "in part for two runaways that he says he will fetch back again, saying he knows where they be," Richards was engaged in negotiating a price for the return of runaways whom leaders at nearby Anomabu offered to deliver. For these, he had "offered . . . 3 angles each head," but the African "captain" with whom he was negotiating would "not deliver . . . any," Richards complained, "if I will not give him 6 angles for each."[69]

Escaped captives were of course most vulnerable to recapture when they were far removed from the physical and social landscape with which they were familiar. Once transported to Cape Coast Castle, for example, men and women originally purchased at the leeward ports were beyond the reach of the towns and communities where they might be able to find assistance. This was in all likelihood the case for a man who escaped from Cape Coast and traveled some forty miles before he was recaptured at Winneba. "Here is a cabosheer not far from hence has stopped a man slave, which on examination is found to run away from Cape Coast Castle," the factor reported in May 1695. According to his testimony, extreme hunger was what compelled him to run. Visible evidence of malnourishment was perhaps also what caught the attention of the cabosheer who seized him.[70] The factor at Winneba offered "the usual allowances" to buy the man back, but the offer was not sufficient; the cabosheer indicated that "he [would] not deliver" the fugitive "for less than his damands." Whatever the company's "usual" price for reclaiming escaped captives, it did not measure up to the two pieces of cloth (one "say" and a "blue perpett") demanded by the cabosheer.

There were other avenues the cabosheer could follow, however, to exploit his opportunity. He might choose to keep the captive, thereby adding to his own retinue of dependents. Alternatively, he might decide to sell the man elsewhere, given the numerous opportunities to do so in the strong domestic market for slaves within Gold Coast society. In this instance, when the factor at Winneba made overtures to comply with the counterdemand, the cabosheer responded that he had already "sold the slave to a Quomboe [Akwamu] man who has carried him away."[71]

Negotiations like those just described demonstrate a truism for all captives at the littoral: escape did not, in itself, alter slaves' status as a market commodity. As long as fugitives remained at large, they could try to put distance between themselves and the European settlements. But as they tried to return, if not "home," then to any alternative place of social belonging, they discovered that time and circumstances were firmly against them. It is not possible to put a figure on the fugitives from European ships and settlements who were retained within the domestic slave market, rather than returned to European ownership. Because the price for slaves was highest along the coast, though, sooner rather than later the commercial tide inexorably returned to the water's edge most of those who had escaped from European captivity.[72]

That was the case for an Arda castle slave who made his escape from the fort at Accra in June 1695. The man had been part of a group of four slaves brought westward to the Gold Coast from Benin in an African trading canoe accompanying a European slaver. Sold to the factor by an African dealer, the man ran away soon after being put to work at the fort. By sending the three others up to the castle, the factor at Accra prevented them from executing their plan to escape as well, and meanwhile tried to obtain information regarding the fugitive. At the time that he reported the incident, no news had materialized.[73] The fugitive had successfully escaped the European settlement, but eventually he was returned to James Fort at Accra. Perhaps the new owner had made an arbitrary decision to convert the man into currency; perhaps debt made his sale a necessity; or perhaps the reason for it, as before, was that he had committed some crime or misdemeanor. Whatever the circumstances, in April 1697, two years after his escape, the man was returned to European possession in exchange for an ounce of gold. The factor considered it "better to be at the charge than to lose him, was it only for example for the rest."[74] The market was everywhere, always shining a light on the captive's "exchangeability."

The collective assault of the practices used to herd together captives at the littoral was greater than the sum of its parts. Physical incarceration and social alienation played a role; but ultimately the power of these and other constraints lay not in their immediate material effect but in the overarching system justifying the commodification of Africans. The most powerful instrument locking captives in as commodities for Atlantic trade was the culture of the market itself. On the coast captives were marked as commodities both physically and figuratively, for the market forged power relations that bound "chaine slaves," more securely than irons could do, to the European ships waiting offshore. As a result, captives and those who claimed to own them understood that saltwater slavery menaced them with "social death" of unprecedented proportions.

After an attempt at mutiny failed, for instance, slaving captain

William Snelgrave engaged the cohort of Gold Coast captives who had tried to escape from his slave ship in a dialogue about what had occurred. Through the linguists posted aboard the ship during its stay on the coast, Snelgrave asked "what had induced them to mutiny," to which they replied that he "was a great Rogue to buy them, in order to carry them away from their own Country; and that they were resolved to regain their Liberty if possible." Snelgrave's reply, that the captives "had forfeited their Freedom before [he] bought them," articulated the standard European reasoning. "They being now my Property, I was resolved," Snelgrave said, "to let them feel my Resentment, if they abused my Kindness: Asking at the same time, Whether they had been ill used by the white Men, or had wanted for any thing the Ship afforded?" When the captives conceded, according to Snelgrave, that "they had nothing to complain of," he then "observ'd to them, 'That if they should gain their Point and get on Shore, it would be no Advantage to them, because their Countrymen would catch them, and sell them to other Ships.'"[75]

Indeed, what was at stake here was the possession of captive people. For just as the singular interest of African and European traders was to own captives as exchangeable commodities, so too was ownership the idiom in which communities laid claim to the persons incarcerated at the waterside market. Because kinship ties were the institutional glue that most immediately bound the self to society, the disappearance of a community member left an absence that portended consequences both for the individual and for those left behind. The scale of geographic displacement and the state power that underwrote the exchange of people on the Atlantic market made it impossible for most to "regain their Liberty": somewhere a family or community cried out for the return of every person made to disappear aboard a slave ship.

Among Akan-speaking communities, for instance, the man called to leave home to go to war did not relinquish the roles that most fundamentally defined his individual and social identity. Temporarily made to wear the uniform of the soldier, he did not cease to be a "mother's brother" [wɔfa], or "head of the house" [(ɔ)fie panin], if he was the eldest brother. On his safe return, he brought honor and possibly material spoils to his sisters and their offspring. At the other extreme, however, his disappearance into the Atlantic market meant that one or more women and their offspring were suddenly deprived of their most immediate source of patriarchal support.[76] The indelible bonds of kinship meant that once out of sight, a departed kinsman could never be out of mind.

When Ayuba ("Job") Ben Solomon returned to his home in Senegambia, an acquaintance recruited to send word of his arrival "expressed great joy at seeing him in safety returned from slavery, he being the only man (except one) that was ever known to come back to this country, after having been once carried a slave out of it by white men." His return being an anomaly—a piece of good fortune enjoyed by none of the thousands of families and communities that had lost members to the Atlantic market for captives—it had become a communally held assumption that "all who were sold for slaves, were generally either eaten or murdered, since none ever returned."[77]

It was appropriate that the departures that resulted from sale into the Atlantic market be explained in the idiom of death, for in precolonial West African cultures (and many other premodern systems of belief), death was understood to engender a leave-taking of the most profound sort. Through the soul's departure from the body and migration to the realm of the ancestors, death entailed a change that resulted not in disconnection or disappearance but rather in its antithesis: a new kind of connection in the form of ancestral involvement in the life of kin and community. In this sense, the departure and displacement of the dead produced migrations that sustained connection, by carrying the soul of the deceased to the realm of the ancestors and returning the personality of the deceased to the realm of the living, reincarnated in the body of a newborn. Death thereby preserved and indeed strengthened an unbroken continuity (indeed, such circularity was central to many precolonial African conceptualizations of time).

Enslavement also resulted in departure and migration, and in this and many other respects, the slave experienced something akin to death. Indeed, the classic situation of the slave is that of the "socially dead person." But if religion, in the form of ancestor worship, "explains how it is possible to relate to the dead who still live," how, asks the sociologist Orlando Patterson, ought society to "relate to the living who are dead," that is to say, to the socially dead?[78]

Patterson has insisted that the social death imposed by slavery entails a process involving the two contradictory principles of marginality and integration. Thus, the slave, like the ancestor, is a "liminal" being, one who is in society but cannot ever be fully of society. "In his social death," Patterson asserts, "the slave . . . lives on the margin between community and chaos, life and death, the sacred and the secular." Patterson suggests, moreover, that in many slaveholding societies the social death of the slave functioned precisely to empower him to navigate, in his liminality, through betwixt-and-between places where full members of society could not. In some societies, the liminal status of the slave empowered him to undertake roles in the spiritual world, such as handling the bodies of the deceased, that were dangerous to full members of society. "Being socially dead, the captives were able to move between the living and the dead without suffering the supernatural harm inevitably experienced by the socially alive in such boundary crossing."[79]

Among precolonial African societies, Patterson has observed, ritual practices associated with enslavement also worked to "give symbolic expression to the slave's social death and new status." But here, Patterson suggests, "the emphasis was less on personal and spiritual labor and more on the social use of the slave incorporated as a permanent marginal into a network of affiliation after ritual break with his old kin ties and ancestral protectors." Among the Imbangala peoples of Angola, for example, the ritual creation of the slave entailed his or her symbolic severing of ties with familial relations, followed by a period of kinlessness and subsequent introduction and attachment to the owner's network of kin. Indeed, throughout precolonial sub-Saharan Africa, where slavery functioned generally as a means of acquiring dependents and incorporating them into the family or community, "the newcomer, unless he was a 'trade slave' destined for resale, was forced to deny his natal kin ties and acquire certain fictive kin bonds to the master and his family."[80]

Nonetheless, insofar as this was a process—a rite of passage—the social death represented in slavery gave rise both to the pain and suffering of social abnegation and to its corollary, the anticipated relief and catharsis of rebirth. To be sure, this was not a return to full personhood. Indeed, it was precisely the function of the slave to inhabit forever a place of liminality: the socially dead did not, could not, ever return fully to social life. But the crucial point is that the slave did return to some measure of social personhood. She moved through the purgatory of virtual kinlessness toward some kind of social belonging.

Insofar as the captives siphoned into the Atlantic too were socially dead, their dilemma was the same as that of all who suffered the marginalization of enslavement: the alienation from their society of birth. In all the ways it robbed them of the markers of their social existence, the violence of commodification signaled to captives—stripped of material adornment, physically displaced, torn from the social embrace of kin and community—that they had been doomed to social annihilation. But for the saltwater slave the social death was something more, something horrifyingly different.

As those who witnessed Job Ben Solomon's departure aboard a

slave ship attested concerning those who disappeared into the Atlantic market, because they were never seen or heard from again, theirs was understood to be the uniquely dishonorable death associated with murder or cannibalism—the antithesis of a proper demise: those who left on the slavers were neither venerated, like the deceased, nor suspended in the balance between marginalization and integration, like local slaves, but rather consigned to an interminable purgatory. If the slave's bane in general was the limiting of his capacity for full social life, the saltwater slave was menaced with a fate more ominous still, the perpetual purgatory of virtual kinlessness.

Saltwater slaves were thus threatened in their capacity to die honorably and thereby continue to exist meaningfully, as dead kin connected with the community of the living, as beings able to make a transition to their proper ancestral roles. Their disappearance threatened to put saltwater slaves beyond both the physical and metaphysical reach of kin. Would the exiles be able to return home to offer protective intervention, to promote the integrity and continuing prosperity of the kinship group? Would their deaths take place in isolation? Would their spirits wander aimlessly, unable to find their way home to the realm of the ancestors?

We cannot know how communities made sense of the loss of family members to the slave trade, how various coastal African communities incorporated such departures into their intellectual systems. Yet some of the scattered evidence is striking for the clarity of the conceptualization of African commodified beings that were its product. In some Atlantic African communities it was believed that persons who departed in this way did in fact return but traveled not on the metaphysical plane of the ancestors but rather, transmuted as wine and gunpowder, on the material plane of commodities—an idea suggesting that the special violence of commodification produced not only social death, but more ominous still a kind of total annihilation of the human subject.[81]

Undoing their objectivization as goods to be bought and sold, therefore, required not only that captives escape the physical hold exerted on them by the forts, factories, and other coastal facilities used to incarcerate them but, more difficult still, that they reverse their own transformation into commodities, by returning to a web of social bonds that would tether them safely to the African landscape, within the fold of kinship and community. For most, as we have seen, distance made return to their home communities impossible. The market, they learned, made return to any form of social belonging impossible as well. If they managed to escape from the waterside forts and factories, their value resided not in their potential to join communities as slave laborers, wives, soldiers, or in some other capacity, but rather in their market price.

For most, the power of the market made it impossible to return to their previous state, that of belonging to (being "owned" by) a community—to being possessed, that is, of an identity as a subject. Rather, the strangers the runaways encountered shared the vision of the officials at Cape Coast Castle: the laws of the market made fellow human beings see it as their primary interest to own as commodities the escaped captives, rather than to connect with them as social subjects. More often than not, then, captives escaped only to be sold again.

As Snelgrave's language articulated so clearly, the logic of the market meant that enslavement was a misfortune for which no buyer needed to feel the burden of accountability. Indeed, according to the mercantile logic in force, buyers (of whatever nationality) *could* not bear the weight of political accountability. Buying people who had no evident social value was not a violation or an act of questionable morality but rather a keen and appropriate response to opportunity; for this was precisely what one was supposed to do in the market: create value by exchange, recycle someone else's castoffs into objects of worth.

Thus, then, did the market exert its power—through its language, its categories, its logic. The alchemy of the market derived from its effectiveness in producing a counterfeit representation; it had become plausible that human beings could be so completely drained of social value, so severed from the community, that their lives were no longer beyond price: they could be made freely available in exchange for currency. The market painted in colors sufficiently believable as to seem true the appalling notion that "a human being could fail to be a person."[82]

Something akin to this understanding perhaps motivated the actions of a man newly purchased who, "of his owne will sprange into the tank" while a group of castle slaves were drawing water from the cistern at Charles Fort in Anomabu, in May 1687. Two men from the garrison plunged in to try to retrieve the captive, but his will prevailed: "After some tyme brought him up but dead though endeavourd what we could to gett life in him by rouleing him on a cask and hanging him by the [ankles] but all in vaine." He "had not been 1/2 an hour in irons" when he committed the act. One measure of the loss comes from Ralph Hassell, the agent who, describing the dead man as "one of the lustiest men slaves I have seen [in] a long time," stated the magnitude of the loss as he conceived it, in the idiom of the market. Of course we cannot know fully what impression the slave intended his self-inflicted death to leave. But we do know something of the effect it did have: by making his "lusty" body lifeless, the man through his decisive act undid what the market quite deliberately had sought to produce and robbed it of the considerable quotient of labor power embodied in his person.[83]

Here at the littoral, then, individual paths of misfortune merged into the commodifying Atlantic apparatus—the material, economic, and social mechanisms by which the market molded subjects into beings that more closely resembled objects—beings that existed solely for the use of those who claimed to hold them as possessions. Once they reached the shore, captives either succeeded in their efforts to retreat back into the protective web of kinship and community, moved forward into the slave ship's landscape of terror, or died there at the water's edge. The terrible lesson all the captives learned was that the system in place put them up against nearly impossible odds. For most captives there was no way out of the one-way current moving inexorably, like a rip current's undertow, away from the water's edge, carrying its saltwater slaves out to sea and beyond the horizon. At the littoral, captives discovered that they had passed the point of no return.

3

The Political Economy of the Slave Ship

Laden with guns and gunpowder, iron bars, knives, and, most important, a half-dozen varieties of textiles, the *Sarah Bonadventure* was a floating marketplace. Its cargo of trade goods, valued at 2,351 pounds sterling when loaded on board in London in November 1676, had been carefully sorted to draw Gold Coast merchants on deck to negotiate terms of exchange. Trade commenced on 28 February 1677, and thereafter varying quantities and assortments of goods changed hands between the ship's captain, Thomas Woodfine, and his African counterparts. When Woodfine prepared to depart five months later, among the items he had purchased from the African traders were 134 marks, 6 ounces, 15.5 angles of "good Arcaney Gold" (Fig 3.1).[1]

Captive people also had come aboard: like the precious metal, they had been bartered; they had been offered as commodities by African traders who would not, or could not, use gold to buy European goods. One transaction yielded two Perpetuanos (a variety of woolen cloth), three paper Bralls (a variety of Indian cotton), and one sheet in exchange for two persons; another converted seven persons into seven Perpetuanos, six paper Bralls, two sheets, and fourteen knives; a third put four Nittones (Indian cotton), five muskets, and a half a barrel of gunpowder in the possession of a trader who left three persons behind and weighed out three angles to com-

3.1 Account of Slaves aboard the *Sarah Bonadventure*, 1677, T70/1212.

plete the deal. The captives boarded in small groups of only two to eight at a time. But the twenty-two transactions completed over five months of trading there collected one hundred people aboard the *Sarah Bonadventure*—a sizable contribution toward the aggregate known to European slaving captains as a "full complement of Negroes."

The gold taken aboard the *Sarah Bonadventure* was likely to have been contained in a single chest, divided perhaps among seven sacks holding twenty marks each.[2] Given the enormously high value of gold in relation to its volume and weight, the cost for its transport amounted to only a fraction of its purchase price on the African coast. As a result, gold was among the least expensive items to carry in Atlantic shipping lanes in the early modern period.[3]

People stood at the other end of the spectrum, their bulk going a long way toward producing a very different equation. Shipping across the Atlantic "doubled the price of slaves," and this, together with the fact that the same doubling was incurred in the shipment of trade goods from Europe to Africa, meant that overall, "the transportation component of converting goods in Europe into slaves in the Americas comprised approximately three-quarters of the selling price of an African in the Americas."[4] If captive people and gold could be substituted one for the other with relative ease in the African marketplace, they occupied dramatically different positions once ships transported them to markets outside Africa.

As shipping costs were the greatest part of the price of goods transported to overseas markets in the Atlantic world, maritime trade proved commercially viable only to the extent that it was possible to compensate for those costs. Opportunities to buy people cheaply on the African coast contributed one part to the slave trade equation. Achieving unprecedented economies of scale contributed another: crowded ships "translated into large savings based on the number of migrants carried per ton of the vessel." In fact, European migrants would have been less costly to transport than Africans if ships carrying Europeans had been as crowded as slaving vessels. For this reason, David Eltis has insisted that "from the strictly economic standpoint there were strong arguments in support of using European rather than African slave labor."[5]

Like De Marees's earlier observation that the Gold Coast at the turn of the seventeenth century lacked the "multitude of Captives" necessary "to load ships . . . with blacks," the slave traders' talk of "full complements" or "quantitys of blacks" reflected the imperatives that gave the African side of the Atlantic market for slaves its distinctive character[6]—for these phrases articulated the truism on which transatlantic slave trading turned: namely, that the operative unit of the slave ship was not the individual captive person, but rather the aggregate that formed the "complete" human cargo. The slave ship, then, could not proceed on its way toward American retail markets until its decks were crowded with the requisite number of captives.

Slaves became, for the purpose of transatlantic shipment, mere physical units that could be arranged and molded at will—whether folded together spoonlike in rows or flattened side by side in a plane. Because human beings were treated as inanimate objects, the number of bodies stowed aboard a ship was limited only by the physical dimensions and configuration of those bodies. "Transportation history provides no parallel," writes David Eltis, "to the transatlantic slave ship."[7]

"How Many Negroes You Propose to Carry"

For the ship to be capable of accommodating a "full complement," preparations had to begin well before the commencement of a slaving voyage.[8] Responding to an enquiry regarding the use of his ship, the *Barbados Merchant,* for a slaving voyage, the company secretary informed Joseph Bingham on 20 June 1706: "In answer to yo.rs of ye 16th Curr.t I have proposed yo.r ship to ye Roy.ll African Comp.a & they have ordered me to write you to make answer to ye p.ticulars herewith sent you & they will entertaine yo.r ship into their service for Guiney & the West Indias." In addition to "How many Negroes you propose to Carry," the company wanted to ascertain what the exact dimensions of the ship's available deck space were: "what heighth between Decks abast ye Main Mast & allso what heighth from mainmast to foremast, from Plank to Planke w.th ye breadth from inside to inside, & length from ye Bulke head of the Gunroome to ye foremast between Decks."[9]

The cargo hold was the area normally used for storage of goods purchased on a trading voyage, but this narrow, irregularly shaped space below the waterline could not be readily adapted to the needs of the slave ship's human cargo. On average some three hundred or more people were intended to occupy the space of a slave ship. Only the long, flat surfaces formed by the decks were suitable for stowage of so many, and those only after the addition of platforms between decks to double the available surface area.[10]

The slave hold was thus a space specially designed for the transport of captive people. In addition to shackles and bolts, material for constructing platforms was among the items the Royal African Company required shipowners to provide before their departure for the African coast. The company's agreement regarding Bingham's ship stipulated, for example: "The owners [are] to provide ye s.d ship w.th a sufficient Quantity of Deals for platforms for ye Negroes, Shackles, bolts, firewood, a bean room large enough to stow such a quantity of beans as is sufficient for provisions for ye Negroes w.ch is ab.t 20 quarter p. 100 Negroes w.th a sword & fire lock, Muskett & amunition for each of ye ships Comp.a &c."[11]

After several months of correspondence regarding the use of Bingham's vessel, the company had offered a proposal in July 1706 to hire the *Barbados Merchant* "to perform a Voyage from Portsm.o to ye South parts of Guinea & thence to Jamaica." The ship's human cargo was to be 350 slaves "or 50 more if can take them in."[12]

One month later Bingham had accepted the offer, and accordingly the company's Governor had "ordered a Copy of a Charterpartye to be gott ready" before the Committee of Shipping's next meeting. In essence a script outlining how the slaving voyage was to proceed, the "charterparty" was a standard contract stipulating such factors as "the size of the crew, the number of passengers, cargo to be carried on each stage of the voyage, places of lading and discharge and the time to be spent at each, and the freight charges."[13]

Apparently, Bingham was not satisfied with the number of slaves his ship was assigned to carry, for his efforts to amend the charterparty prompted two rounds of further negotiation. The company secretary wrote to notify Bingham on 15 August 1706, "[The company officials] have considered your last proposall and are come to a Resolution that your Ship shall take in 450 Negroes and no more by reason she is a Crank [top-heavy] Ship." Having secured license to carry a hundred more slaves than originally agreed, Bingham appears to have tried to raise the number higher still. In September, the company wrote to Bingham again, acknowledging the "alterations" he had made in the charterparty, but stipulating that "for answer, they agree to take your ship at 450 Negroes certain and no more."[14]

As a ship's physical dimensions were fixed, crowding ever more bodies onto its decks was the only means to extend the limits of its carrying capacity. On more than one level, stretching that capacity to the utmost was key to a slave ship's profitability. Maximizing the size of slave cargoes maintained the rate of return that investors demanded. Moreover, it answered the captain's self-interest, as the greater share of his compensation depended on the number of persons delivered alive to the American market, not the price at which they sold on the market. The contract for the *Barbados Merchant* included the standard provision: "The Captain to have four Negroes by lott out of each one hundred & four for a gratuity provided he take particular care of ye Negroes during ye Voyage & observe the Company's instructions during the Voyage & the Doctor to be allowed by ye Company's agent at Jamaica £12 per head for all Negroes delivered alive at Jamaica upon making account of the Mortallity."[15]

The voyages undertaken on behalf of the Royal African Company before 1714 carried 330 persons on average, or 2.3 slaves per ton. "We calculate he can take 300," Royal African Company officials wrote regarding Robert Groome's impending voyage in command of the 122-ton *Cape Coast Frigate* in May 1701, for instance.[16] The specific equation the company used to make such calculations is not known, but we do know the result. Noting their comparative economic "efficiency," Eltis found that these numbers put English slavers ahead of both Dutch and French competitors in the late-seventeenth and early-eighteenth centuries, for the English ships were carrying "50 percent more slaves per ton and twice as many slaves per crew member" than the others.[17]

Whatever the number of captives a ship was allowed to carry, it was routine to permit and indeed to encourage ship owners and their captains to squeeze more bodies into their human cargoes. Though the *Spanish Merchant* was "freighted" to carry 550, the company agents at Whydah had leave to put ten to twenty more persons aboard if they thought it "convenient" to do so.[18] The company's instructions regarding the *William & Jane* likewise noted that the ship was "contracted to take in 230 slaves and 20 more if you can conveniently put them aboard."[19] And it was with approval that officials in London noted the use of children as filler to top off the cargoes put aboard the company's ships. "We like well yo.r method," the missive to Cape Coast read, "of putting some small boys & girls of 10 years of age and upwards abd. our own ships over & above ye complement we intended them for."[20]

Captives languishing at the Gold Coast littoral in 1702 stood to gain, however, if their departure from the forts landed them aboard the *Royal Africa*. When that ship was dispatched to Cape

Coast Castle in September it carried instructions to pursue an alternate approach to attain the same end that crowding was meant to achieve. The *Royal Africa* was to carry six hundred persons to Barbados. "But if you have near his complement ready," the officials advised, "would not have the ship sent to seek for 50 to 100 Negroes but rather dispatch him directly for Barbados, for more money may be gott tho not so fully slaved by a short voyage then to run the hazard of the inconveniencys of a long one."[21]

When the company sent the frigate *Somers* to Cape Coast for a second slaving voyage in September 1700, it was "judge[d]" that the 240-ton ship would "conveniently take 500 slaves." The vessel had carried an even greater number on its preceding voyage; "but wee fear," the company's London officials explained, "the crouding too many into her might be the occasion of a greater mortality, which wee would study all wayes possible to prevent, and being fewer wee hope you will more readily purchase them and further her dispatch."[22] Only when the human cargo was thought to be large enough to raise the probability of death and the attendant loss of property could the slave ship be deemed "full," its complement of captives "complete."[23]

The vessels used in the English trade before the late eighteenth century were not specifically built to carry slaves. Captains were therefore obliged to design novel ways to organize space aboard their ships to accommodate human cargo. Peter Blake's journal aboard the *James* illustrates how captains transformed the decks of standard merchant ships into quarters meant to stow a "full complement" of captive people.

Small numbers of Africans already had come aboard the *James* when Blake began preparations to put his vessel into full-time service as a slave ship in November 1675. The first step was to divide the space of the vessel's lower gun deck.[24] While anchored off

Anomabu and Agga in late November, Blake sent some crewmen ashore in the ship's boat to cut long wooden poles for "stanchions to make up my bulk head upon ye Gunn Deck." Once in place, this partition would serve as a barrier to "keep our Negroes apart from our white men."[25] Conventions of social hierarchy ordered English life aboard ship no less than they did on land. This space below the main deck was the domain of the crewmen, while their superior officers resided in the more comfortable quarters up above.[26] For the duration of the Atlantic crossing, crewmen and the Africans they held captive would be neighbors in this space belowdecks.

Once the stowage of captives belowdecks commenced, officers required that the hatchways remain covered at all times for the safety of the ship. Yet these three openings cut into the mid-, aft-, and forepart of the main deck, together perhaps with a few smaller openings or "scuttles," were the only means by which air reached the close quarters below. In outfitting a vessel to transport human cargo, it was necessary to keep the hatch openings covered, so as not to thwart security, while still allowing air to flow through to the Africans incarcerated below.

In the seventeenth-century, ship captains engineered a makeshift solution to the problem by making use of the narrow beams that formed the under-support of the decks. Ledges installed across the hatchways formed a makeshift grate that kept the openings secured without impeding the supply of air to the quarters below, while so-called carlings were used to build up "raised borders about the edges of the hatches and scuttles," to prevent water from running down below.[27] Blake undertook this task while anchored off "Amissa" (Amersa), a few miles east of Kormantin, after going ashore accompanied by his carpenter "to cutt wood to make head ledges and Comings" for a grating to "let down the aire among the Slaves."[28]

At this time Blake also commenced the most labor-intensive of the alterations to the ship: construction of platforms to add surface area that would be needed to stow his human cargo. While ashore at Amersa, Blake enlisted the assistance of the local captain, or "Meerine," whose party of workers "cutt me 100 great poles to make stanchions for my platforms."[29] With the ship's lower deck suitably partitioned to separate white from black, its ventilation system in place, and platforms under construction, the *James* was prepared for its role as slave ship.

On 9 January 1676, Blake received orders "to sail for Wyemba [Winneba] and there take in what slaves" the company agent had acquired.[30] The orders disappointed Blake, for having viewed the captives held at both Winneba and Accra already, he hoped to win permission to "goe for Accra and take in those good slaves, because I was afraid," he explained, "of having a parcell of thin slaves from Wyemba."[31] The castle's orders stood, however, and Blake made his way to Winneba.

Once he was there, it would be necessary to feed the African captives that began to board in large numbers, and in this regard Blake's efforts to make his ship ready to receive its human cargo had fallen short. The "furnace," or cooking apparatus, that would be used to boil food for the slaves was damaged, having "burnt out and a great hole in ye bottome," though Blake had repeatedly requested permission to go to Cape Coast Castle "to have my Slaves Furnace sett up" and unload the trade goods that continued to occupy much-needed space in the ship. The requests had been denied, however, and the agent at the castle had sent Blake "from place to place with all ye goods in ye ship." As a result, Blake complained, "I am forced to carry a great part of my water upon my upper deck." As the ship's store of fresh water was consumed, he was hard pressed to find a place to store the empty casks and was resolved, therefore, "to hang them alongst [his] quarters" on both sides of the ship.[32]

Given that a large contingent of African captives was due to come aboard, a solution had to be found immediately. While Blake remained on shore to confer with the company agent at Winneba, his crewmen were busy assembling a makeshift apparatus for preparing the slaves' food. At daybreak on the morning of 11 January, a party of seamen went ashore in the ship's longboat to collect sand "to fill a great square hearth, to make fyer on to boile ye Neagg.rs Furnace," and returned to the ship later that morning with both sand and "40 men slaves." Meanwhile, Blake ordered the other of the ship's two small boats, the pinnace, to bring aboard "as many slaves as she would conveniently carry." Later that afternoon Blake returned to the ship himself, "to see if ye great Furnace would boyle," and on the following morning, "finding our Furnace to boyle very well," Blake went back on shore and ordered the remainder of the slaves to be sent aboard the ship, confident that his jury-rigged setup would enable him to feed the 167 men, women, and children from Winneba in his charge.[33]

The condition of these captives was no better than that of the people Blake had seen several months before. This group being "for ye most part very thin slaves," their emaciated frames told of severe deprivation in the two months or more they had spent incarcerated there. What was more, among those sold as adult males were "severall boys for men," whom the local king had insisted the company take toward payment of a debt.[34] Blake remained for one day after getting this group aboard, "in expectation of more slaves" the king had promised to deliver the following morning, "which he said would be Choice slaves." But the additional captives were not forthcoming, and so before daylight on 14 January, when a favorable land breeze began to blow, Blake unfurled his sails and raised anchor.[35] For some ten days he was forced to rely on the makeshift furnace, not finding opportunity to set up the "Slaves Furnace" until 21 January, when he was able finally to put ashore all of the trade goods from the ship at Cape Coast Castle.[36]

Even with the nearly doubled surface area created by platforms, the lower deck alone could not accommodate a "full complement" of captives. It would be necessary also to make use of the upper deck. With at least 167 slaves aboard already and many more still to come, Blake once again sent ashore for stanchions "to make an end of setting up my platforms upon the Gunn Deck," and also to complete platforms "in the Forecastle."[37] With the forepart of the ship's upper deck occupied by African captives, only the quarter-deck and captain's cabin remained available for Blake and his officers' exclusive use.

Once captives went aboard the slave ship, their management continued to be governed by the alienating agenda of commodification. Captives were segregated by sex in the quarters belowdecks when they came aboard, and it was common to erect barricades to separate men and women during time spent abovedeck as well—a strictly observed policy that reflected the captain's concern to disable normal social relations among the human cargo. Bosman reported that "their Lodging-place is divided into two parts; one of which is appointed for the Men the other for the Women; each Sex being kept a-part."[38] Likewise, according to Barbot, "the men and women are usually separated, the men being placed in the forepart beyond the main mast, and the women towards the stern, with a stout barrier between them, otherwise," he explained, "there would be dreadful confusion."[39] Thomas Phillips acknowledged the difficulty with which captains enforced such efforts at social control. "Tho' we separate the men and women aboard by partitions and bulk-heads, to prevent quarrels and wranglings among them, yet do what we can," he wrote, "they will come together."[40]

"By Degrees and Good Industry"

Captains' aim to increase the volume and hence the profitability of slave cargoes entailed considerable time and a complex coordination of efforts. Of the numerous variables sea captains tried to control, none was more important than time, as the men who succeeded in the business of human trafficking well knew. Both their safe return to European home ports and their proceeds depended on the speed with which they could conclude their business on the African coast. Their task was to obtain the best collection of people the market could offer in a limited window of time. Because this was a market, the contest was competitive between European buyers engaged in an anxious race against time and African sellers, who exploited this and other European dependencies with great finesse.

European buyers came into direct contact with the slave supply system at the Atlantic littoral, where African sellers accumulated captives and determined who would be sold, and when, to nourish the growth of European slave cargoes. Always watching the market carefully, the African owners exploited captives' labor until such time as a visit from a dealer trading directly with European buyers, or from a European factor himself, signaled that the time was right to consign some of the captives at their disposal to the commercial channels leading toward the water's edge. Or perhaps word reached the sellers' ears that a newly arrived slave ship was anchored offshore. In regions that lacked European settlements, African brokers held slaves until European ship captains were ready to begin receiving them aboard their vessels. Even in regions that did host European settlements where captives could be held while awaiting debarkation, African brokers preferred to hold captives until the arrival of European slave ships, in hopes of commanding higher prices.[41]

In the closing decades of the seventeenth century, the victims of Akwamu's expansion in the eastern Gold Coast were the human face of the slave economy. The correspondence of the Royal African Company factors allows us to trace the flow of people, as those reduced to captivity by Akwamu's wars were funneled to the major eastern Gold Coast ports in the closing decades of the seventeenth century; and subject polities were called upon to release people whenever demand was high, such as when several ships were trading in the vicinity of a port at the same time, all anxiously seeking captives to fill their decks.

The Atlantic market's pull on the eastern Gold Coast becomes evident in the disposition of people seized in Akwamu's campaigns against Agona, for instance. The Agona kingdom was a regular target of Akwamu aggression during an eight-month period from January through August 1686—the prelude to Akwamu's defeat of the kingdom in 1688–1689.[42] Though the gold trade was severely damaged by the fighting throughout the period, opportunities to buy captives generally were plentiful. Whereas captives had been "very scarce" in January, by 2 March there was a "good quantity of very good slaves" in the fort at Accra, and the factor was able to put twenty-five men and twenty-one women aboard the slave ship *George* two weeks later.[43]

Captives continued in good supply in the following months. Though "very little gold" had been purchased "because of the war between the Arguines [Agona] and Ahenesa [Akwamuhene Ansa Sasraku]," the factor reported in June, "I have now by me 30 very good slaves," and he was rejecting opportunities to buy more because he did not have sufficient provisions to feed them.[44] On 18 July, twenty-five captives were sent up to Cape Coast Castle, and almost four weeks later another forty-seven were dispatched to the castle. Meanwhile, the Dutch also were buying "great quantities of slaves," and the factor at Accra had been "informed [that] slaves are plenty which cannot be brought here by reason Ahenesa [is] having war with Arguina [Agona]."[45] Captives continued to flow in for the following six weeks, the factor at Accra purchasing at least eighty-six from mid-August to the end of September.[46]

By the end of September 1686, a new round of fighting was under way in the Akwapim hills northeast of Accra. Akwamu had made tributaries of the small polities nestled behind the escarpment and drew heavily on the hill communities to supply the Atlantic market for captive people.[47] "Trade is gone very low again by reason

Ahenesa warring Occrepon [Akropong]," reported the factor at Accra at the end of September, further noting, "Slaves also are gone very scarce."[48] On 21 October Ahenesa reportedly was ready to head into battle. Only ten days later, the news of his victory aroused anticipation regarding the human traffic that was likely to follow. "Ahenesa having beaten Ocrepon will not be long ere slaves and gold will be more plenty, being now very scarce," read the report from Accra.[49]

Sixteen captives were in the fort when the factor at Accra penned his report on 31 October. When he requested additional provisions "for slaves use" one week later, their number had grown to twenty-five. "I know not how suddenly may come a great quantity," he wrote, "they coming daily more and more very good Gold Coast slaves from Ahenesa."[50] Another week passed, and the factor reported, "I have now by me 40 slaves, most men."[51] One week later there was talk that Ansa Sasraku was finally preparing to bring his troops, together with the spoils of their warmongering, back home to the Akwamu capital at Nyanaoase. "Trade is now very dull for gold and little better for slaves," the factor at Accra reported, "which must be expected until the return of the said Ahenesa from the field which I hope will not be long he is daily expected." By the first week of December, more than 105 enslaved men and women had been brought down to the Royal African Company fort at Accra, while others went to the neighboring Dutch fort.[52] In contrast to the steady stream of war captives, very little gold came down from Akwamu. "I suppose," concluded the factor, "[it] cannot be expected before they have discharged themselves of their slaves."[53]

At the end of December there were enough captives in the fort for forty-six men and twenty-one women to be put aboard the slave ship *Dragon*.[54] The surplus of Akwamu captives appears to have been expended at last by the early months of the new year. Having guessed in December that he might be able to purchase "in a month's time maybe 100 or 150" slaves, the English factor offered a different assessment on 1 February. "I cannot tell you how many slaves I could procure in a month's time," he wrote, "in these parts the trade is very dull at present for that commodity and cannot give you the least encouragement."[55]

When there was no specific need to off-load large numbers of war captives, it was the arrival of ships that triggered the flow of people toward the water's edge. In January 1680, the arrival of the hundred-ton *John Bonadventure* at Cape Coast Castle set the machinery in motion. A vessel employed by the castle, the *Isabella,* was already out buying slaves at Allampo and put a parcel of fifty-two captives onshore at the company's fort at Accra. In the meantime, the *John Bonadventure* sailed to windward (west) of the castle in search of a supply of corn.[56] The following month the *Isabella* ferried another fifty-eight captives from Allampo to Accra, and another sloop was dispatched from the castle to buy slaves at Winneba.

The activity continued in March, the *Isabella,* the castle's sloop, and the *John Bonadventure* all being sent out to collect slaves at Winneba and Allampo.[57] Also in March, the company agents at the castle offered "a dashey" of "4 yards scarlett broad cloth and 5 ½ gallons brandy" to one "Attabarba," in the hope that he would "open the trade with Angina [Agona] to bring downe slaves to give Capt. Woodfine the speedier dispatch."[58] The gesture appears to have had the desired effect: seventy-one captives were bartered for goods at the castle in the following month.[59] "Aboard Capt. Woodfine wee have put his full complement of Slaves according to his owne Liking," read the report from agents at the castle dated 20 April 1680.[60] When the ship departed at the end of the month, its human cargo consisted of 560 captives "taken in on the Gold Coast & Alampo."[61]

Details regarding the market for captives at the time the *John Bonadventure* was seeking its cargo on the Gold Coast suggest that

Woodfine's "liking" fell considerably short of ideal expectations. The standard instructions to ship captains called for twice as many men to be put aboard as women and further stipulated that none in obviously poor health or outside the prescribed age limits—"from the age of 15 years not exceeding 40"—were to be accepted.[62] Over against this abstraction of the ideal slave cargo, however, stood the material realities of acquiring sufficient captives to assemble a ship's complement on the African coast. More than half of the adults purchased for the *John Bonadventure* on the castle's account were women, and nearly a quarter of these removed themselves, by death or escape, before the group boarded the ship. The *John Bonadventure*'s cargo was known to fall below prescribed standards on at least two counts: the high proportion of women, and indications of epidemic disease among the captives put aboard.

In fact, the dire condition of some of the captives assembled for the *John Bonadventure*'s cargo was plainly apparent, so much so that agents at the castle removed from the group "noe less then Forty" whose illness was too evident to be ignored. According to Nathaniel Bradley, chief merchant at the castle at the time, it was his policy to take such precautions on the company's behalf. "At their going away if they had Poor & sickly slaves which wee thought would not stand wee have changed them thinking it more for Your Interest that they dye on shoare then that they go away sick & infect the good slaves."[63] When the appearance of ill health was serious enough to suggest the probability of imminent death, captives might thus avoid the slave ship. But it was the fate of many captives, having passed inspection by European eyes trained on the need for a full complement of captive people, to face death amid the terrors of the slave ship.

The qualities that mattered most in the African markets were different from those of greatest concern to buyers in the Americas. The ship captain's most pressing concern was not his captives' qualifications for plantation labor; rather, what mattered most to the ship captain was whether captives would survive their passage aboard the slave ship. The business of the Atlantic market in Africa, in other words, was production not of bonded laborers but of human commodities—units of merchandise that became an acceptable cargo by attaining the desired number and rough demographic specifications.

Given the imperative to acquire an aggregate of bodies in a timely fashion, it was often necessary to approach the assembly of the slave cargo with considerable flexibility. The "lusty" man cost more in the African market for slave exports than his ordinary counterpart, the woman with blemish-free skin drew a higher price than one whose body was marked by smallpox scars, and the "man slave who wanted the first joint of his thumb" could be purchased for three ounces of gold instead of the four ounces paid "per head" for a captive in possession of all ten fingers.[64] On the slave ship's invoice or in the castle's "account" of "shipping slaves," however, all these became commensurate units in the same commercial categories—"men" or "women." Here on the African side of the Atlantic market, the value of the "chain slave" resided in her contribution to the volume of the aggregate. Quality was necessarily subordinate to quantity, which was required for the slave ship's speedy departure.

The imperative for European captains to acquire large numbers of captives in a short period of time put African sellers in a position of considerable advantage. Although European buyers preferred for their cargoes more males than females, the stronger over those weakened by illness and deprivation, those in the prime of adulthood over the very young and elderly, African sellers recognized and exploited the market reality that pressured European buyers to accept whatever was made available to them. Forced to concede to African commercial interests if they wished to "complete" a cargo at all, European buyers accepted women as substitutes for men, the very young and old as substitutes for adults in their prime. In all these ways, the political economy of the slave ship produced a market for captives on the African coast that was markedly indiscriminate.

Company officials in London regularly wrote to their factors on the African coast to complain that the quality of the slaves purchased did not meet the company's standards: the cargoes included too many women, too many "superannuated" or very young people, and worst of all, cargoes where the death rate exceeded the "common mortality" or whose survivors were in a state so pitiful on reaching American markets that agents there suspected the captives must have been noticeably ill when put aboard on the African coast.[65] Likewise, officials at Cape Coast Castle might chide subordinates at the trading factories for buying captives who did not fit the profile agents were charged to produce. The agent at Anomabu, for instance, acknowledged the complaint from the castle that of the thirty persons he sent up to Cape Coast, "4 are mentioned as old" and promised that "for the future shall take great care to buy none but what I shall be well satisfied will answer your expectations."[66] If the recurrent themes in the dialogue between London, Cape Coast Castle, and the factories on the Gold Coast are any indication, though there was consistent pressure to mold slave cargoes in the image metropolitan investors and American buyers considered ideal, the cargoes assembled on the African coast regularly fell short of that standard.

A particular source of dissatisfaction was the appearance of women in numbers greater than the company desired.[67] Women were more valuable than men on the African market for slaves, but women were also easier both to obtain and to dispose of. The productive and reproductive capital they represented was the primary concern of kinship institutions, and women circulated with relative frequency and ease in the exchange networks that framed kinship relations. Moreover, women did not present the threat to security that male captives posed, and as easily as they could be incorporated into urban domestic households or village compounds as wives and agricultural laborers, they could be released at a moment's notice when lucrative opportunity arose. Describing the production of cargoes at the neighboring Bight of Benin, for example, English slaving captain Thomas Phillips reported, "The present king often, when ships are in a great strait for slaves, and cannot be supply'd otherwise, will sell 3 or 400 of his wives to compleat their number."[68]

Bringing men to the coast in large numbers, by contrast, entailed planning and organization. In the aftermath of war, traders regularly marched groups of male captives to the coastal forts; or if ships were on the coast seeking human cargoes, traders happily negotiated directly with European captains. Whereas men appeared in irregular bursts, women were easily corralled for sale to European buyers anxious to "complete" a ship's human cargo.

"Here is no trade come from Quomboe [Akwamu] as yet," the factor at Accra reported in July 1683. "His son and the man which always was our messenger is up in the Country but when it doth come it is all at once." The factor had purchased seven captives "and could have had more," he wrote, "but we stand for one man and one woman, men slaves being very scarce here."[69] Writing to update agents at Cape Coast Castle on his progress buying slaves at Allampo in September 1683, John Groome reported that he had twenty-eight aboard his ketch the *Merchants Adventure:* twelve men, thirteen women, two boys, one girl, "and may purchase more women but I do not forbear because I would have them bring one man with one woman." He would begin the return voyage to the castle when wind and current conditions turned favorable, and he hoped by that time to have "50 or 60 slaves in or more." The local broker from whom he had purchased his first group of captives at Allampo had "sent his men with ye goods up in ye Country for ye purchasing of more slaves, & are not come downe as yett, but I am in hopes," Groome continued, "that this weeke may proove better than ye Rest of the time has." But he closed his missive with a proviso: the African traders here were asking "very high rates" for the captives they offered for sale, "and specially them that are good."[70] Ten days later, the result of his negotiations reflected his earlier warning. The number of captives aboard the *Merchants Adventure* had grown, there now being forty-five aboard the vessel, but, Groome confessed, they were "not according to your desire, for men are verry scarce & especially those that are good."[71] One month later, Hugh Shears offered a similar report of his progress procuring a cargo for the *Cape Coast Brigantine*. At anchor a few miles east of Accra, Shears had purchased eighty-seven captives, of whom there were more women (forty-four) than men (thirty-eight) among the adults.[72]

A large part of the challenge European buyers faced on the Gold Coast in the seventeenth century had to do with prices. Captives could be obtained at lower prices in the neighboring Bight of Benin and in the Bight of Biafra, and European traders' command of maritime technology enabled ships to approach Atlantic Africa as an integrated commercial zone. European investors in slave cargoes relied on the ability to gather information on prices everywhere in Atlantic Africa and to direct their slaving vessels accordingly. African investors did not share that advantage: they could not know the price of human commodities in markets elsewhere on the coast. Eltis has pointed out that "if Africans had sold their slaves on the coast for twice their actual price in the last quarter of the seventeenth century, say, £8 instead of £4, then quite possibly little slave trading would have occurred."[73]

In the Gold Coast in the seventeenth century, however, bullion was available in sufficient quantities to merchants engaged in Atlantic commerce to mitigate European demand for human commodities. The evidence suggests that African merchants were expert at making European buyers pay for the human specimens they most valued and pushing European buyers to take lesser captives in order to realize an affordable cargo. In the absence of data on local prices for slaves, it is not possible to pursue comparative analysis of the domestic and Atlantic export markets. But the advantage African sellers enjoyed in a market shaped by stringent time constraints and fierce competition between and among national groups of European buyers is clear. It appears likely that the astute African broker of human commodities had the potential to sell people in the Atlantic market for a price in excess of the captives' value on the domestic market for slaves.

This, at least, was how European factors viewed the African sellers' power to unload all manner of captives at a profit. A woman "not thought Merchantable" was removed from the *Dorothy & Anna* and "put a Shore" at Cape Coast Castle in September 1715, and subsequently returned to the factor who had purchased her at Anomabu. "I asked advice of severall what I should doe with her and what was Customaraly done with Slaves returned not fitt for the Company's Service," he wrote. "Every one I demanded advice on told me," he continued, "they Sold them where they Could, and that the Gentlemen at Cape Coast did the same, with Sick & bad Slaves they had often at Cape Coast." Accordingly, "the Woman I sold to one Capt. John Green for 48 Gallons Rum," he reported.[74] Likewise, he "sold severall of the sickly Slaves to Capt. Morgan of the *Tunbridge Gally*," according to his report regarding a group of captives too ill to pass muster aboard a Royal African Company ship in January 1721.[75] Only by death, escape, or redemption did captives—even those deemed not "merchantable"—evade the market's grasp.

Although it was possible to fill slave ships at the Gold Coast, the demand for slave exports far outpaced the supply of captive people made available by the local merchant class in the second half of the seventeenth century. Though ships usually could obtain at least some portion of their human freight on the Gold Coast, often months of coasting back and forth among the leeward ports were required to accumulate enough captives to "complete" a cargo. By the 1680s, the Royal African Company, realizing the efficiency of treating the Gold Coast and the Bight of Benin as a single region for slaving, ordered ship captains to obtain what they could at Gold Coast markets and then sail eastward past the Volta River to the ports serving Whydah and Allada in the Bight of Benin, where a seemingly limitless supply of slaves was available.[76] Though some number of vessels departed every year with a cargo procured primarily between Cape Three Points and Allampo, it became increasingly common to "complete" cargoes by pooling captives from the Akan- and Ga-speaking communities of the Gold Coast together with large contingents of Ewe-speaking people obtained from communities that funneled slaves toward the Bight of Benin ports.[77] As a market for people, the Gold Coast came to be a constituent part of a larger integrated whole, comprising the continuous four-hundred-mile stretch of coast from Axim to Whydah.

When the *Edgar* arrived there in January 1681, outfitted to take on a cargo of 320 captives, 32 people were counted among the "Inventory of goods in Cape Coast Castle," including 18 "poore old refuse" men and women, a woman employed in the garden who was "sick of the smallpox," and 10 "very sicke and weake" men and women who had been brought up to Cape Coast from Allampo the previous month.[78] Four "Arda" men (castle slaves) together with 9 women and 2 boys were at the factory at Agga, and no human commodities had been housed at Anomabu and Anishan. Finally, though there were 37 people at Accra, only 8 were men, and 3 of these were "Arda bumboys."[79] Already on the coast when the *Edgar* arrived was Captain Henry Clark in the *Prosperous,* en route to procure his cargo of slaves at Angola, and also the *Mary,* under the command of Captain Robert Smith. Having arrived in November 1680, the *Mary* was to receive its full cargo as well, and she was still taking in slaves when the *Edgar* arrived. When the

Mary finally departed, probably sometime the following month or early in March, more than five hundred persons had compressed themselves between the ship's decks.[80] Following so close on her heels, the *Edgar*'s captain Charles Bowler would find his task procuring a cargo on the coast that much more difficult.

One month after the ship's arrival, thirty captives (ten men, nineteen women, and one boy) were aboard the *Edgar*. The group included the three men, eight women, and one boy put aboard while the ship was sent to gather shells at Amersa, along with perhaps the two men and eight women who had been purchased at the castle during the month of February, and probably also a man who, having run away from one of the company settlements, had recently been taken again.[81] Now Bowler made his way out of the roadstead at Cape Coast Castle, en route to "purchase his complement of slaves at Winneba and along the coast to Allampo."[82]

By 9 March the *Edgar* had reached Winneba, the primary Atlantic outlet for the Agona kingdom.[83] Here, thirteen boarded the vessel, apparently all that remained of the captives available for export at the time, as "all the slaves that was at the waterside" there already had gone aboard the "two English interlopers" also trading in the area. Well aware of the advantage that fell to African sellers when slaving captains were trying to fill their ships, the queen of Agona, sending word that she would come down to the waterside herself, with a parcel of captives to sell, now held the *Edgar* at anchor several days more. But the "great trade for slaves" that was promised never materialized. When the ship departed a few days later, none but those first thirteen had joined the cargo.[84]

As the forty-three captives now aboard the *Edgar* felt the ship under way once more, Captain Bowler set his course for Accra. There, the company agent presented the group of captives he had accumulated, giving the ship's factor "the Choyce of Nineteene Negroe Slaves." Most of these having made a poor visual impression, only a handful boarded the ship, and the factor reported that among this group he "could hardly find Seaven fitt to be putt aboard Shipp." These seven having brought the number of captives aboard to fifty, the *Edgar* put back to sea, now headed for Allampo.[85]

As had been the case at Winneba, there were no onshore settlements, so the ship's factor, James Nightingale, negotiated directly with the local African traders and an official appointed by the king "to fix the price of slaves going on board, one by one, according to sex and age . . . as they are delivered from the mountains."[86] While Nightingale remained onshore, trying to secure agreements with the African merchants against competition from English interlopers as well as Portuguese and Dutch traders (all of whom offered higher prices than he), an assistant, Robert Hollings, stayed aboard the vessel, sending ashore whatever trade goods Nightingale requested.[87]

On 25 March, there were "but one hundred & one negroe Slaves" aboard the ship, which number made up "not one third part of our complement," Bowler complained. Having sent up into the hills to acquire more captives, the Allampo merchants had "promised the rest in five weeks time." There was good cause for concern, however, for when Nightingale had gone ashore to trade, he had discovered that many of his goods were "not vendible." If the officials at the castle did not respond to the current list by sending trade goods he requested, whatever captives might appear would be sold to other ships.[88]

The passage of time was yet another challenge they faced, for in seven days the *Edgar* would enter into a twenty-day "demurrage" period, beyond which time additional freight charges would be levied against the Royal African Company by the vessel's owners if the ship had not yet left the African coast.[89] Nightingale did his best on shore to purchase what he could over the following several weeks, but by 6 April, only thirty additional captives had been added to the group; the *Edgar* now had "not above 135 Negroes aboard." Nonetheless, he remained hopeful. "The people of the Countrey which are gone for Slaves are not come downe . . . Wee doe expect them dayly with a good quantity, and then will doe my indeavour," he wrote optimistically.[90]

Now almost a full week into the ship's demurrage period, it was necessary to decide whether to dispatch the *Edgar* or to keep the vessel beyond the twenty-day window, to try to complete its cargo. Nightingale offered his "small opinion" that if the proper trade goods were sent up from the castle and the vessel was permitted to remain, "[I] do believe by degrees and good industry we may get your ship's complement of slaves or thereabout in six weeks time." Meanwhile, he had sent a parcel of goods not selling well at Allampo back up to Winneba, in hopes that they might procure some slaves there. "I doe assure your Honour and Councills," he wrote, "that I study every way to gitt Slaves for ye Ship."[91]

One week passed, and Nightingale had heard nothing from the castle, but the number of captives in the slave hold had grown slightly, to 140 persons, and Nightingale promised, "We do what we can to procure more with those goods which are vendible."[92] Another two weeks elapsed with no assistance from the castle, and Bowler finally elected to weigh anchor and return to Winneba, where he intended to procure his store of water and leave the coast. Despite the unsatisfactory cargo of trade goods, 140 captives had boarded the *Edgar* during these four to five weeks at Allampo. As the ship set sail, now tacking against the current and prevailing winds, some 200 captive people filled her decks.[93]

On 25 April, the *Edgar* stood off Accra, where word came that a fifteen-man canoe that had set forth from the castle with trade goods and captives to assist the vessel had been lost near Amersa, and nearly all of its passengers, both black and white, drowned. News also arrived that, additional charges to the company notwithstanding, Bowler was ordered to remain on the coast to complete his intended cargo of 320 slaves. As a result, he sailed westward, back to Winneba, where his crew would obtain fresh water to fill the vessel's casks and the officers hoped to find a more favorable market for slaves.[94]

Again, they were disappointed in their efforts. The queen of Agona came down to the coast and promised to pay part of a debt she owed to the Royal African Company, supply pawns for the establishment of an English factory there, and even give "the best of her endeavours" to procure captives for the *Edgar*. But despite her promises, all available slaves went aboard interlopers that lay waiting a few miles offshore on either side of the town.[95] Like most of the local rulers with whom the company traded, the queen had received goods without providing either gold or slaves to pay for them. The company absorbed such debts as a matter of course, as it was necessary to placate local rulers, to ensure the free passage of upland merchants, from whom the bulk of the large quantities of gold came. After nearly three weeks, "no more than 6 slaves" had joined the others in the *Edgar*'s hold.[96] In the meantime, thirty-nine were sent up by canoe from the castle and the factory at Anomabu, of whom two were rejected by Bowler. These brought the number of captives aboard to 243.[97]

The situation aboard ship turned critical at this juncture. Those in the group who had boarded the vessel at Cape Coast Castle had spent more than two months on the ship. The inevitable motion sickness that came with windy weather or riding at anchor in the ocean swells perhaps would have subsided, as the constant rolling and creaking of the vessel became familiar.[98] Now, however, the smallpox virus was spreading in the hold, and already seven had died.[99]

Meanwhile, the captain had "not above 4 months provisions left" for his crewmen, and concern regarding the ship's store of provisions for the slaves was mounting, as well.[100] A hogshead of "negro brandy" had been lost, and Bowler had been forced to throw a large portion of the "negro bread" overboard, "it being old bread when bought in England . . . and not fit for use." The loss of the brandy particularly distressed the captain, who anticipated the great need that would arise during the long Atlantic passage, for it was necessary to dull the slaves' senses against their pain and anguish, and to foster an illusory sensation of warmth against the damp and chill of the sea. "There is an absolute necessity for a recruite of Brandy for the Negroes," Nightingale wrote on the captain's behalf, "without which if wee depart the Coast it may be the loss of many of our Negroes in the voyage."[101]

Having weighed all these factors, Bowler announced that unless the company could assist him in procuring the rest of his cargo, he was determined to quit the African coast with those already aboard. The two canoes sent to assist the *Edgar* had depleted the store of captives at the castle, and only four men and nine women remained in chains at Cape Coast at the end of May.[102] Nor were the trading factories able to supply him. On 25 April, the factor at Accra had reported that no new slaves had been purchased there, "but what you left are still remaining."[103] The factor at Anomabu, following orders to send what captives he held to Winneba, had already supplied seven of the slaves sent up by canoe in May.[104]

Some captives were available at Winneba and Allampo, but the *Edgar* lacked the proper assortment of goods to trade successfully at either market. The *Edgar* was laden with a supply of "sayes," but the textiles required to do business at Winneba were "broad Tapseeles," "Brawles," and "Sheets," while at Allampo the "Tapseeles" together with "long clothes" were popular. Neither did the vessel have the "bright Musquetts" that also were in demand at Winneba, or the cowrie shells needed to advance trade at Allampo.[105]

Though a speedy departure might preserve lives (including those of the ship's captain and crew), leaving the coast altogether was not a viable option, for it would indicate failure to comply with one of the most important provisions in the contract that bound the ship's captain, its owners, and the Royal African Company in a relationship of mutual obligation. Departure at this juncture would mean the captain had not managed to procure a "complete" cargo. His protests silenced, Bowler agreed to pursue the alternative and prepared to proceed two hundred miles farther east to the company's factory at the Bight of Benin.[106] On 20 May, Bowler left Winneba and headed back down to Accra to deposit the remains of his Gold Coast trading cargo and take aboard whatever captives might appear in the three days he expected to be there.[107] By this point, eight men and eleven women had died among the 252 persons taken aboard. When the *Edgar* set sail again, it carried 233 captives who had been turned into commodities in the Gold Coast market.[108]

The first small contingent had boarded the *Edgar* in February, at the beginning of the Harmattan season, when winds blowing down from the Sahara Desert produced particularly hot, dry conditions on the coast. Even during this time of year, however, the night always brought cool air. A century later, an eighteenth-century slave ship captain, Robert Norris, would obliquely acknowledge the extremes of temperature—whether cold at that point or the excessive heat characteristic of a crowded hold—in observing that "when a Ship had only Half its Complement of Cargo on Board, those Negroes then there lay as close to each other, by Choice, as afterwards in a Case of Necessity." Those confined aboard the *Edgar* during the weeks before the vessel was crowded with captives, therefore, may have found it useful at times to huddle close, even next to a stranger, in search of warmth against the damp, drafty chill of the slave hold.[109]

As their number had increased during these three months, however, the heat generated by the growing number of bodies, together with the dry heat of the Harmattan season, made conditions in the hold increasingly difficult. Every new delivery of captives added to the effluvia of sweat, vomit, urine, and excrement that painted the decks where the captives lay; each new body required space where now none was to be had. Overwhelmed already by their collective number, the slaves strained to receive what breeze was produced by the vessel's forward motion, as Bowler proceeded along the coast toward Allada, "wanting 87 slaves" to complete the population of that stifling world.[110]

Aided by the eastward flow of the current and prevailing winds, a ship could reach the Bight of Benin from Accra in three to four days.[111] When the *Edgar* arrived, rebuilding of the company's factory at Offra (adjacent to Jakin) was almost complete, after a fire in March had destroyed much of this waterside town where the company conducted the majority of its trade with the Allada kingdom.[112] The new factory, one of the factors boasted, included a "very secure Trunck" in which to store goods and collect captives for export.[113] Twenty-two captives were sent from the nearby factory at Whydah on 7 July. Assuming that this shipment was sent to help bring the process to a close, the *Edgar* probably was ready to depart no later than the end of the month. The company's factor at Offra reported in his August accounts that he had "dispatched Capt. Bowler from here with 87 slaves according to your order." At last the *Edgar* held a quantity of people deemed sufficient for it to begin the ocean crossing to an American destination.[114]

The annual loss of 1,500–2,000 persons to the slave trade in the last decades of the seventeenth century could hardly have seemed demographically significant in a Gold Coast population estimated to have numbered over a million.[115] But those who inhabited the waterside towns where the business of slave trading was conducted must have looked on warily, wondering what might develop out of this change in direction of slave traffic across the littoral. The demands of the slave ship's political economy established the rhythm of incarceration at the littoral, and that relationship was not lost on the captives themselves. They observed the regular arrival of new prisoners in the coastal factories, the disappearance of those who died or escaped, and periodically, the departure of those who were led out by the castle slaves and never returned again—the last being those selected to board one or another slave ship waiting offshore.

"6000 Slaves Yearly, If They Can Be Gott"

Events in England, America, and the Gold Coast contributed toward a notable shift in the rhythm and the geography of the market for captives at the turn of the eighteenth century. In England, advocates of free trade began to gain ground in their efforts to dismantle the Royal African Company's monopoly on trade with Africa. After 1698, any and all English traders were free to mount voyages to the African coast, provided they paid a 10 percent duty on the value of their outgoing cargo of trade goods.

Noncompany vessels trading in violation of the monopoly—interlopers—had long been a regular presence on the African coast; with this first step toward formal erosion of the company's privileges, "10 percent men" began to appear on the African coast in large number. Joining the fast-growing number of English ships seeking human cargoes was an increasing array of Dutch, French, Portuguese, and Brazilian merchants, all responding to the burgeoning demand for labor in the American colonies. New gold mines in the Minas Gerais region of Brazil, cane fields spreading to all corners of the Caribbean basin, tobacco fields in Virginia, and rice swamps in the Carolina low country contributed to an overall trend of ever-expanding colonial production and the attendant demand for steady supplies of cheap, servile labor.

No African region was more firmly tied to the Atlantic market at the turn of the eighteenth century than the Gold Coast. Though societies in no fewer than eight distinct regions of coastal Africa regularly received merchandise from European ships, analysis of the cargoes assembled for export to African markets paints a strikingly skewed picture of the distribution of European goods. According to Eltis, "at least two-thirds of all merchandise arriving and leaving sub-Saharan Africa in the second half of the seventeenth century passed through the Gold Coast."[116] When gold deposits that had for centuries supplied the world market for bullion along trans-Saharan and trans-Atlantic routes began to dwindle by the turn of the eighteenth century, the incentive to respond to the fast-growing demand for captive people was powerful.

The Gold Coast was chief among Atlantic African regions that responded to the slave ships plying the coast in ever-larger numbers. Whereas the company agents had struggled to maintain a steady flow of captives in the last quarter of the seventeenth century, officials in London were writing to agents at Cape Coast in May 1699 with these instructions: Be prepared to provide for "our ships, and ships we take to freight, which we compute may be for 5 to 6000 Slaves yearly, if they can be gott."[117] Similarly, the chief factor at Cape Coast reported in February 1706 "that 10,198 Slaves have been purchased in 2 years & 6 Months."[118] Stiff competition from "10 percent ships" occasionally prompted the Royal African Company to pursue its former practice of sending ships to the Bight of Benin to round out cargoes that agents had begun to assemble on the Gold Coast.[119] But the enormous rise in the volume of captive people departing from the region after 1700 suggests that it was possible to fill many, many, ships with human cargoes there in the first quarter of the eighteenth century.[120]

The concentration of political and military power in Asante brought the threat of saltwater slavery to new communities in the central and western hinterlands of the Gold Coast. The changing political geography was reflected in the patterns of Atlantic captivity. At that point people began to appear for sale in those same central and western Gold Coast outlets that had put the greater part of the region's gold exports into Atlantic circulation in the preceding century. The flood of traffic in human commodities now shifted to such outlets as Anomabu and Dixcove—ports that had never been a site of mass slave departures in the preceding century. "We are informed that the chief trade of the 10% men for rum is at Annamabo and that from thence they slave most of their vessels," read a missive from company officials in London that concluded with this directive: "We would have you take that place into consideration that it be supplied with proper persons and plenty of rum to gain that trade and to purchase for our acc.ts all the negroes that is there to be had."[121] By this time the sellers were largely traders from Asante, and among the captives were people from Denkyira and other polities that had come under Asante's dominion.[122]

Drawing from a store of tobacco to purchase two men on 29 January 1712, an agent at Cape Coast Castle put the facility's account for "shipping slaves" in debt to the account for "Port[uguese] Tobaccoe" in the amount of six ounces of gold. On 26 April, gunpowder exchanged for one boy made the account for "shipping slaves" beholden to the account for "powder" in the amount of one ounce, fourteen ackies of gold. Four days later the "shipping slaves" account became indebted directly to the account for gold by the one mark and four ounces given in exchange for four men added to the castle's stock of slaves "in chains." Such were the transactions documented on the left-hand, or debit, side of the "shipping slaves" ledger for the year 1712, where factors recorded the exchanges that brought people into the castle's prison. For every captive acquired, one or more "accounts" lost value, by giving up something against which people were exchanged. People, tobacco, gold, and gunpowder, all mutually exchangeable against one another, were able to pass smoothly across the transactional lines that separated one account from another. Having begun with a balance of 1 man, 6 women, 1 boy, and 1 girl, in the "shipping slaves" account on 1 January, the account shows that seven months of transactions brought the number to 443 captives as of 1 September: 226 men, 111 women, 78 boys, and 28 girls (Fig. 3.2).[123]

As the "debt" owed by the "account of chain slaves" grew, the human collective swelled, one body at a time, until its size reached the requisite number—250, 400, 650—to fill the space of a slave ship. Only once that aggregate of captive people became a "full complement of Negroes" did it enter the right-facing, or credit, side of the ledger. Now moving out of the castle as a group, shipping slaves paid off their "debt" to the various accounts that had been drained by their purchase. Accordingly, when a large contingent left Cape Coast Castle on 30 June 1712, its departure caused the "shipping slaves" column to be credited by the company's general account, for 300 persons "Shipt on board *Pindar* Gally."[124]

Lifted from the ledger's pages and entered into the company's profit and loss books in London, the numeric values in the ledger were the raw data that supplied the official account of the slave trade. From the ledger's figures metropolitan investors evaluated the company's success and the Board of Trade compiled its reports. The numbers did more than record quantitative values, however. As important as their empirical content is the form and structure of the ledgers, invoices, and other instruments of accounting that documented the traffic in human commodities.[125]

The ledger's double-entry pages and the neat grid of the invoice gave purposeful shape to the story they told. Through their graphic simplicity and economy, invoices and ledgers effaced the personal histories that fueled the slaving economy. Containing only what could fit within the clean lines of their columns and rows, they reduced an enormous system of traffic in human commodities to a concise chronicle of quantitative "facts." Thus, Mary Poovey writes, "like the closet, the conventions of double-entry bookkeeping were intended to manage or contain excess."[126] Instruments such as these did their work, then, while concealing the messiness of history, erasing from view the politics that underlay the neat account keeping.

The slave traders (and much of the modern economic literature on the slave trade) regarded the slave ship's need for volume as a self-evident "fact" of economic rationalization: the Board of Trade's reports, the balance pursued in the Royal African Company's double-entry ledgers, the calculations that determined how

3.2 Account of "Shipping Slaves," Cape Coast Castle, 1712, T70/664.

many captive bodies a ship could "conveniently stow," the simple equation by which an agent at the company's factory at Whydah promised "to Complie with delivering in every ten days 100 Negroes."[127] But the perceptions of the African captives themselves differed from the slave trader's economies of scale and rationalized efficiency of production. What appears in the European quantitative account as a seamless expansion in the volume of slave exports—evidence of the natural workings of the market—took the form of violent rifts in the political geography of the Gold Coast. People for whom the Atlantic market had been a distant and hazy presence with little direct consequence for their lives now found themselves swept up in wars and siphoned into a type of captivity without precedent.

4

The Anomalous Intimacies of the Slave Cargo

If the operative unit of the slave trade was the slave cargo, the constitutive element of that cargo was the single captive body. In this sense, the slave trade produced something besides the generic aggregate of human commodities described in the slave trader's ledger. Commodification did not change the basic fact that residing in the slave dungeon of the castle and aboard the coasting ships were individual subjects. Each person pulled onto the slave ship embodied a social history: one or more distinctive places that were called "home" and an indelible web of relationships comprising ties with immediate family and the extended network of kin. A collective of people suddenly torn from participation in these and other domains of social life, the slave cargo was, necessarily, a novel and problematic social configuration.

Atlantic commodification meant not only exclusion from that which was recognizable as community, but also immersion in a collective whose most distinguishing feature was its unnatural constitution: it brought strangers together in anomalous intimacy. A product of violence, the slave cargo constituted the antithesis of community.

How did captives negotiate the unfamiliar social landscape of the slave ship? In essence, this question about group identity has most commonly been directed toward the end of the ocean crossing—

toward relations that developed in the terrain of New World slavery.[1] But we cannot adequately frame questions about who Africans
became in diaspora without first asking who they understood themselves to be before falling victim to Atlantic dispersal. Definitive answers to these questions, of course, are not possible in the absence
of captives' own representations of self and community. Piecing together evidence drawn from the accounts of contemporary European observers and recorded indigenous traditions makes it possible, however, to weave together some notion of the kinds of
affinities and fault lines that shaped the social landscape of the Gold
Coast, and therefore also the unique social tapestry of the slave
cargo. Examining how the peoples of the Gold Coast approached
language, ethnicity, and cultural practice, and how the social con-
figurations created by Atlantic commodification challenged those
norms, helps define the boundaries of the captives' group identity.

"Of Several Nations & Languages"

For their part, ship captains and European agents in African and
American ports well understood that the cargoes they assembled
exhibited varying degrees of social and ethnic complexity. Indeed,
traders were acutely aware that their well-being depended, at the
very least, on awareness of the political dimensions of ethnicity
among the persons placed in their possession. Aboard the *America,*
for instance, unusually acute ethnic division appears to have been
implicated in both an attempted shipboard uprising and its ultimate
defeat. Sent to obtain a cargo of slaves from the Gambia River, the
ship's captain, John Brome, sailed from the region in April 1693 en
route to Jamaica with 461 captives on board: 421 of these came
from trading networks developed by English factories along the
Gambia River; the remaining 40 had been captured during an English assault on French trading posts at Gorée Island, situated some
two hundred miles to the north, and Saint Louis, another two hun-

dred miles beyond it, in the mouth of the Senegal River.[2] As the vessel was preparing to leave the English fort at Gambia, the factor there reported "an insurrection amongst Bromes Negroes," in which "the Jellofes [Jolofs] rose" and "the Bambaras sided with the Master."[3]

The term "Bambara," which entered the slaving lexicon of the region in the late seventeenth century, designated "interior people" (probably Malinke-speaking) who reached the coast via the Soninke trading state Gajaaga and are likely to have been the constituents of the *America*'s cargo assembled at the Gambia River. The Wolof-speaking peoples of the Jolof kingdom, a coastal state situated in the well-watered lands just south of the Senegal River, were important partners in Afro-European commercial networks throughout the slave-trading era, and as such they never figured prominently in slave exports after that region's contribution to the Atlantic traffic in people peaked in the sixteenth century.[4] It is quite possible, in fact, that the rebels identified as "Jellofes" aboard the *America* had been domestic slaves employed at Gorée and Saint Louis, rather than captives held there to await export.

At the other end of the spectrum was the *Ferrers,* whose captain, a first-time commander of a slaving vessel, put in at Cape Coast Castle in 1722 boasting of the "good fortune" he met with in obtaining a cargo, having "purchased near 300 Negroes in a few Days, at a place called Cetre-Crue," on the Windward Coast. When the *Ferrers* arrived, the coastal people of the town had just completed a successful military assault on an enemy inland polity.[5]

His seemingly fortuitous timing gave the captain "the opportunity of purchasing a great many of the Captives at an easy rate. For the Conquerors were glad to get something for them, at that instant, since, if a Ship had not been in the Road, they would have been obliged to have killed most of the Men-Captives, for their own Security." On hearing the captain's story, veteran slaving captain William Snelgrave cautioned the novice. "Understanding from him, that he had never been on the Coast of Guinea, before, I took the liberty to observe to him, 'That as he had on board so many Negroes of one Town and Language, it required the utmost Care and Management to keep them from mutinying.'" Worse yet, though the captives' staple diet consisted of rice, the captain had not purchased any of that commodity while on the Windward Coast, and he was now unable to come by anything like a sufficient quantity on the Gold Coast. Months later, when he reached Jamaica, Snelgrave received word that the slaves aboard the *Ferrers* had indeed staged a revolt, one that had taken the ship captain's life as well as the lives of eighty captives ten days following their departure from the African coast. Undeterred by their losses, the captives went on to attempt a rebellion on two separate occasions between the vessel's arrival in Jamaica and the cargo's sale to local planters.[6]

Between these two extremes—the *America* representing a sharply drawn ethnic fault line aboard ship, the *Ferrers* representing ethnic affinity within the narrow compass of a single town—could be found most cargoes assembled in Atlantic Africa's eight major slave-exporting regions, including the Gold Coast. All the regions that exported people in the Atlantic market—Senegambia, Sierra Leone, the Windward Coast, the Gold Coast, the Bight of Benin, the Bight of Biafra, West-Central Africa, and southeast Africa—encompassed a plurality of ethnicities and speech communities. Some were more ethnically or linguistically heterogeneous than others, and in most the presence of powerful states figured heavily in their capacity to supply slaves in the first place. But in none of these regions did states yet correspond to national bodies in the eighteenth century.[7] And although it is true that most ships obtained their entire cargo from only one or two ports, an equally important point is precisely that these were ports: collection sites, central places to which goods—in this case, people—flowed from afar and were collected for shipment.[8]

Cargoes traveled from African to American ports bearing labels derived from the regional place names on the European map of Africa. Ships departing from the Gambia River carried "Gambian" slaves, while those from what modern historians now call West-Central Africa were described by the generic rubric "Angolans." Akin to a clothing tag that reads "made in the Gold Coast," this deliberately vague bit of information was all prospective buyers needed to know. But as they reflected a European rather than an African geography, the labels that attached to slave ships as they maneuvered into the transatlantic shipping lanes obscured the diversity actually represented in the cargoes they carried.

With regard to the Gold Coast, the regional system of supply enabled slave traders to "complete" cargoes by drawing from a stretch of territory along the coast that followed the east-west geography of port towns and their corresponding hinterlands, from Cape Three Points (the western border of the "Gold Coast" proper) as far as the Volta River, two hundred miles to the east. This, coupled with the fact that in the seventeenth century many cargoes whose production began on the Gold Coast were completed at ports in the Bight of Benin, meant that during this period, "Gold Coast" cargoes regularly comprised multiple ethnicities and often many linguistic and cultural threads as well.

Cargoes assembled at Gold Coast ports exhibited a diversity that can be measured by reference to the distinct languages represented among the slaves. Given that the slavers drew men and women from the length of the Gold Coast littoral, and in many cases from the Bight of Benin, the presence of three and sometimes four different major languages can be assumed. Two dialects of Akan were spoken along a hundred-mile stretch from Axim to Kormantin (the Anyi-Baule dialect from Axim as far as Shama, the Twi dialect from there to Kormantin). Guan—the language of the region's pre-Akan settlers—remained dominant around Winneba and Beraku, as well as among communities such as Latebi, in the Akwapim hills behind Accra.[9] Ga was the language of the coastal Accra region, and closely related Adangbe was spoken by coastal communities just to the east at Ningo and Allampo. Captives from communities located on either side of the Volta River added Ewe-speakers to the mix; and those coming through the major Slave Coast ports at Whydah, Offra, and Jakin contributed Aja, Fon, and other variants of Gbe to the languages heard aboard ships like the *Edgar*.[10]

Many of the captives that Akan-speaking traders from Akwamu sold into the Atlantic market were a by-product of the state's depredations against such small hill polities as Latebi, so Guan was probably the language spoken by those whom the factor at Accra purchased in 1693, for example. Describing social complexities that were plain to those responsible for the day-to-day work of slave trafficking, the factor stationed there explained: "The slaves we buy here are not all Quamboers [Akwamus] but I know they are natives not far from thence altho they speak another lingua. However," he continued, getting to the fundamental point, "they do not cost the Company £4 sterling per head which the Captains are allowed for Whydah negroes."[11]

It was thus that the cargo put aboard the *Coast* frigate elicited the following complaint upon the arrival of the ship in Barbados in February 1686. "Those . . . by you stild [styled] good Gold Coast negroes we here found not to be so," the company agent wrote, "but of several nations and languages as Alampo the worst of Negroes, Papas & some of unknown parts & few right Gold Coast negroes amongst them."[12] By the latter term the agents referred to those known to American buyers as "Coromantis" and as Akan-speakers distinguished from others by language.[13] If the *Coast* stood out among astute American buyers for its near-absence of "right Gold Coast negroes" evidence indicates that, on the whole, the group aboard this ship was more typical than not.

When the Asante state entered into the orbit of the Atlantic market in the eighteenth century, and what had been a modest tributary became a fast-moving torrent of people that could be culled to make up slave cargoes at the coastal ports, Asante's reach into its northern hinterland reconfigured the slave ship's ethnic profile. In the absence of the kind of documentary material for the earlier period, it is not possible to map those historically shifting contours in detail, but some sense of the ethnic politics of captivity can be discerned in European observations. A group of Asante merchants came to the Royal African Company's fort at Komenda in August 1715, for instance, with the news that the "great many more" traders who were yet on their way "have abundance of both gold & teeth but no slaves, what they have caught in their last battel with Gingebea, a countrey beyond Ashantee, being so very maugre & lean that are not as yet able to undergo the fatigue of so farr a journey to be vendable when come here."[14] As the "Gold Coast" from which captives departed in 1715 was a place different from that of a few decades earlier, so too were the social contours of the cargoes they constituted. The trajectory of historical change in the region thus contributed additional layers of complexity to the diaspora of captives from the region.

Identifying the ethnic composition of the Gold Coast peoples raises still further questions. What meaning did ethnic labels actually have in people's daily lives? At what level(s) of social and political organization did "identity" reside? Here again, contemporary European representations of the region's geography offer a useful point of departure. Europeans defined their "Gold Coast" by mapping it, marking the details deemed relevant to the European agenda of commercial expropriation: which people had gold and which did not; which were known to steal gold from merchants seeking to trade with Europeans at the coast and which were reliable partners in economic exchange; and so on. Cartographic representations of what Europeans needed to know about the region's politico-economic landscape provide a useful framework for exploring questions about the socioethnic landscape of the Gold Coast.[15]

One of the earliest extant European maps of the region is a 1629 Dutch rendering of "the Regions of the G[old] C[oast] in Guinea." Its layout defined spatially by forty-three *landschapen* (territorial units), the map told its viewers that the territory called Aquemboe stood adjacent to the territory called Akim or Great Acanij; that the inhabitants of the former were "Thievish people" but those of the latter were "Very delicate people and rich in slaves"; and that abutting "Akim or Great Acanij" was the territory called simply Acanij. "Here," the map's notation explained, "live the most principal merchants who trade gold with us."[16]

Gold Coast historian Ray Kea has interpreted the Dutch term *landschapen* as "a Dutch rendering of two Akan terms: *oman* (in the plural, *aman*), which refers to political units, and *afamu*, which refers to geographical ones." The Gold Coast on this map, then, comprised polities or states *(aman)* whose limits were neatly defined by corresponding territorial boundaries. Comparing this map with two others, one drawn in 1602 and another prepared around 1720 (but dated 1746), Kea has observed that all but two of the territorial units depicted on the later map are found also on the 1629 map, and many also appear on the earliest of the three. Through this correspondence, "the spatial and historical continuity of political and geographical units over a period of 170 years (1550–1720) is clearly affirmed," writes Kea. Indeed, he continues, the three maps "indicate a historical and spatial continuity of towns, and, by extension, of settlement systems, both on the coast and in the interior."[17]

But if indeed the boundaries of political authority corresponded neatly to geographic boundaries, did these correspond in turn to the other varied elements of ethnic belonging that define group identity? In other words, to what extent did states (such as Wassa, or Acquemboe, or Acanij) correspond to ethnic groups, and if so, to which people did such neatly correlated social-political-geographic identities extend? Who among the inhabitants of the place called

Bonnoe identified themselves exclusively or primarily as "the Bonnoe" people? To put it somewhat more abstractly, what complex factors shaped the relationship between place and people—correspondence to a speech community, a ruling group, a community of original settlers, a recent migration, displacement and assimilation by way of enslavement?

The nation-state, with its posited correspondence of social, political, and territorial boundaries, was emerging at this time as Europe's approach to the problematic interplay of identity, place, and assent to political authority; but as the literature on early modern Europe continues to make ever clearer, there the nation-state turned on correspondences as much imagined as real, produced as much by coercion from above as by processes from below.[18] It is no surprise that viewed through another lens, a different geography for the peoples of the Gold Coast can be discerned from the one mapped by narrow European interest in the region's "subterraneous treasures."[19]

Invisible to Europeans until the unfortunates appeared at the littoral to be sold, the anonymous thousands who came together aboard slave ships had inhabited a social landscape whose contours we must attempt to map, even if only in rudimentary fashion. Of greatest concern here is not which places possessed gold and which did not, but rather who occupied this landscape from which captive people were expelled to fill the holds of European ships, and how did those inhabitants define themselves? Stories of origin provide a means for prying open another window onto the region's social landscape.

"Who Are You?"

Among the seemingly nonsensical things Dutch trader Willem Bosman heard when he visited the Gold Coast at the turn of the eighteenth century were stories about "first Men" who "came out of Holes and Pits."[20] In Asante tradition, Ankyewa Nyame, the original ancestress of the royal Oyoko clan, is remembered to have appeared in the forest country that became the Gold Coast from the sky: let down by "a long gold chain [that] descend[ed] from heaven to the earth."[21] Part of the narrative repertoire through which eighteenth-century Akan-speaking communities articulated their historical consciousness (one that has continued into the twenty-first century), stories featuring ancestors who emerged from holes in the ground or descended from the sky, can be understood as accounts of historical processes recounted in mythic form.[22] Stories such as these can be understood, in other words, as "dramatic ways of conveying very important information."[23] They illuminate something of the social life underlying the political geography of the Gold Coast, for they reflect collective consciousness of the role genealogy and kinship played in shaping the region's social and ethnic history.[24]

In both their eighteenth-century and modern iterations, the traditional histories conveyed, among other things, claims to the status of indigenous settlers. The Oyoko, that is, distinguish their own historical presence in the region from that of other Akan-speaking groups. Claiming to be the primordial settlers of a designated site, the Oyoko define themselves as a group whose history begins here, in this place. Other groups are defined, necessarily, as subsequent arrivals. They are remembered, that is, as overland migrants—people who came on foot, from some other place. As the Oyoko claim to have ties to no other place than this one, they remember that their ancestress Ankyewa Nyame did not migrate to the forest region that became the Gold Coast from some other place; rather, she simply appeared. The stories of the Oyoko clan thus record that she came from the sky "because they have nowhere else to say that [she] came from."[25]

Stories such as these recall the origin of the matriclans and the matrilineal system of descent common to the region's Akan-speaking groups (in this case, specifically the clan that later became associated with possession of the golden stool of Asante). Among Akan-speaking groups, the matriclan was one of three levels of kinship organization that structured the individual's relationship to arenas of social and politico-economic power, the matriclan *(abusua kɛsɛɛ)* being the largest. The other two were the matrilineage *(abusua)*, and the lineage segment *(ɔyafunu koro)*.[26] Thus, every person was integrally bound, in the first instance, to an extended family, and in the second instance, to a matrilineage *(abusua)*, the institution that "functioned throughout much of Asante history as 'the highest level of effective social organization.'" Hence T. C. McCaskie's observation that the matriclan was becoming "vestigial" by the seventeenth century. "The 'big lineage' or matriclan *(abusua kɛsɛɛ)*," writes McCaskie, "was an organizational unit appropriate in scale for the effective mobilization of the massive labour inputs required by the formidable economic tasks of the fifteenth and sixteenth centuries—clearing the forest and initiating agriculture." By the turn of the seventeenth century, however, settled agricultural society was well established and the once high demand for labor began to recede. "As a result," McCaskie goes on to explain, "the much more restricted matrilineage *(abusua)* came to replace the matriclan as the appropriate unit of subsistence organization. The matriclan—having been supplanted in its primary economic function—over time became vestigial."[27]

The matriclan in early Akan societies was an institution that imposed the temporal thread of kinship ties on relationships that had no actual basis, or only a limited one, in shared genealogy; the function of the matriclan was to facilitate the integration and social cohesion of societies shaped by incorporation on a large scale of immigrant strangers. Thus, groups that had been brought together through recent migration (movement in space) were fictively integrated as though embodying the genealogical integrity of continuity over time.[28] To put it more simply, the traditional histories remember the role genealogy—the reach of blood and kinship ties through time—played in legitimating territorial claims to authority in the spatial terrain of the region. These traditions articulate the principle that genealogy was an important vector of ethnic distinction within the cultural landscape of the Akan-speaking peoples: genealogical ties to primordial settler groups were an important legitimizing determinant of territorial authority in the present and therefore constituted a salient thread of ethnic identity.

The story of Ankyewa Nyame commemorates the cycles of migration in which Akan-speaking peoples gradually blanketed the forest belt that became the Gold Coast. Her descent from the sky first brought Ankyewa Nyame to a site called Asiakwa (in present-day Akyem Abuakwa), but this place was not to her liking. "'I only mistakenly come here. Here is not the place I mean to come,'" she announced, and then "disappeared and went to a district called Asumyia Santimansū (Asantemanso). And there certain [people] from the ground appeared near her and the 10 family Royal [all] also appeared from the ground in different parts."[29]

Ankyewa Nyame's story also calls to mind the role of kinship and clan membership in the historical production of politically meaningful ethnic differences. Subsequent to the establishment of her people at Asantemanso, for example, Ankyewa Nyame was approached by another group also claiming to be Oyoko. The encounter is narrated thus: "When these Yukun [Oyoko] came near to her she asked one 'Who are you?' and they said we are [part] member of your Yukun: and she told them 'if you are Yukus, then I am Yuku-Kor-Kor-Kon, i.e., I am more Yuku than you.'"[30]

Significantly, it is not the dispersal and settlement of the Akan that is described in Ankyewa Nyame's story, but rather that of the matriclan, "the Oyoko." And the matriclan itself is in turn remembered as an institution comprising lineage segments linked over spans of time and space in relationships of conflict and competition no less than in amiable articulations of shared genealogy. The oral traditions thus illustrate the antiquity of kinship institutions (matriclans, or *abusua*) that sustained vertical social integration through genealogical time, the emergence of centralized territorial institutions (the polity, or *oman*) that aimed at horizontal social integration across space, and the historical interplay between the two.[31]

Ankyewa Nyame was the founding ancestress of a royal clan (Oyoko), and thus her story (and other Asante stool traditions) served the same political agenda as did the ideological underpinnings of the European nation-state: their function was precisely to posit (or enforce) the orderly integration of distinct institutions of belonging and axes of political power. In the case of Ankyewa Nyame's story, the narrative posits an easy correspondence between the authority and affinities that derived from allegiance to the institution of the matriclan (the idiom of kinship) and those which derived from allegiance to the institution of the state, or *oman* (the idiom of kingship).

To the elite, then, fell the privilege of exerting some measure of direction and control over migratory movements. In the royal clan traditions, every move is undertaken by a coherent body—a collection of nuclear families, for example—and corresponds to a remembered moment in time. It is thus that the migrations of the elite can easily be woven into a narrative describing subjects whose movements are genealogically integrated in time, and tracing connected arcs of dispersal (first "we" came "here," then "we" went "there").

It was precisely this integration of clan- and state-derived bases of identity that was not possible for the nonelite in Akan societies. Indeed, for most, it was precisely in the contested interplay between these that identity resided and therefore could find articulation in any number of contingent forms: migrations produced by the violent upheavals of warfare, refugee displacement, or slavery, for example, sundered the political significance of kinship ties and the thematic emphasis on the genealogical thread of time and foregrounded instead identities rooted more firmly in the spatial relations of residence. Therefore, for the commoners and slaves history and genealogy were not particularly reliable or useful anchors of identity. Identity involved complex choices rather than a narrowly defined and prescribed script, and only the privileged were in a position to benefit from choosing to focus on the historical linkages of real genealogy as opposed to the situational linkages of fictive kinship.

The oral traditions illustrate a dimension of the region's social terrain that European maps of the political landscape could not: matriclans and their kinship-based claims to authority that posited group membership through the idiom of blood were as significant as states and their kingship-based claims to authority that framed assumptions about group membership and demands for allegiance in the idiom of commercial influence and military might. The cultural centrality and historical weight of kinship institutions meant that the state was not necessarily also a national body (it had no necessary correlate in national or ethnic membership). At play among communities in the Gold Coast in the seventeenth and eighteenth centuries were the shifting and competing affinities subsumed under these two distinct axes of authority: kinship (matriclan) on the one hand, and kingship (state) on the other. The varied and contingent threads of ethnic identity ran through the interplay of these two.

The recorded oral traditions convey movement that belies the static picture drawn in European maps. They set the still image of the map into dynamic historical motion. The oral traditions allow us to perceive, however faintly, something of the complex social topography of the region, in both its spatial and temporal dimensions. In a spatial sense, the oral traditions reveal something about the ethnic diversity of the community; temporally, they illustrate the historical dimension of ethnicity. In this sense, the social geography of the region cannot be adequately understood as the history of an ethnically homogeneous people who called themselves the Akan. Rather, it must be understood as a history of competitive claims to resources and power waged by groups whose identities were rooted not in a shared language or "culture" per se, but in the interplay of local, historically contingent markers of affiliation. "Identity" in other words, was multivalent.

"Another King's Country"

Though European cartographers had drawn the purported boundaries of the region's politico-economic geography, it behooved Europeans operating on-site to attend to the fuller complexity of the region's social geography, if only because of its impact on commercial opportunities and outcomes—when or whether gold or slaves would be forthcoming from their African trading partners. It was just such awareness that allowed the Royal African Company agent at Anomabu to explain an event that caused his less informed superiors at Cape Coast Castle some confusion.

The incident involved warfare between two polities near Anomabu in August 1682. Though captives were known to have been taken, none appeared for sale at the English fort after the battle was concluded—a result that elicited a query from officials at the castle. The following reply came from Richard Thelwall, the factor at Anomabu: "As concerning slaves, though the Abbraers panyard the Cormanteen people yet they dare not sell them for they are all of one Country."[32] Still not satisfied, officials at Cape Coast apparently asked for additional clarification. "As to the custom of the Country," Thelwall elaborated, "if they had been taken in Fettue Country then but a peaze but if in another King's Country they sell them; so they say is the Custom."[33]

Here was a case in which warring states shared ties of affinity that prohibited sale of captives to the Atlantic market. Shared "country" affiliation between victor and vanquished (in this case between polities that shared membership in the Fantine confederation of states) was sufficient to prohibit sale of captives to Europeans eager to buy them. But what was the content of such affiliations? What constituted a "country" in the seventeenth-century Gold Coast? What was the nature of the simultaneous difference and sameness that governed relations between these groups?

Contemporary European sources are replete with such references to "countries" and the "kings" who ruled them, and often European elites, like the officials at Cape Coast Castle, sought to define "kings" and "countries" in a way that mirrored the image of the European nation-state, with its correspondence between territorial, political, and sociocultural elements (for instance, the idea that "England" designated a place inhabited by the English people). Viewed in this way, the socioethnic geography of the Gold Coast could be grafted onto the politico-economic maps produced by European cartographers, to weave a tapestry of "imagined communities" of the kind claimed by European sovereigns. But just as the European "nation" was a community whose integration of territorial, political, and cultural boundaries indeed was more imagined than fully realized, so too did ethnic belonging in the Gold Coast reside in a multiplicity of groupings. In this sense, it becomes crucially important to recognize that Gold Coast "countries" were not nations in the modern Western sense of the term.

In the case of polities located in the vicinity of Anomabu in the seventeenth century, the boundaries of "countries" were coterminous not with the territorially inscribed reach of states, but rather with the kin-based authority of the matrilineage. The matrilineage constituted the "country" to which the two warring polities belonged. For the Fantine confederacy in the seventeenth century, then, states effectively defined themselves within kinship-based ethnic belonging. In this place and time, ethnic identity resided betwixt and between the overlapping and contested claims of state and clan: the ethnic affinity that inhered in shared kinship could yield to political conflict between states and could simultaneously intercede, in delimiting what was permissible in the treatment of defeated people in the aftermath of war. It was thus that the same polities willing to perpetrate violence or wage war against one another "dare[d] not sell their captives" into the Atlantic market when the war ended.

In the seventeenth century, the authority of kingship was not sufficient to thoroughly override that of kinship. In marked contrast, in the case of Asante in the eighteenth century, the architects of the state worked hard to craft political symbols of the state that imposed a measure of national belonging on the varied ethnic communities contained within its imperial bounds. In between these two extremes stood a reality in which the state existed both within and between communities of ethnic belonging, a situation that made the relations between war, captivity, and the market dynamic and historically contingent.[34]

For European would-be buyers of captive people, the lesson was that although large supplies of slaves became available only in the aftermath of war, the reverse did not always hold true. To the frustration of officials at Cape Coast Castle, not all armed conflict produced captives available for export. For the peoples of the Gold Coast themselves, the lesson was that although the market hungered to seize all who fell into the unfortunate situation of captivity, politics determined whose captivity would in fact end in their export aboard European slave ships. In the seventeenth century, captives who could be offered as commodities on the Atlantic market for slave labor, with all the horror that entailed, were those for whom ethnic difference derived from the absence of shared kinship affiliation. This situation would change, however, as the institution of the state acquired sufficient legitimacy to give kings and statecraft authority and sway greater than it had ever been possible to exercise effectively when political power was based on kinship. It would thus become possible, and increasingly common, to treat kinsmen as though they were from "another king's country" in the eighteenth century, as the boundaries of "countries" came to be defined by the boundaries of the state.

The ethnic and linguistic diversity on the slave ship did not mean that people could not communicate with one another. In many instances, Akan speakers boarded the slave ships alongside others who also spoke one of the Akan dialects, and speakers of the other major languages also often found that they could understand close dialects. Moreover, a measure of bilingualism was common among people residing on the borders between different speech communities, and widely used lingua francas often softened the edges between speech communities.[35] Beyond that, marriages, work, wars, and other events regularly put people in motion within the broader landscape. Women moved from their villages of origin to those of their husbands, sometimes crossing dialect boundaries; occupational mobility resulted in a degree of linguistic dexterity among such laborers as traders and fishermen; war prisoners were resettled in territories ruled by their captors; and sometimes whole groups uprooted themselves to flee scenes of military conflict and took up residence in new host communities.

Although it would be misguided to assume that linguistic differences posed barriers to social cohesion, it would be equally erroneous to assume that linguistic similarities necessarily enabled easy relations. Ethnic belonging bears no set correspondence to linguistic, political, territorial, or other cultural boundaries. At this remove, we cannot know with any certainty what the ethnic and cultural mix generally present in the slave cargoes meant for the captives themselves. To reduce the communities that inhabited the Gold Coast or any of the other slave-exporting regions of Africa to such

monolithic groups as *the* Akan, *the* Angolans, or *the* Biafrans
would be to obscure socioethnic complexities that are likely to have
mattered a great deal to the inhabitants themselves.

This suggests that the social formations that took shape at the
littoral and continued to evolve during the diaspora of Atlantic
migration and slavery cannot be adequately understood either
as fully integrated "groups" or as entirely randomly constituted
"crowds."[36] Neither concept captures the variety and complexity of
possibilities for affiliation and conflict among the persons assembled into the "cargoes" and "lots" that were the migratory units in
the African diaspora. Most important, neither category embraces
Africans in diaspora as historical actors—people making decisions
in the moment about who to claim themselves to be, how to negotiate the novel and uniquely multivalent social formations their Atlantic commodification produced. Identity being multilayered and
contingent, the captives funneled into the Atlantic market for people lived within many different bodies of affinity all at once, making
and remaking strategic choices as opportunity or misfortune dic-
tated.

What, then, does our picture of the African landscape tell us
about the nature of the slave cargo as a social formation? This question has most commonly been approached as a cultural one: If Africans from a particular region can be said to have a common culture
(usually defined so broadly that it is based solely on historically related languages), they are presumed to represent a coherent community of actors entering the Atlantic world together, as if people
who *could* talk to each other can be assumed to have *wanted* to talk
to each other. This premise rests, however, on the erroneous assumption that shared cultural traits automatically constitute community.

Africans did not enter the Atlantic market as members of the cultural groups that populate modern Western anthropological (that
is, colonial) constructions of "Africa," but rather as ragtag collec-

tives—persons whose most evident commonality was their isolation from the kin and ethnic communities of origin that determined both individual and group identity. As captives left the slave ship through the portal of the market, they entered the terrain of American slavery in similarly disaggregated "lots" that resulted from their sale to owners eager to profit from their labor.

The slaves collected at the waterside produced anomalous intimacies out of the social geography of the Gold Coast and also the seed of community within the African Atlantic diaspora of which they now were a part. The slave cargo put captives into a setting where communication was a necessity and interaction took on an unparalleled intimacy and urgency: shackles, for instance, threw people into bodily contact whose closeness was matched only by that of sexual union. As they engaged with these exigencies, the captives laid the groundwork for a new kind of diasporic identity. But the existence and dimensions of that diaspora would become known to them only in the setting of the Americas. For now, the only social geography the exiles knew was that of the Gold Coast. So as they entered the ships and the Atlantic, they stood in an intermediary space—conscious of localized ethnic identities and the peculiar heterogeneity of the slave cargo, yet prompted by the crisis in their circumstances to engage with that diversity for its human possibilities, regardless of the obvious limitations.

Recognizing that the peoples of the Gold Coast (like those everywhere in the early modern world) occupied a complex and multilayered social and political landscape goes a long way toward helping us imagine that captives in diaspora actively called on their understanding of the relationship of people to place no less than they had done before their exile from the fluid and contingent social landscape of the Gold Coast.

As Africans sold into Atlantic slavery endured this time in the European settlements and coasting slave ships, each drew his or her own conclusions regarding the meaning of this particular type of

captivity. But certain truisms regarding the nature of their crisis became painfully clear to all. When they turned to look back toward
the African landscape, these men and women sold into Atlantic
slavery faced a coastal marketplace increasingly committed to the
exchange of people for goods. When they looked in the opposite direction, they saw only the terror of the open sea, and the unnatural
society of the slave ship. Whether they turned their gaze toward the
coastline or out toward the open sea, the horizon was forbidding,
for beyond the waterside markets, the social fabric of African communities was rent by the disappearance of kinfolk. And on the
ocean's horizon the captives encountered only the social world of
the slave ship, a similarly mutilated assemblage that was not a func-
tioning whole but rather an arbitrary collective of isolated and
alienated persons. This motley collective of missing people taken
together constituted a novel social formation that bore no correlation to the communities they left behind, and therefore no recognizable meaning or order. The captives' understanding of what their
own isolation and displacement portended was mirrored in the disturbing social composition of the slave cargo. In one another's eyes
they saw the reflection of their own traumatic alienation.

5

The Living Dead aboard the Slave Ship at Sea

Like the Atlantic market of which it was a part, the slave ship at sea produced two competing narratives of the experience of the transatlantic voyage. The dominant European narrative—that of merchant investors—represented the ship as the height of maritime commercial endeavor: a useful conveyance that linked markets in a known seascape, an instrument of commerce that carried human cargoes from African sites of production to American sites of consumption.

As the African captives lacked a culture of maritime travel, the ship produced in them an experience of motion without discernible direction or destination. On the ship at sea the logic of commodification reached its nadir. It was here, on the ocean crossing, that the practices of commodification most effectively muted the agency of the African subject and thereby produced their desired object: an African body fully alienated and available for exploitation in the American marketplace.

The slave ship at sea produced an African narrative of persistent and often lonely attempts among the captives to continue to function as subjective beings—persons possessing independent will and agency. Women who exhausted themselves to death in their futile efforts to attend to the needs of their infants; captives who helped care for one another when disease invariably struck; and strangers who facilitated communication between speakers of mutually unintelligible languages—by such simple acts, all demonstrated the determination required to live as a human being rather than exist as an object aboard the slave ship at sea.

"This Hollow Place"

Remembering his childhood experience of slavery, Olaudah Equiano recalled the slave ship at sea as a site of profound displacement. Trying to make sense of his captivity aboard an English ship, he asked others older and ostensibly more knowledgeable than he a simple question: "What was to be done with us?" They told him, he wrote many years later, "We were to be carried to these white people's country to work for them." Equiano tried to quiet his fears of imminent death and struggled to convince himself, "If it were no worse than working, my situation was not so desperate." But these assurances did not get to the root of his anxiety. "I asked them," he wrote, whether "these people had no country, but *lived* in this hollow place?"[1] News that his captors indeed hailed from a "distant" land prompted more queries:

"Then," said I, "how comes it in all our country we never heard of them?" They told me because they lived so very far off. I then asked where were their women? Had they any like themselves? I was told that they had. "And why," said I, "do we not see them?" They answered, because they were left behind. I asked how the vessel could go? They told me they could not tell; but that there was cloth put upon the masts by the help of the ropes I saw, and then the vessel went on; and the white men had some spell or magic they put in the water when they liked, in order to stop the vessel. I was exceedingly amazed at this account, and really thought they were spirits. I therefore wished much to be from amongst them, for I expected they would sacrifice me; but my wishes were vain—for we were so quartered that it was impossible for any of us to make our escape.[2]

In this often-cited passage from his *Narrative,* Equiano's language compels understanding through its analytical precision. For whatever the balance of personal experience, ethnographic report, and imagination in his published account, Equiano's description of the ship at sea is strikingly specific in its analysis of the puzzle the slave ship at sea represented for African captives.[3] In the first instance, there was the persistent problem of European intentions— "What was to be done with us?" If slave ships carried some who confidently claimed to know that the slavers were an instrument of labor recruitment, surely for others (no doubt even from among the sophisticated Akan) the weight of inexperience was too great to counter fear and anxiety. And though we cannot know, we must suspect that even those who began the crossing in confidence struggled to square what they could claim to know with what they encountered as the slave ship carried them deeper into Atlantic waters.

Additionally, African captives confronted the problem of the European merchant ship itself, which presented them with challenges both physical and metaphysical. With regard to physical challenges, its cavernous form signaled an eerie emptiness demanding to be filled, a powerful and dangerous capacity to consume. As for the metaphysical aspect, the very habitat of the ship—the open sea— challenged African cosmographies, for the landless realm of the deep ocean did not figure in precolonial West African societies as a domain of human (as opposed to divine) activity—just as it had not figured as such in medieval European systems of knowledge.[4] In its guiding principle—the proposition that life can be lived at sea—the ship presented an oxymoron.

Now that land not only lay far distant but had, more ominously, vanished from the horizon altogether, the ship's relentless motion pulled the captives ever deeper into temporal and spatial entrapment. The sheer scale of the unknown element disabled many of the cognitive tools supplied by African epistemologies, which attributed dangerous supernatural powers to the watery realm.[5] The slave ship at sea reduced African captives to an existence so physically atomized as to silence all but the most elemental bodily articulation, so socially impoverished as to threaten annihilation of the self, the complete disintegration of personhood. Here their commodification built toward a crescendo that threatened never to arrive, but to leave the African captives suspended in an agony whose language no one knew.

Where, then, was agency to be found—or some affirmation that there yet remained a self to be preserved? Of the relationship of pain to language, Elaine Scarry writes, "Through his ability to project words and sounds out into his environment, a human being inhabits, humanizes, and makes his own a space much larger than that occupied by his body alone." Indeed, the only means to survive in this realm was to divine a means to explain it, to define and delimit it. And the only means to achieve that was to speak of it—to probe its contours with words spoken among strangers. Words were the glue that made the crowd to which Equiano belonged into a collective "us," whose fate stood in the balance during the journey. Agency aboard the slave ship took refuge above all in the voice, the means by which the "self" finds realization "across the bridge of the body in the world."[6]

For African captives, it was their wholeness as fully embodied subjects that was at stake in the Atlantic setting. Entering the open sea signaled the end of one contest—*whether* captives would go into circulation as commodities in the Atlantic market—and the beginning of another—*how* captives would sustain their humanity in the uniquely inhumane spatial and temporal setting of the slave ship at sea. This truth lends substance to Equiano's poetic insight that the ship packed beyond capacity with a "full complement" of African captives was a "hollow place": a place distinguished by its many lacks—its material and social poverty, its cognitive dissonance, and its defenselessness in the face of the supernatural.

Atlantic Time-Space and Its Reckoning

Having had no reason to develop a body of knowledge and ideas about the sea as an arena for the activities of the living (as opposed to those of the ancestors—the dead living), enslaved Africans entered the Atlantic without the information and background that enabled their European captors to navigate the open sea. When confronted with the phenomenon, African captives responded to the Atlantic as Europeans had done: they made it knowable in their own terms. But the conditions of their Atlantic experience shaped that process, just as the particular conditions of maritime exploration had shaped the integration of the Atlantic into European culture and consciousness.

With their charts of winds and currents, chronicling of important events such as storms and encounters with enemy vessels, and accounts of daily activities at sea, artifacts such as Captain Peter Blake's "Journall" of his voyage aboard the *James* provide abundant evidence of the ways European mariners made sense of the Atlantic. Applied statistical analysis, epidemiology, and modern biological science, too, have proved important tools for historical interpretation of the ocean crossing. But neither the European nautical instruments of that era nor modern Western historical explanations can help us fathom Africans' own understanding of the Atlantic and the slave ship traversing it. We can be sure, however, that for early modern peoples everywhere in the Atlantic basin, the initial encounter with the Atlantic as an arena for human activity was profoundly transformative.

The ship under sail was a world unto itself, where the passengers had to rely only on the expertise of the sailors aboard—and on whatever spiritual power they might be able to summon. No group of early modern Atlantic sea travelers had greater experience of the Atlantic than European mariners. Over the long course of Europe's gradual reach into the Atlantic, generations of sailors developed a rich maritime culture all their own. From the knowledge and skills of observation and interpretation that enabled the "old salts" to find meaning in the mysterious events at sea, the navigational science of maps, charts, and tools of measurement was distilled—an acquired body of knowledge without which the European westward expansion would not have been possible. "Seamen," as historian Marcus Rediker has explained, "created a rich store of knowledge, much of it genuinely scientific and reliably predictive, from the heavens and the earth."[7]

European travelers—those who did not build their lives around life at sea but chose to take up life as emigrants to the Americas—also accumulated a different kind of knowledge about the Atlantic. Describing the seventeenth-century Puritan migrations to New England, David Cressy writes, "English migrants to North America often approached their journey with apprehension and fear. Stories of storms and wrecks effectively dissuaded some prospective migrants from voyaging to America; others battled anxieties as they encountered the strange and terrifying world of the sea." With regard to the ambience on the oceangoing vessel, Cressy notes, "Skeins, coils and tangles of rope hung with mysterious complexity. Unfamiliar nautical tackle and the puzzling seafarer's vocabulary sparked both wariness and curiosity."[8]

Indeed, "apprehensions about 'the casualties of the seas, which none can be freed from' and 'the length of the voyage . . . such as the weak bodies of women and other persons worn out with age and travail . . . could never be able to endure,' had turned some of William Bradford's associates away from the Pilgrim venture." Even after English colonization of North America was well under way, "similar concerns dissuaded some prospective emigrants" from leaving England. "Good workmen . . . are fearful to go to sea for fear they shall not live to come to your land," one writer observed in 1639. "'Were it not for the danger of the seas you might have enough,'" he went on, explaining the challenge of drawing newcomers to Connecticut. Similarly, a writer from Newcastle, England, lamented that "'the sad discouragement in coming by sea [was] enough to hinder'" his return to join his family in New England."[9]

The point, too easily glossed over in familiar narrative formulations attributing to all Europeans the mariner's hard-won mastery of the sea, is that "before the great migration of the 1630s only professional travellers, merchants and mariners knew the ropes of blue-water sailing." Many of the English emigrants came from coastal communities possessed of a rich maritime tradition based on the navigation and exploitation of inshore waters. But that store of knowledge did not mitigate English fears. "The ocean was another matter, unknown and therefore feared," writes Cressy, noting further that "to the popular imagination the ocean suggested hazard and uncertainty. It conjured an alien and frightful environment of commotion and discomfort, fraught with 'daily expectations of swallowing waves and cruel pirates.'" Cressy observes that "as some colonial promoters pointed out, open-water sailing was much less hazardous than coasting," and concludes that "much of this thalassophobia was overblown," as "remarkably few people drowned on the way to New England, and many found the journey more exhilarating than tormenting."[10] But this perhaps misses the point: English emigrants believed transatlantic travel to entail unprecedented hazards, and reports of successful, even "exhilarating," crossings did not necessarily relieve prospective emigrants of their fears.

Through the networks of communication that linked New World colonies to Old World metropolises, various forms of information about the ocean crossing made its way back through European communities. The content of letters written to friends and family back home and of promotional pamphlets designed to entice new migrants coalesced into a kind of rumor-based knowledge—information that was reliable because it came from someone trusted, or someone who spoke with authority. Thus, the prospective European emigrant who could not fathom the idea of crossing the Atlantic could seek information, and find comfort, or not, in the idea that "a ship at sea may well be compared to a cradle rocked by a careful mother's hand, which though it be moved up and down is not in danger of falling."[11]

Like Europeans before the age of Columbus, Africans developed their knowledge of the ocean from familiarity with coastal lands and inshore waters. The sea provided a vital source of animal protein, and the salt deposited on the shore made it possible to preserve food.[12] Most important, Africans knew that the sea was controlled by powerful deities whose benevolence was the real source of the sea's gifts to them, and whose disfavor was the source of the sea's destructive potential.[13]

That the earth and the sea were sacred sites of supernatural power was an African truth that De Marees explained thoroughly, if unwittingly, in his exegesis of African ignorance of the Christian God:

Although they do not know him, he has given them gold, Palm wine, *Millie* and Maize, Chickens and Oxen, Sheep, *Bannanas,* Yams and other Fruits for their upkeep. But this they were not willing to concede, and they could not understand that such things came from God, saying it was not God who gave them the Gold but rather the earth, in which they seek and find it; according to them, God does not give them the *Millie* or Corn which they sow and reap either, but the earth gives them these things. Thirdly, Fruits are given by the Trees which they plant and which were first brought by the Portuguese. Fourthly, young Sheep come from old ones; the Sea gives Fish and they catch them; and there are many such things which they do not wish to acknowledge as coming from God, but rather say they come from the earth and the sea, each giving of its own.[14]

Their relationship to the sea thus reflected the underlying logic found throughout traditional African systems of thought: that the sacred and the secular, the physical and the metaphysical were not separate spheres but rather integrally bound together and manifest in the material world.

Also like European cultures, coastal African communities developed a rumor-based body of knowledge of their own about the Atlantic arena. Though experience in the Atlantic beyond the coastal waters was relatively rare among resident Africans before the nineteenth century, small numbers of them crossed the Atlantic aboard European vessels and subsequently returned to Africa as witnesses to the world beyond inshore waters. Particularly along the Gold Coast, where European settlement was so extensive, African men, occasionally taken to Europe to learn English, returned to the Gold Coast and found employment as interpreters.

Others from the region found their way across the Atlantic and back as accidental passengers aboard slave ships. In 1719, three canoemen and another employed as a "Gold taker" traveled aboard a Royal African Company ship to Barbados, where they passed at least four months before being returned to Africa. "Captain Ayerst brought with him 3 Cannoe Men," the Royal African Company agent at Barbados reported on 7 March 1719, "which shall be return'd by the first as also a Gold taker named Quamina."[15] On 30 June 1719, the company agent at Barbados "shipd on bd. the *John & Elizabeth,* Captain Jacob Burgesson for Cape Coast, the following Slaves, Accraw, Quaw, Cuffee, & Cobiner."[16] Having crossed the Atlantic and spent several months on American territory, these four, when they walked once more on

African soil, shared with others accounts that no doubt spread quickly among Cape Coast residents.

The structure of African involuntary migration was distinguished most by the general impossibility of such informational feedback, for persons who witnessed life in the Atlantic world and returned to Africa to tell about it represented a tiny minority when measured against the millions of deportees whose voices could not reach Africa's shores. With no network of communication linking their experience in the Atlantic world, the African captives who boarded European slave ships carried a range of expectations shaped by the interplay of their own beliefs regarding the men who had purchased them and whatever rumors circulated among the coastal communities about these strangers and the land from which they came.

For African emigrants, as we have seen, the slave ship was not just a setting for brutality and death, but also a locus of unparalleled displacement. As the sight of land grew faint, or as the land disappeared suddenly on the closing of the hatch, the disorientation that for many had begun with the process of procurement on the African coast became more marked. Out of sight of any land, enslaved Africans commenced a march through time and space that stretched their own systems of reckoning to the limits.

By the time Europeans began to colonize the New World, voyagers to the west were confident that their journey would follow a linear path, with known beginning and end points. European seamen translated the land-based systems of time-space reckoning of medieval Europe to the wider temporal and spatial context of life in a "new" Atlantic world. Hourglasses and astrolabes measured time and space; and applied mathematics and geometry turned these into the Cartesian coordinates seamen used to recognize place in the seemingly formless arena of the sea.[17] Ship captains like Peter Blake could know when their ships had reached designated spatial coordinates at sea—virtual landmarks such as the equator; and whether six months or a year had elapsed since their departure from England.[18] Measured against this standard, the dramatic dimensions of the displacement Africans experienced as they moved farther out into the Atlantic, their own knowledge of time and place rapidly losing its utility, can be grasped at least intellectually.[19]

Like many nonliterate peoples, Africans relied on the regular cycle of climatic events to locate themselves in time and space. The dry season of Harmattan winds had begun when most of the Africans on the *James* had come aboard, and if it was the middle of the month of March by European reckoning when Blake removed the slaves' irons, no doubt some among the Africans knew that the planting season now was under way in the communities they had left behind.[20]

Aspects of the calendrical system used by Akan-speaking peoples of the Gold Coast drew the attention of many European visitors to the region in the seventeenth century. At the most superficial level, Europeans recognized that certain days held ritual importance among the coastal Akan communities and noted the day of the week in the Julian calendar to which these days in the Akan system of reckoning time corresponded. In 1603–1604, Ulsheimer observed that the day of the week Europeans identified as Tuesday was significant. "Every Tuesday (which they celebrate as we do Sunday)," he explained, "people must bring the king all the wine from his whole territory, and he in turn must give it out liberally to his people."[21] During his residence at the Dutch fort at Mori, Brun likewise noted, "Tuesday is their sabbath and on this day they do not go out to sea; for their god Fytysi [*fetiso*] had forbidden them to do so."[22] Müller observed the same during his stay among the Fetu of Cape Coast. "Instead of Sunday, Tuesday is celebrated throughout the country," he reported.

> It is called *ohinne da*, the king's day, by them. The fishermen living on the coast hold this day so sacred that they believe a great disaster would befall them if they went to sea to fish with hooks on that day.

Nevertheless they are free to put out and fetch in their nets on Tuesday. This day is celebrated in honour of the *o-bossums* or supposed gods of the sea. When the sea becomes rough, so that the fishermen either suffer loss or cannot even fish, they get the priests to question these gods and appease them with a sacrifice.[23]

In addition to learning the Akan term *ohinne da,* which he translated as "Tuesday," Müller added *Quassi-da* (Sunday), *Egwju da* (Monday), *Ejauda* (Thursday), and *Efi-dà* (Friday) to the vocabulary list he compiled. Müller found that *Adà* represented the unit of time he knew as a "day," and on learning that the Akan employed a larger unit of seven days called *Dansun,* he translated that term as "week." He further identified *Osran,* which he translated as "month," as the Akan word for "moon." Finally, Müller concluded that the Akan word *Affi* corresponded to the European concept of a year.[24]

In the Akan system for reckoning time, the units of temporal measure identified by Müller comprised a forty-day cycle known as *adaduanan* (literally, "forty days").[25] The cycle actually consisted of forty-two days, however, and appears to have derived from the fusion of two systems of temporal measure—one recognizing a six-day week, the other featuring a seven-day week—observed by the different groups that settled the region well before the era of European exploration. From an apparent process of cultural amalgamation a calendrical system had been derived in which the six-day cycle and seven-day cycle ran concurrently, so that "when the six-day week is counted side-by-side with the seven-day week it takes a total of forty-two days to reach all combinations."[26]

Within the forty-day cycles certain days were designated for ritual observance of the ancestors—the special days remarked on by Müller and other seventeenth-century European commentators.[27] Beyond its primary role in ordering the cycle of ritual days associated with ancestor worship, the 40-day *adaduanan* cycles also gave shape to the annual agricultural calendar. Multiple *adaduanan* cycles completed a year, which was marked by the annual harvest festival, *odwira*. The timing of the *odwira* celebration and other annual agricultural rites was determined by priests "in consultation with the gods and ancestors," and also on the basis of the "ripening of the crops." Since the number of *aduadanan* within the year varied between eight and nine such 42-day cycles in a 365-day agricultural calendar, "annually celebrated rites of the different Akan groups . . . are therefore celebrated each year on different days of the year."[28] Within the year, each *adaduanan* cycle was tied to the particular ecological demands of the season. According to one historian who has studied Akan time reckoning,

> the various *adaduanan* cycles within the year are given a number of appellations, which are not the same from place to place, and of course never quite the same from year to year, since there are less than nine and more than eight cycles in any one year. *Opepon* (*Ope* = harmattan, dry season; *pon* = supreme), for example, more or less corresponds to the *adaduanan* which appears about January–February in the middle of the dry season.[29]

Shaped by the seasonal demands of the landscape, the Akan system for reckoning time was no more up to the challenge of giving order and structure to life in a maritime arena than had been those of Europeans prior to their fifteenth century.[30] Even for those among African captives who were accustomed to travel—traders or fishermen, say—Atlantic displacement was unlike anything with which they were familiar. Travel overland, for no matter how great a distance, took place in daily increments: as each day came to a close, the travelers found a place to rest and pass the night before commencing the journey again the following morning. Similarly, fishermen and traders who followed routes connected by coastal waters were accustomed to travel only by daylight, nighttime being the occasion to stop and to rest. Travel aboard the slave ship, however, would require that captives remain as watchful at night as during the daylight hours, for nightfall brought no halt to the forward motion of the ship at sea.[31]

Once they were onboard ship, the African captives measured time at sea as best they could by marking the cycles of the moon.[32] The rising and setting of the sun and the moon's regular appearances were familiar markers, but without a template for ordering time in this maritime arena, so distinct from the landscape from which they had been torn, Africans struggled to maintain their bearings. Counting the moon's cycles, they knew what time it was by the agricultural calendar that had ordered their lives—whether it was time to harvest or time to plant. But that information did not help them know where, precisely, they were, how far they had traveled, how to situate this place in their own mental maps of the world.

Their travel as captives thus made it enormously difficult for Africans to clearly distinguish the phases of their journey, or to anticipate the end of one phase or the beginning of another. The events that gave shape to their time aboard the slave ship at sea were random, indeterminate signs to be observed and interpreted as they appeared. Always in motion but seeming to never reach any destination, the ship plowed forward in time without ever getting anywhere, always seeming to be in the same place as the day before. It was as if time were standing still. Time was lived in motion, but at no discernible rhythm by which Africans could orient their movement in time or readily measure time's passage.

The Accounting of the Dead

In few settings were human beings exposed to a greater number of pathogens in the early modern world than aboard slave ships en route to the Americas.[33] Any sailing vessel was an enclosed space, where it was impossible to create physical distance between the infected and the noninfected, African or European, when disease broke out. But the crowded conditions on slaving vessels made for a level of human density unmatched on other types of oceangoing vessels.[34] With crowding came lack of sanitation, and the enslaved Africans found that none of the familiar habits of personal hygiene could be observed. Thus, illness was nearly impossible to avoid in that setting. Exhaustion, malnutrition, fear, and seasickness resulted in depressed immune systems and increased vulnerability to disease. Particularly among the African prisoners, crowding, poor hygiene, and often contaminated food and water supplies, together made the slave ship a breeding ground for airborne pathogens (smallpox and tuberculosis) as well as those spread via fecal-to-oral pathways (bacillary and amoebic dysentery) or by direct physical contact (yaws).[35] The spatial dimensions of the Atlantic and the relatively slow pace of oceanic travel in the age of sail meant that the assault on health was sustained without relief for the duration of the sea voyage. The Atlantic passage was above all else a test of African endurance, with no known end in sight.

Every African who boarded a European slave ship brought his or her own strengths and weaknesses to the encounter—a reflection of the life that had preceded expulsion into the Atlantic. The basic nutritional profile of the community of origin distinguished inhabitants of the Gold Coast, for example, whose primary staple crop was maize, from those of Biafra, whose primary crop was the less nutritious yam.[36] And the particular events that carried individual men, women, and children aboard the European ships made for varying combinations of exhaustion, injury, hunger, exposure to contagious disease and vulnerability to pathogens that were endemic to local African populations. Within every cargo, some were more physically or emotionally exhausted, some more nutritionally deprived, and some more vulnerable to illness than others.

Conditions thus made the slave ship a deadly place, so much so that in Africa the language of death became part of nomenclature for it. Slave ships were called *tumbeiros* in the eighteenth-century Angolan trade, for example, a term historians have translated as "floating tombs" or "undertakers." The symbolism of the tomb also was used to designate the personnel involved in the activities of slaving, other historians having translated *tumbeiros* to mean "bear[ers] to the tomb," finding it used also to refer to those "who brought slaves down to the coast."[37]

For the most part, though, historians have described the slave ship's lethal nature the same way the slave traders did: by calculating the number of dead. Indeed, as long as the transatlantic slave trade has been a subject of intellectual inquiry, mortality and its quantitative measurement have functioned as a key with which scholars have labored to unlock the secrets of the slave ship and expose to view the stories that played out belowdecks. By tallying the dead to measure the toll the voyage took on African life, we have made that body count the most potent symbolic measure of the horrors of the middle passage. We can gauge the trauma to the extent that we know how many lives it extinguished: the greater the number, the deeper the perceived tragedy.

A great deal has been learned from the data on mortality aboard the slave ship, but overall numbers—and our interpretation of them—correspond only loosely to the ways African captives experienced and understood shipboard mortality. Narrative texts like Blake's journal written aboard the *James* offer another window onto the slave ship at sea, one that helps us recognize the limitations of quantitative analysis. This alternate analysis of shipboard mortality, in alluding to the temporal and spatial realities of African captives' transatlantic voyage, puts the statisticians' numbers back into the context in which death occurred (Fig 5.1).

On 6 September 1675, Peter Blake penned the following in his journal: "This day I had a neagg.r man departed this life whoe died suddenly." Coming just over a week since the first captives had come aboard the vessel on 28 August, this first death of an African

5.1 "Account of the Mortallity" aboard the *James,* 1675–1676, T70/1211.

aboard the *James* occasioned the beginning of a supplemental documentary record Blake would keep within his "Journall." Marking
the first entry in his "Account of Mortallity of Slaves aboard the
Shipp *James*," Blake entered a "1" in the column labeled "Men,"
and in a separate column for explanatory notes, he added the brief
phrase "departed this Life suddenly."[38]

Blake entered numbers and words in his account of mortality
in language adequate to the needs and tasks of a slaving captain.
The numeral stood for the property now lost, and succinct phrases
reducing death to a simple statement of cause and effect were sufficient to explain the event: "departed this Life suddenly," "departed this life of Convulsion fitts," "Received from Wyemba
[Winneba] very thin & wasted to Nothing & soe dyed." Blake's
language not only explained the circumstances of death, but also
identified the agent of death. The captives themselves bore the responsibility and had the agency—it was they who "departed this
life." The language of accounting thus rationalized shipboard mortality, portraying the European agent of commodification as the
passive victim of the Africans who died—as an investor robbed of
his property *by* that property.

But for the person whose earthly life had ended here in the waterborne wooden vessel, the picture was far more complicated and
troubling. Death represented not just a discrete event but rather a
shift in social relations that had wide reverberations. Why did death
weigh more heavily on one group of captives than another? Why
did one man suffering from flux die, while another did not? Whose
supernatural power intervened to save the woman ill with dysentery or smallpox? Why did the white doctor's suspicious-looking
medicine bring relief to one and death to another? Far from simple
equations based on circumstances, the patterns of life and death
aboard ship were complex and mysterious. The circumstances of
death were not explanations in themselves but rather signs—indica-
tors of activity among the supernatural forces that possessed the
real power.

The "departure" that Blake had unambiguously recorded in fact put the departed very much in jeopardy, according to the understanding the African captives brought to the occurrence, for it was marked by the absence of traditional mortuary ritual—a distressing failure to act.[39] If the prescribed ritual was not performed, death threatened to have far-reaching consequences for both the deceased and the living. Nowhere was this truer than in the Atlantic, where the most central element of mortuary practice was lacking: earth.

Properly memorialized, death afforded the opportunity to join the living community through a protective web of connections to the ancestors and the not-yet-born. Mourning and interment mitigated the disruptive threat that death posed, by channeling the sacral power of death into the renewal of life. Suitable rituals thus protected the community from the unmitigated loss of its members and protected the individual from the threat of annihilation; the "necral space" of the burial ground and the rituals associated with it served as the medium through which these vital connections were maintained.[40] Ancestors "consecrated" the ground in which they were buried, "and continuous rituals connecting them with their heirs created a single community consisting of the dead, their heirs, and the soil they shared."[41]

The soul's departure and migration to the realm of the ancestors could only be carried to completion by the performance of mortuary practices that affirmed the close affinity between these two domains. Death without a funeral compromised the journey on to a new realm. With no food and drink to sustain the deceased in the domain of the ancestors, neither clothing nor tools with which to continue the activities of earthly life in the new realm, and no earth to receive the dead bodies, how were the deceased to find their way out of the watery realm to the land of the ancestors? In essence, a fully realized death could not be accomplished alone. Nor was it something one could attain at sea.

Far more than the economic event Blake casually recorded in his journal, this first death of a slave aboard the *James* was an event that held singularly traumatic consequences: for the deceased, death at sea meant an unfulfilled journey to the grave and therefore also to the realm of the ancestors; for the kinsmen of the deceased, his death meant that a thread of the special power and protection only ancestral members of the community could provide was lost to them forever. For the collective of African captives remaining aboard the *James,* the death of one of their number left them with the burden of a tormented soul, trapped here among them because its migration to join the ancestors had been thwarted.

Two more deaths followed in the next eight weeks, a time when only small numbers of captives were onboard. While Blake bartered for gold, his crew prepared the ship to receive the large numbers that would "complete" its human cargo. Once the cargo on the *James* approached capacity in January, the forward motion of the vessel would be charted by the dispersal of bodies committed without ceremony to the sea, an accumulation of displaced souls. One week following receipt of the group of "very thin ordinary slaves" from Winneba (Chapter 3), the death march continued.

20 January: a man, "received from Wyemba thin and Consumed to Nothing & soe dyed."

Then a reprieve of five days.

26 January: a woman, "received from Wyemba very thin & wasted to Nothing & soe dyed."

Then a lapse of twelve days.

8 February: a man, "received from Wyemba very thin & dropsicall & soe departed this life."

Then a full two weeks' respite from the recurrence of death.

23 February: a woman, "bought to Windward & departed this life of a Consumption & Wormes."

24 February: a boy, "received from Wyemba with a dropsy & departed this life of ye same disease."

26 February: a woman, "received from Wyemba thin & soe Continued Untill death."

And then a break of six days.

5 March: a woman, "miscarryed & the Child dead within her & Rotten & dyed 2 days after delivery."[42]

On 6 March, Blake prepared to leave the African coast, his supplies of food, water, and fuel finally complete. His ship was now, he observed, "put . . . in a posture to sail tomorrow morning with the land breeze." That following day, the *James* thus began its transatlantic voyage toward Barbados.[43]

With land fast disappearing in its wake, the *James* carried its cargo of captives forward into the open sea. The last point of spatial reference vanished once the ship was surrounded by an empty horizon on all sides; only the vessel itself offered fixity and the sense of place. Its scale dwarfed by the unbounded expanse of ocean, the ship became, in this astonishingly unearthly realm, a world unto itself.

Following the death of the pregnant woman on 5 March, the captives' first month at sea continued with a stretch of seven days during which no one perished aboard the *James.* No longer was death at sea a novel occurrence, but thus far it had targeted the people from Winneba with a persistence that could not have gone unnoticed. The pattern continued when the procession of departing souls resumed.

13 March: a man "received from Wyembah."

15 March: a man, "received from Wyembah very thin & fell into a flux."

As the slave ship made its way into deeper waters, the daily cycles of land and sea breezes gave way to the more random, and power-ful, winds and ocean swells on the open sea. Not long after the land disappeared from view, crewmen aboard most slave ships began to remove the iron shackles that the enslaved men had worn for weeks and sometimes months by this time. "When our slaves are aboard," wrote Thomas Phillips, "we shackle the men two and two, while we lie in port, and in sight of their own country, for 'tis then they at-tempt to make their escape, and mutiny." But "when we come to sea," he explained, "we let them all out of irons, they never at-tempting then to rebel, considering that should they kill or master us, they could not tell how to manage the ship, or must trust us, who would carry them where we pleas'd."[44] Likewise, Jean Barbot reported that women were allowed to move about freely on deck, while "many of the males had the same liberty by turns, succes-sively; few or none being fetter'd or kept in shackles, and that only on account of some disturbances, or injuries, offer'd to their fellow-captives, as will unavoidably happen among a numerous crowd of such savage people."[45]

It was one week following the ship's departure from the Afri-can coast before captives aboard the *James* regained the use of their limbs. In the midst of a storm of two days' duration and sufficient strength to cause the main topsail yard to break, Blake decided to remove the shackles that bound their arms and legs. "This day," Blake wrote, as the "turnadoe" continued with "much thund'r lightening and raine" on 16 March, "I putt all my slaves out of Irons."[46]

Removal of iron restraints restored tiny freedoms that brought captives enormous relief. Whereas before actions as simple as roll-ing onto one's side had required coordination with another person, now a measure of independent movement was possible. Even so, movements larger than small bodily gestures demanded choreo-graphed effort. The reduction of so many bodies alive with kinetic energy to disquieting stillness was among the worst of the violence done to slaves on board ship.

> *18 March:* a man, "received from Wyembah very thin & soe fell into a Consumption & departed this life."

On 22 March, Blake recorded that the *James* had crossed to the south of the equator. This event, significant as an indication of the ship's progress toward its destination, supplies a spatial referent not even perceptible to the African captives aboard the *James*.

Of great meaning for the captives was the freshly caught fish Blake added to their diet. Having promised on 28 March to reward his crew with one pint of brandy "for every 10 fish" caught, he henceforth made albacore a regular part of the rations his captives received. Notations like the one he entered on 28 March, "Gave my slaves 10 fish in ye Suppie [Supper]," started to appear routinely in Blake's journal.

The eleven days beginning 19 March passed without event when it came to death, making this the longest such stretch of days during the entire voyage thus far. The loss of a captive from Winneba broke the lull.

> *30 March:* a man, "received from Wyembah very thin & soe Continued Wasting Untill death."

> *31 March:* a "very sick" boy "fell overboard in the night & was Lost."

> *6 April:* a man, "received from Wyembah thin & Consumed very low & after dyed of a Great swelling of his face & head."

> *14 April:* a man, "received from Wyemba thin & dyed of a flux."

> *15 April:* a woman, "received from Wyemba Sickened & would not eat nor take anything."

16 April: a man, "bought by mee & dyed of a flux."

17 April: two men, "the one received from Wyembah & dyed of a flux. The other received ditto who Leaped over board & drowned himself."

The second man chose his moment to act in the afternoon hours. The ship's boat quickly pursued him, a "stout manslave" to a trader's eye, but "just as they came upp with him," Blake wrote, "hee sunke downe," and when the coxswain "runn downe his oare betweene his armes," the man "would not take hould of it & soe drowned himselfe."

Thirteen weeks had passed since he had boarded the ship, and in this time he had seen seventeen bodies committed to the sea, thirteen of which belonged to people who also had boarded at Winneba. Why did that slave choose to take his own life? Did he seek to follow someone to whom he was connected by kinship? Did he somehow trust that his journey beyond the ship would lead to communion with his ancestors, although he had violated prohibitions against suicide? Or was it his choice to accept a different fate: Was his refusal to take the oar extended to bring him back to the ship a choice to risk the eternal wandering of his soul, rather than remain in the limbo of a ship that could sustain neither life nor death?

20 April: a woman, "received thin att Wyembah & dyed of a Consumption."

21 April: a boy, "received from Wyemba with a dropsey & soe dyed."

26 April: a woman, "bought by my selfe & being very fond of her Child Carrying her up & downe Wore her [self] to nothing by which meanes [she] fell into a feavour & dyed."

On 27 April, the ship crossed the equator for the second time. Sailing once again in northern latitudes, the *James* had reached another milestone in its transatlantic voyage: on a westerly tack, the ship now approached the Americas.

Captives who had not lost track of the moon's phases knew that the ship was entering its third month at sea; meanwhile, Blake turned his calendar to the month of May. At that point, those who had boarded the ship at other Gold Coast ports—Amersa, Anomabu, and Agga—began to join the community of the deceased.

1 May: a man and woman, both "received from Anamaboe departed this life of a flux."

2 May: a woman, "received from Agga & departed this life of a flux."

3 May: a man, "received from Wyembah & departed this life of a dropsey."

4 May: a man, "received from Mr. Ballwood att Amyssa [Amersa] & dyed of a feavour by Lying in the [ship's] Longboat in the rain in the night which noe man knew of for hee went into her privately."

5 May: a woman, "received from Wyembah very thin & old & departed this Life of the flux."

6 May: a man, from Anomabu, who likewise "departed this life of a flux."

8 May: a woman, "received from Wyembah with a Dropsey & departed this life of the same disease."

9 May: a man, "bought by mee at Anamaboe & departed this life of the flux."

12 May: a woman, "received from Wyembah thin & consumed away untill life departed from her."

13 May: three men, one "received from Wyembah thin & departed of a flux"; another "received from Anamaboe & dyed of the Cramp in all his joynts & all over his body, being lately recovered of the flux"; and the third "bought my mee" and also "dyed of the Cramp."

Also on this day, Blake began to close in on his destination. "I directed my course Northwest and then by West distance 55.5 miles until 10 o clock, and then supposed myself to be near the latitude of the Island," Blake recorded in his journal. Sixteen days after crossing back into the northern hemisphere, he was on the lookout for the tiny island of Barbados.

14 May: two women, "the one received from Wyembah very thin & departed this life of the flux" and "the other received from Anamaboe & departed this life of ye flux."

16 May: a man, "received from Anamaboe & departed this life of a flux."

On 18 May the *James* was passed by a ship from New York, traffic that confirmed for Blake his proximity to the island. For the captives on board the *James,* signs that change was imminent were less clear. "Wee put our Slaves to noe allowance of Water" was the additional notation Blake entered into his journal that day.[47] Meanwhile, the most oppressive of the ship's rhythms continued with a steady and relentless beat.

20 May: a woman purchased by Blake "departed this life of Convultions."

21 May: a man "received from Agga & departed this life of a flux."

Also on this day, the island of Barbados finally appeared on the horizon in the early hours of the morning, a Sunday on Blake's calendar.[48]

Steering a course for Barbados was not an easy task. The seventeenth-century traveler Sir Henry Colt likened it to finding "sixpence throwne downe uppon newmarkett heath." The easternmost of the Lesser Antilles by a distance of ninety miles, Barbados stands alone in the southwestern corner of the North Atlantic, marking the first doorway to the Caribbean Sea for those who could find the tiny island at all.[49] Seventeenth-century sailors, who possessed not much more ability to determine their position in the Atlantic than Columbus had three hundred years earlier, relied on a combination of guesswork, science, and luck to find their way to the Caribbean islands. Latitude was relatively easy to calculate with some degree of accuracy. With the help of the astrolabe, mariners were able to determine their place on the vertical axis connecting the North and South Poles. The measurement of longitude, however, remained an extremely imprecise matter. Without an accurate measure of distance traveled east or west, mariners were forced to guess at their longitudinal position.

Knowing the average crossing time from his African port of departure to the Caribbean, a skilled ship captain paid close attention to the passage of time in the Atlantic and aligned his vessel with the latitude of Barbados when the calendar indicated that it was time to begin searching for the tiny island's silhouette on the western horizon. Once the ship was in the vicinity of the island (if calculations and guesswork had proved accurate), a well-trained watchman's eye would enable him to complete the navigational task. Even after it was positioned in the correct latitude, the vessel that carried Colt to Barbados in 1631 "tacked warily for several days" before the island was sighted "in the small hours of the morning" by a lookout whose cry of "Land!" signaled the successful completion of the voyage, forty days after the departure from England.[50]

Barbados, because of its easterly position, was the first available landfall in the Americas. For this reason, whatever the final destination, most slavers crossing the Atlantic sailed first to Barbados. There, captains, even if bound for Jamaica or the Chesapeake colonies, could take on provisions when their own supplies were either spent or too spoiled to use. When the *Lady Francis* reached Barbados from New Calabar in 1678, for instance, the slaves aboard were given 1,000 pounds of potatoes, 4,000 limes, and 84 gallons of rum before putting out to sea again en route to Virginia.[51] The 240 Africans aboard the *Marygold* received 2,450 pounds of potatoes, 28 gallons of rum, and an allotment of tobacco when the vessel arrived at Barbados in May 1677.[52] Even vessels headed for the nearby Leeward Islands might occasionally stop first at Barbados. The *Dragon* took onboard 31 bushels of peas, 1,288 pounds of fish, 425 pounds of potatoes, 63 gallons of rum, and 4,000 limes at Barbados before sailing for Nevis in 1680.[53]

The stop at Barbados was often especially necessary when ship captains had not taken advantage of the opportunity to fortify their store of provisions at São Tomé or one of the other islands in the Gulf of Guinea, before undertaking to cross the long stretch of open sea to the west. After a voyage of nine weeks from Cape Coast Castle, the *Blossom* reached Barbados on 29 May 1679, "in pretty good Condition," but in need of "water and Refreshments for the Negroes, not having touched at the Islands." After one week's stay, the vessel continued on its way to Virginia with 244 Africans aboard.[54]

Just days after the *Blossom* departed, another Virginia-bound vessel entered the harbor. Once laden with 179 Africans at New Calabar, the *Swallow* had "touched for refreshments" at Annabon Island (southwest of São Tomé). Nonetheless, the "yeams being all rotten" by the time the captain reached the Americas, he was forced to stop at Barbados. There, company agents agreed to "furnish them with all speed with such provisions as this country at present affords, and . . . dispatch them with all speed to their designed port of Virginia," putting on board 52 bushels of peas, 2,278 pounds of flour, and 96.5 gallons of rum.[55]

Standing alone in the eastern Caribbean Sea and having a markedly low "silhouette," Barbados might easily be missed by European mariners anxiously searching the horizon for its outline. So Africans perhaps did not take note of the impending landfall until the island swung into view. By the time daylight came, the startling sight of the coastline, "a white line of breakers, sand, and rocks, with wooded land rising steeply beyond," had replaced the endless expanse of the open sea.[56]

As the sun climbed in its familiar path, the panorama spread out before the captives aboard the *James* filled with detail. From the sparsely inhabited eastern shore of the island, the ship passed around Easting's Point, and the shoreline grew thicker with dwellings, until finally the ship stood athwart a busy waterside town hugging the edge of a wide bay, called by the English after the Earl of Carlisle.[57]

Sale of the captives delivered on the *James* began four days after the ship's arrival on 25 May, by which date four more captives were dead. By the time the seventeen unsold "refuse" slaves left the ship on 6 June, another seven persons had expired. In all, fifty-one had perished aboard the *James* during the nine months it had served as a waterborne prison for African captives.

On average, 20 percent of the Africans carried into the Atlantic in the seventeenth century died at sea, and 40 percent of cargoes experienced mortality levels *above* that benchmark.[58] Seen through this lens, mortality among the captives aboard the *James* appears notably benign. Since captivity on the *James* proved considerably less deadly than aboard other ships navigating the Atlantic at this time, the fifty-one people who died on the ship leave only a faint mark in the slave traders' comparative calculation of loss.

But look again. Equally convincing was the competing narrative framed by the captives themselves, those aboard the slave ship in transatlantic motion. They also evaluated death on the Atlantic, but by very different systems of value and measurement. Through the words he entered in his journal and his account of mortality, Blake unwittingly offers a glimpse of the captives' experience. Like epitaphs, his words convey the traumatic content that shaped the captives' own "account"—a man's determination to commit his own body to the sea (and confront the danger that action entailed for his soul), a woman's unwillingness to abandon her duties as a mother aboard ship, a man's desperate search for a private place to endure his illness, and others' profound inability to heal their disintegrating bodies or counter the overwhelming forces that made them so ill.

European investors in African human cargoes focused constant attention on the conditions of the slave ship under sail. They tried different strategies for providing food sufficient in quantity and quality, worried about the purity of water supplies, fretted about crowding ("tight packing"), disease, depression, and physical atrophy. Each of these being a problem demanding a rational solution, the investors devised strategies to cope with all these concerns: extra provisions, methods for protecting water from contamination, mandatory exercise, regulations on the number of captives a ship could carry, inoculation against smallpox when the procedure became available early in the eighteenth century, and even recourse to indigenous African healing practices.

Indeed, so pressing was European anxiety and effort to manage the innumerable risks that attended the business of slaving that it is easy to confuse European interest in preserving life to prevent economic loss with positive concern for the captives' human welfare. But to interpret the regime of the slave ship in that way is to be duped by the slave traders' rhetoric—a language of concealment that allowed European slaving concerns to portray themselves as passive and powerless before the array of forces (including the agency of the captives themselves) outside their control.[59] Slave merchants and their backers disguised from themselves the ugly truth that the Atlantic regime of commodification took captives from fully realized humanity and suspended them in a purgatory in between tenuous life and dishonorable death. The *James* held a collective of 423 people in psychic terror over a journey in which some-*one* died fifty-one times. Each thwarted life, each departure, was distinct in its details, and each was connected to and compounded by the accumulating residue of those which had preceded and by those which would follow.

Mortality on the Atlantic produced a crisis of enormous proportions, as Africans labored under the cumulative weight of these deaths that remained unresolved. For the Akan captives, the *James* was the site of a relentless accumulation of incomplete deaths, each one holding its own tragic meanings. Entrapped, Africans confronted a dual crisis: the trauma of death, and the inability to respond appropriately to death. This indirect violence, arguably, was the most abject experience of the captives' Atlantic crossing. The cost for Africans of that crossing cannot be adequately represented by any statistics. More fundamentally, on the sea voyage, even the African dead were enslaved and commodified, trapped in a time-space regime in which they were unable fully to die.

6

*Turning Atlantic Commodities
into American Slaves*

Having already been bought and sold at least once in Africa, captives deported across the Atlantic aboard European ships again became the object of calculated attention and scrutiny on arrival in the Americas. In superficial details, the New World setting where the slave ship ended its transatlantic journey appeared more similar than not to the African setting where the voyage had begun. Just as that coastal market was the portal through which captives had entered into the slave ship, only through the portal of another market could they leave the slave ship alive.

Beneath the surface, however, the American market was different from that on the African coast in important respects. Buyers and sellers engaged in competitive valuation focused on the African captives, but the agendas that drove that contest were distinct from those which had driven market activity on the African coast. The merchant or commercial concern that had been represented as a buyer of people on the African coast was in this context a seller of human commodities. Here the wholesale production of slave cargoes that was the business of the supply-side market on the African coast met its correlate: the American market was the final site of retail transaction. The agenda behind this market was the sale of commodified labor: it was here that human commodities became American slaves.

As in Africa, in America those responsible for documenting the activities of the market produced two categories of textual "accounts," the one an official account recorded in the ledgers and remittances of sales, the other a more informal account recorded in the running commentary of correspondence and marginalia, where anecdotal observations appeared. And here again it is in the dissonances between these two accounts that we can discern something of the captives' own testimony.

"Account of Sales of Negroes by the *James*"

It was in the English merchants' interest to effect an easy complementarity between African and American markets—to ensure that the merchandise acquired on the African coast corresponded as closely as possible to what Americans wanted to buy. The end point of the dealers' efforts was the accounts and invoices that agents prepared when the sale of a cargo was completed. Upon concluding the sale of captives delivered to Barbados aboard the *James,* for instance, the company agents on hand drafted an "Account of Sales of Negroes by the *James,* Capt. Peter Blake"(Fig. 6.1).[1] Together with Blake's "Account of Mortallity," the summary of transactions over the constituent bodies in the cargo produced the numbers that would define the outcome of the voyage in narrowly quantitative terms of profit and loss.

In a few lines scribbled at the bottom of the invoice they prepared, the Royal African Company agents at Barbados did the arithmetic for the voyage of the *James:* 372 captives sold by the company agents, 51 dead on the voyage from Africa to America, 7 delivered to Blake for payment of his commission. In all, 430 units of human property purchased on the African coast with the company's goods now were accounted for. Sale of the 372 men, women, and children, distributed to buyers in fifty transactions over the course of three days, produced "nett proceed" in currency credit and sugar in the amount of "four Thousand eight hundred thirty

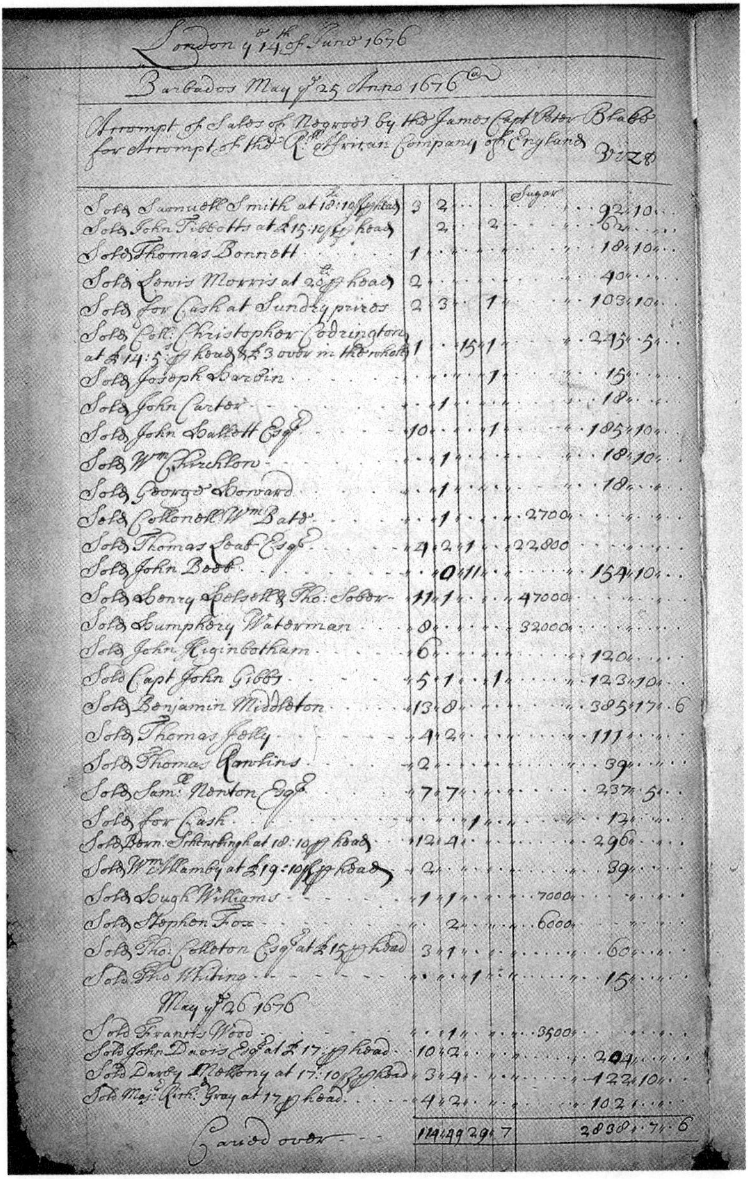
London ye 14th of June 1676

Barbados May ye 25 Anno 1676

Accompt of Sales of Negroes by the James Capt Peter Blake for Accompt of the Rll African Company of England Vizt

					Sugar			
Sold Samuell Smith at 18:10 per head	3	2				92	10	
Sold John Tibbotts at £15:10 per head		2		2		62		
Sold Thomas Bonnett	1					18	10	
Sold Lewis Morris at 20£ per head	2					40		
Sold for Cash at Sundry prices	2	3		1		103	10	
Sold Coll: Christopher Codrington at £14:5s per head & £3 over in the whole	1		15	1		245	5	
Sold Joseph Harbin				1		15		
Sold John Carter		1				18		
Sold John Hallett Esq	10			1		185	10	
Sold Wm Chrichlow		1				18	10	
Sold George Howard		1				18		
Sold Collonell Wm Bate		1			2700			
Sold Thomas Leab Esq	4	2	1		22800			
Sold John Boot		0	11			154	10	
Sold Henry Helsell & Tho: Sober	11	1			47000			
Sold Humphery Waterman	8				32000			
Sold John Higinbotham	6					120		
Sold Capt John Gibbs	5	1		1		123	10	
Sold Benjamin Middleton	13	8				385	17	6
Sold Thomas Jolly	4	2				111		
Sold Thomas Rawlins	2					39		
Sold Samll Newton Esq	7	7				237	5	
Sold for Cash			1			13		
Sold Bern: Schenckingh at 18:10 per head	12	4				296		
Sold Wm Allamby at £19:10 per head	2					39		
Sold Hugh Williams	1	1			7000			
Sold Stephen Fox		2			6000			
Sold Tho: Colleton Esq at £15 per head	3	1				60		
Sold Tho Whiting			1			15		
May ye 26 1676								
Sold Frantis Wood		1			3500			
Sold John Davis Esq at £17 per head	10	2				204		
Sold Darby Mahony at 17:10 per head	3	4				122	10	
Sold Majr Rich: Gray at 17 per head	4	2				102		
Carried over	114	49	29	7		2838	7	6

6.1 "Account of Sales of Negroes by the *James*," May 1676, T70/937.

four pounds five Shillings Six pence Sterling and one hundred fifty six thousand four hundred pounds of Muscavado Sugar."[2]

In the correspondence that accompanied the invoices, the sellers of human cargoes on the American market left another transcript as well, one that reveals some of the details of this final stage in the commodification of African captives. In this as in any retail market, the fit between supply and demand was not self-evident but rather was developed in the interplay between sellers, buyers, and the commodities themselves. The invoices produced in the American market, like the equivalent records of the African coastal market, present sales of slaves only as a series of quantitative facts, a reflection of purely mercantile preoccupations. The agents' correspondence, however, opens a window onto the social world that animated the American market.[3]

When Captain John Woodfine brought his ship the *John Bonadventure* to anchor at Jamaica on 7 June 1682, 521 African captives were aboard. All appeared to be "good slaves" whom the agents intended to "expose to sale" eight days from that date. Ten Africans died in the intervening week, and the agents accordingly delivered 116 persons to Captain Woodfine for his commission and freight on delivery of 511 slaves. Once the sale was under way, however, another man perished. Since this death occurred after commission and freight charges had been calculated, the agents had to record the loss in the invoice they forwarded to London. They absolved themselves of responsibility for the miscalculation by explaining that the man in question had been "a very Likely Negroe to the eye."[4] Did the agents speak truthfully, or were their words a mere deceit? Did this captive's outward appearance in fact convince the company agents that he was in good health, or had they cynically paid commission and freight on a man whose imminent death they could foresee? It does not matter for our purposes any more than it did for theirs, for what their words clearly convey is that the end of the ocean crossing returned captives to the regime of the marketplace, where another's gaze held the power to define them.

In purely commercial terms, it was in the interests of the English merchants, whose aim had been to buy cheap on the African coast, to sell dear in America. Their task was complicated, however, by two factors. First, the commodities they sold to American buyers were not the same commodities purchased on the African coast. In Africa, European traders obtained lots of human freight adequate to constitute a complete cargo. In the Americas, the desired commodity was the ideal embodiment of labor power. Second, as success for English mercantile concerns hinged on their earning a profit on their investment in human trafficking, it was the American agent's job to exact a price for the human commodities sold on the American market that would exceed the costs associated with their production. As "carrying merchandise to the African coast from Europe doubled the price of that merchandise and carrying slaves from Africa to the Americas also doubled the price of slaves," the costs built into the price agents needed to obtain for the people they sold were high.[5] The equation rested on a contradiction, though: the transport system that doubled the price of human commodities when they reached America also greatly diminished their quality. Having been physically and psychologically traumatized by the violence of their commodification, the people who disembarked from slave ships in the Americas were the antithesis of what planters wanted to buy.

Making the African supply side correspond to the American demand side of the market, in other words, involved more than simply transporting goods from one side of the Atlantic to the other. It required also a transformative power of representation—marketing. Commercial success in the American market hinged on a trick: if agents in the American markets were successful, it was because they convincingly represented the exceedingly damaged goods they received as the ideal embodiment of labor power that their customers were looking to buy.

Following English cultural assumptions regarding the appropriate division of labor among the sexes, the planters came hoping to find twice as many men as women. And in further consideration of the physical demands they expected to impose, the planters had no interest, when inspecting the African cargoes, in specimens that were either small children or adults past their prime. The sellers' rhetoric and zeal notwithstanding, neat correspondence between African supply and American demand was unrealizable: it was not possible in any consistent way to obtain twice as many men as women in the African market; it was not possible to obtain only captives in the prime of their productive years; it was not possible to obtain only captives in good health.

In actual practice, then, the value that captive people had in the African market necessarily diverged from their worth in the American market where they were to be sold. Negotiations between English mercantile concerns and Anglo-American purchasers over their respective interests determined where and under what conditions African captives could leave the slave ship.

"They Choose Them as They Do Horses in a Market"

"When they are brought to us," Richard Ligon of Barbados said in the mid-seventeenth century, "the Planters buy them out of the Ship, where they find them stark naked, and therefore cannot be deceived in any outward infirmity. They choose them," he continued, "as they do Horses in a Market; the strongest, youthfullest, and most beautiful, yield the greatest prices."[6] Yet of course these commodities were not horses, but people about whom there was much more to know than what the eye could register about sex, age, strength, or "beauty." Attaching value to superficial visual cues in this way, prospective buyers gambled that visual inspection of the naked bodies offered sufficient confirmation of what they wanted and needed to know. They pinned their hopes on what few details they could glean about the captives' background and qualities.

In this regard, the American slave market was as compelling a theatrical stage as any to be found in Renaissance England; for here, where the commodification of Africans bore fruit in the sale of their bodies for profit, packaging and the power of illusion held sway. On the American market the sellers broke the composite—the cargo—down into the individual units of human property that would be offered for sale to planters. There the captives were convincingly fashioned into slaves—the human machinery that would plant and harvest the crops of sugar, rice, and tobacco that drove the colonial American economy.

"The 17th & 18th wee appointed for theire Sales."[7] With these words, the agents of the Royal African Company on Jamaica set the wheels in motion. Both the *Sarah Bonadventure* and the *Allepine* had arrived from Africa on Sunday, 9 July 1682, the former in the morning, the latter in the afternoon.

The arrival of a slave ship commenced a period of roughly a week during which agents prepared to stage their show: the presentation of African cargoes to prospective American buyers. The preparations began with food. The fresh food and water agents generally sent aboard newly arrived slave ships provided a welcome change, intended to "refresh" the slaves before sale. Starchy foods that would be the mainstay of the slaves' diet on the plantation, potatoes, yams, plantains, or peas, gave the undernourished Africans a much-needed nutritional boost before they went ashore.[8]

The quantity and type of food provided varied according to the perceived need of the Africans on each ship. The 207 people who reached Jamaica aboard the *London Merchant* in 1675 received a full range of provisions. Limes and tobacco were sent aboard "for ye Negroes refreshment," along with a barrel of mackerel, twelve bushels of peas, and 2,170 pounds of potatoes, whereas the 299 captives aboard the *Phineas & Margaret* received 6,060 pounds of potatoes and five bushels of peas when that vessel arrived in 1681.[9] Agents spent five pounds and ten shillings on provisions for the 550 Africans aboard the *Sarah Bonadventure* when they arrived in Jamaica in November 1677, the captain's own provisions for them having been "spent."[10] Many "leane and sickly ones" were among the 490 Africans who reached Jamaica aboard the *Sarah Bonadventure* in 1680. Their hunger and illness had been "occasioned from the want of Provisions throughout the voyage" from Angola, so potatoes, limes, 4,644 pounds of yams, and more than 14 bushels of peas were sent aboard upon the arrival of the vessel.[11]

Next, attention turned to the factor that would matter most in the captives' upcoming performance: their physical appearance. The aesthetic preliminaries for marketing African captives as slave laborers went beyond what could be achieved with a brief reprieve from the extreme nutritional deprivation on shipboard. Hoping to divert the audience's eye from the all too noticeable ravages of the Atlantic voyage, captains and agents made sure that heads were shaved and bodies were bathed, in order that lice-infested hair, skin stained with bodily fluids, or other such undesired testimony to the violence and unsanitary conditions of the slave ship would be concealed from view.

So important was the appearance of physical vitality that oil of one kind or another was used to give captives' skin a superficial luster and mask the depletion, weakness, and exhaustion that would otherwise have been evident. This was not a gratuitous embellishment but rather an indispensable element in the preparation for sale. Peter Blake gave the captives aboard the *James* "Fresh water to wash & palme oyle & tobacco and Pipes," and on one occasion when palm oil was not available, the company agents in Antigua used "mantigo" (probably from Spanish *manteca,* meaning "lard") instead, to "rubb them before Sale."[12] When the *Elizabeth* reached Barbados in August 1688, among the expenditures made in association with the sale of the slaves was two pounds, ten shillings paid in cash for one barrel of generic "Negro Oyle."[13]

Finally, about one week after the ship had come to anchor, the day of sale arrived, bringing buyers and sellers into negotiation over the assemblage of human wares on display. Sellers, of course, aimed to project onto the captives those values that would allow the cargo as a whole to "sell to Advantage."[14]

At the carefully staged performance surrounding the sale of captive Africans, the agents responsible for overseeing the process were keen to cater to their audience's comfort and pleasure. In the seventeenth century, when slave sales in the English Caribbean generally took place on shipboard, prospective buyers were ferried out to the slave ships in boats provided by the company. The norms of hospitality required agents to serve wine and "refreshments" to prospective buyers, to keep the mood jovial and the atmosphere pleasant.

The money spent for "boathire on board & on shoare" in the sale of slaves delivered to Barbados was a standard item included in nearly all the accounts remitted to London by company agents in Barbados—in the case of the *Lenox* in May 1677, ten shillings—as was the amount, two pounds and change, expended for "wine, brandy, [and] mobby Sugar" to serve the buyers.[15] After the *Convert* arrived in July 1680, the agents spent one pound for "boathire on board to muster the negroes at arrivall & to deliver the Commission & Freight Negroes & the 3 daies of Sales," as well as six pounds, one shilling, and nine pence, for "provisions with wine, Brandy, Sugar etc. the 3 daies of Sales."[16]

Similarly, when the Africans aboard the *William* were sold in Jamaica in November 1674, the agents spent ten shillings to send a messenger to Yallahs Bay "to give notice of ships arrivall and sale," six pounds for "wine, Brandy and Victualls on board at the sale day to Entertaine the Country," and fourteen shillings, sixpence for "boat huyre to and from the Ship on sale day."[17] In selling the Africans aboard the *Vyne* in February 1680, the agents paid one pound "for boathire untill all Sold" and four pounds, one shilling "for a Treat aboard at Sales."[18] Wine, bread, and olives were the fare served on the "day of Sale" when the slaves crowded aboard the *Mary & Margaret* were sold on 24 May 1699.[19]

In the American market, Anglo-American planters were motivated by the universal buyer's aim, to acquire maximum value at minimal cost. For the planters who came down to the harborside seeking to purchase new slave laborers, the threat of making a bad investment loomed large. Like buyers in any market, they had to weigh the commodities on display against the ideal in their minds' eye.

The physical condition in which many of the Africans entered the marketplace proved an even greater disappointment to the buyers than the scarcity of young males for sale. Bodies shaved, washed, and oiled to supply the illusion of health could not completely conceal the truth. Of the 214 persons who departed from the Gambia River aboard the *Coaster* on 1 July 1680, 34 had been lost by the time the ship reached Barbados at the end of the month. By marketplace standards, they were an ideal assemblage of Africans: there were nearly twice as many adult men as adult women, and men and boys together made up two-thirds of the cargo. But their bodies betrayed both the usual sufferings of the middle passage and the violence meted out to those who had tried to change their course in the Atlantic. "Some good men amongst them," the agents reported, "but the Women very bad and as wee conceive many of the men are much the worse for being soe Loaded with Irons as they have been all the voyage the Captaine saying they are very unrully and once designed to Rise and Cutt him and his People off, so durst not trust them otherwise."[20]

The bodies of some appeared swollen with dropsy when they were put up for sale. Such was the condition too of those who reached Nevis aboard the *Supply* in September 1681. On arrival, of the 235 purchased at Calabar, only 59 remained, and those "very dropsicall, soe that wee were glad to put them off as well as wee could," the agents explained.[21] Others bore the painful evidence of unhealed maladies suffered on the long journey. Many of the captives who reached Barbados in July 1684 aboard the *Coaster* were judged to be "elderly," and their skin was "bursten" with sores.[22]

Cargoes that included too many women, too many children, too many older people, or too many ravaged by hunger and dysentery appeared with such regularity that the agents came to refer to them as "ordinary." It was a label that was applied to many slave cargoes that deviated in one way or another from the ideal sought by buyers. When the *Welcome* reached Barbados on the morning of 12 May 1681, the cargo earned the description "very Ordinary Negroes, being most of them women & very Old Slaves." The vessel had departed Old Calabar on 12 February with 227 Africans aboard; exactly three months later, fewer than 70 percent of their number remained: 51 men, 90 women, 12 boys, and 8 girls.[23] The "very Ordinary" cargo of Senegambians aboard the *Ann* when that vessel reached Barbados in October 1680 included people who were not only "old" but also "Poore & Blind and many burst ones." Their condition, together with "the little esteeme those Negroes have here," kept many prospective buyers away, causing the slaves to "Ly Long on our hands & goe off att Low prizes."[24]

On all accounts, the planters frequently were disappointed, as they were when the *Hannah* reached Barbados in June 1688. Reportedly, the cargo of 416 Africans purchased at Whydah lost no more than 13 on the ocean crossing and arrived "in good condition." But with 187 women and only 172 men, the cargo was "ill sorted as to males and females" among the adults: according to the company agents, such an "extraordinary" number of women would "much impaire the sales."[25] Indeed, when Edwyn Stede sent the invoice for the sale of the cargo to company officials, he reminded them, "Its the company's interest to give a consideracion to have 2/3 men."[26] When the *Elizabeth* arrived later that summer, having also departed from the company's factory at Whydah, there were again more women than men aboard the vessel. While the 154 women constituted 45 percent of the 345 Africans made available for sale, only 124 men among that group (36 percent) were put up for sale.[27] Worse still, the Barbados agents complained that "above thirty men" in the cargo were deemed to be "superannuated."[28] Similarly, the Angolan cargo of slaves aboard the *Carlisle* included more women (188) than men (157) when it reached Jamaica in September 1681.[29] Though the Africans aboard this vessel appeared "indifferently well flesht" when they arrived, the agents complained that "there were a great many old ones amongst them," and two slaves, the one "mad," the other "bursten," brought complaints from disgruntled buyers.[30] The repeated arrival of cargoes dispatched from Whydah with "as many Woemen as men" moved the company officials to remind the agent hired to manage the factory there of the conditions of his contract, and to clarify its meaning. "Your articles," they wrote, "sayes the Major part men, and you drive it soe hard [as] to make that Major part not to be above one person, the number of Women exceeding doeth much disparayes [disparage] the whole cargoe."[31] A simple majority of men was not sufficient to meet the company's goal.

Apart from the great proportion of women who helped sustain the flow of enslaved migrants to the Americas were many whose small size betrayed their extreme youth and many whose advanced age was too obvious to be concealed. Indeed, children—those judged to be less than fourteen years old—made up 27 percent of the Africans shipped aboard Royal African Company ships in the years 1673–1725.[32] After viewing the 415 Africans who arrived at Nevis aboard the *George & Betty* on 3 December 1681, the agents reported that the cargo was "most women, amongst which was about 40 children under the age of 8 Yeares to our best Judgements." For his part, the captain, protesting that the matter was outside his control, explained that "they could not buy soe many men & women without that number of Children" on the African coast. For their part, the agents suspected that the captain had concealed other slaves aboard the ship, in the intention of smuggling them ashore. "Wee believe something elce in it, which wee hope in Little time to discover," they wrote.[33] Once the agents accounted for 17 Africans who had died at the port and for those given over to the captain in partial payment of his commission and freight charges, there remained 301 slaves to be sold for the company's profit, of whom more than a third (34 percent) were judged to be children: the count was 87 men, 111 women, 69 boys, and 34 girls.[34] Two days later the *Alexander* entered the harbor at Nevis carrying a cargo of 311 slaves purchased on the Gold Coast and in the Bight of Benin that included more women (115) than men (74), and also a rather high proportion of children (41), who accounted for 18 percent of the 230 persons sold by the company's agents.[35] When the *Prosperous* reached Barbados in September 1681 carrying 476 slaves from Angola, the 142 children aboard made up 30 percent of that number, while the largest group comprised the 189 women, accounting for 40 percent of the cargo.[36]

When the *Two Friends* arrived at Barbados on 17 March 1683, the agents complained that the Africans aboard were "but indifferent being many elderly amongst them nigh ½ of the men being of 40 to 50 yeares old or more."[37] And when the *Coaster* arrived nine months later, the 172 persons who appeared before the agents "proved but very Indifferent Slaves many being very old & poore & others Burst decreipt & Lame & Blind."[38] The agents responsible for the sale of the company's slave cargoes recognized four demographic categories in their presentation of the human commodities for the slave marketplace: men, women, boys, and girls. Thus, while it has been possible to analyze the proportion of children represented among the Africans reaching the English West Indies in the seventeenth century, it is not possible to do the same with regard to those who occupied the other end of the age spectrum. Frequent complaints about "superannuated" slaves among the cargoes, however, remind us that in the transatlantic flow of migrants the presence of another category of people further eroded the number that could be counted as male adults in their prime: the elderly and emigrants already in late middle age.[39]

The Geography of the American Slave Market

Out of the interplay of American demands and African supply emerged a geographical hierarchy of value: place of origin could figure heavily in determining where captives would end up entering their American enslavement. At one end of the spectrum stood Africans from the Gold Coast, the most coveted of all Africans who came to the Anglo-Atlantic world. The wealthy and powerful Barbados planters exerted their buying power to attract to their tiny island about half the ships departing from the Gold Coast, while their counterparts in Jamaica and the Leeward Islands took what they could get of the remainder, and fewer than a thousand went to the Chesapeake colonies. At the other end of the spectrum stood the Biafrans. Though they were not well liked, they were cheap and plentiful on the African coast, and thus Anglo-American colonists who wished to participate in the slave trade could not entirely avoid purchasing them.

It was only by an accident of timing that the captives aboard the *Sarah* went to York River in Virginia in June 1721. The orders that had accompanied the ship when it had left London the previous September directed the agents at Cape Coast Castle to "freight her with negroes and consign to Franklin Willis and Charles Chiswell, our agents at Virginia."[40] But new orders were sent in December, when the *Cape Coast* frigate was dispatched to obtain a cargo on the Gold Coast and deliver it to Barbados: "Regarding *Sarah*, Capt.

Bulcock, which we ordered you to slave for Virginia. If this reaches you in time, we would have her cargo also consigned to Barbados."[41] As it was June by the time the revised instructions reached Cape Coast Castle, news that the 250 captives aboard the *Sarah* were intended for the cane fields of Barbados reached the agents' hands just as the cargo arrived in Virginia, to be dispersed instead into the world of tobacco farming.[42]

The consignment to Virginia took the slaves aboard the *Sarah* out of the mainstream that carried more than 60 percent of cargoes from the Gold Coast to Barbados or Jamaica in the late seventeenth and early eighteenth centuries. Like buyers in any marketplace, Anglo-American planters were quick to develop a set of assumptions about the relative quality of the human commodities they purchased, and slaves from the Gold Coast—referred to as Cormantines in the English Americas—were consistently and highly praised by Caribbean planters throughout the seventeenth and eighteenth centuries.[43] The market strength of Barbadian planters in the seventeenth century, and of their Jamaican counterparts in the eighteenth century, ensured that their preferences were honored.

The opening decades of sustained slave exports from the Gold Coast tied the region at first nearly exclusively to Barbados in the 1660s and then to Jamaica and Nevis in the following decade. Occasional cargoes from the region began to appear in the other major areas of European colonization in the last quarter of the seventeenth century: sites of Dutch, Danish, and French colonizing efforts in the Caribbean, areas of English expansion in the Leeward Islands, and Virginia, whose planter elite reshaped the course of that English North American colony's labor regime by turning abruptly and decisively away from English indentured servants toward African captives.

At the turn of the eighteenth century Jamaica rose to prominence, eclipsing the claim Barbados had made in the preceding century on one of every two who survived the ocean crossing from the Gold Coast. The numbers of slaves pouring into Virginia and core areas of the Caribbean grew. Over the first quarter of the new century, the American market scattered Gold Coast peoples throughout the circum-Caribbean region, from the Chesapeake Bay to the Carolinas to the shores of the Rio de la Plata in South America; from Veracruz in the Gulf of Mexico to Portobelo, Panama, on the southern curve of the Caribbean Sea; from Saint Domingue to Guadeloupe, both sites of rapidly expanding slaveholding in the French Caribbean.

With a jump start of some twenty years on the other English colonies in the exploitation of slave labor, Barbados was already deeply committed to slavery by the 1660s and was home to no fewer than 175 "big planters"—those who owned sixty slaves or more—in 1680.[44] Thus, at the Barbados slave market there was no shortage of buyers to purchase from the Royal African Company's ships, and many of them were financially solvent enough to be a safe credit risk for the company. The exercise of market controls was deemed unnecessary there, meaning that the island's planters were free to pick and choose at will among the human commodities on display.[45]

Both wealthy and poorer planters in Barbados came aboard the ships eager to buy enslaved laborers, and by the time a day's business was concluded, buyers had negotiated the individual terms by which their transactions would be governed. For example, the first transaction concerning the 202 Africans delivered to Barbados by the *Arthur* in May 1678 assigned ownership of one woman to Richard Salter, in exchange for 3,000 pounds of sugar. In the second transaction, Richard Farr chose four men at a cost of 3,800 pounds of sugar per head "to pay by March." He was followed by Colonel James Carter, who claimed thirteen men, five women, and one girl, "ye men at £20, ye woemen at £18, the Girle at £11," to be paid in bills of exchange by 1 May of the following year.[46]

The transactions—forty-eight in all—continued aboard the *Arthur* for two days, as buyers negotiated the best terms they could, given their resources. A few were able to pay in "ready mony," but most relied on the company's willingness to invest in their future prospects. Wealthier members of the planter class could buy large groups of slaves on generous terms of credit; for instance, Doctor Thomas Cole and Elisha Mellowes together purchased twelve men and four women, paid for with bills of exchange due "½ in 6 months, the other ½ at 12 months." But Lawrence Rees was to pay the sixteen pounds charged for the woman he took home in three months, and William Alamby was to deliver out of his current harvest the 2,800 pounds of sugar due in exchange for one girl.[47] When the negotiations were complete, the planters returned to shore alone. Within a few days, the slaves they had picked out would follow. Having completed transactions for all but twenty-odd "refuse" slaves on Saturday, 27 May, for example, the agents at Barbados went aboard the *James* the following Monday, where they removed "& delivered 80 slaves which were part of the 118 which were sould on Satturday."[48]

The size and demographic composition of groups sold in Barbados ranged widely, and most of the early transactions in slave sales involved significantly more men than women, as the island's wealthiest planters picked out the most highly valued slaves—the adult men—first. The demographic description of the groups in which Africans left the slave ship tended to vary according to the timing of the sale transaction. Indeed, women were "more than 2.5 times more likely to be sold in the second half" of the sale.[49] For those aboard the *Arthur,* for example, the first twenty-four of forty-eight transactions were pretty much skewed in favor of men. Just over half the cargo (53 percent) was sold, but twenty-four groups included 67 percent of the cargo's men and only 34 percent of the women aboard the ship.[50]

When Barbados was already England's colonial crown jewel, in the second half of the seventeenth century, Jamaica was a diamond in the rough, whose full potential had yet to be realized. Seized from the Spanish crown in 1655, the island had as an English colony experienced little plantation development by the time the Royal African Company was chartered in 1672. By comparison with Barbados's 175 "big planters," slaveholders in young Jamaica were less wealthy. Though consolidation of large estates was well under way, Jamaica's planter class was "still in embryo," and most were "fairly small entrepreneurs by Barbados standards."[51]

Jamaica was fast becoming an island of extremes, however, where most sugar planters owned a sizeable number of slaves and relatively few small slaveowners could be found. Of fifty-four Jamaica sugar planters whose estates were inventoried in the last quarter of the seventeenth century, only six owned fewer than twenty slaves, and, more to the point, "the great majority had at least forty, and seven of them more than a hundred slaves."[52] The development of such large slaveholdings was reflected in the buying patterns of Jamaican planters when they attended the Royal African Company's sales. In a sample of 3,693 Africans sold in Jamaica in the years 1674–1693, only 20 percent were sold in groups numbering fewer than five slaves, and only 5 percent were sold singly.[53]

The burgeoning Jamaican plantocracy, though its numbers and slaveholdings remained small by comparison with those of its Barbadian counterpart, was eager to follow in the footsteps of Barbados. The Royal African Company could rely upon these large planters to visit Port Royal harbor often and to purchase larger rather than smaller groups of slaves. But these men alone could not sustain a viable market for slaves. The market in Jamaica, unlike the older one in Barbados, still lacked the capacity to absorb an entire cargo once the most highly valued slaves were taken. Moreover, Jamaican slaveholders did not have sufficient credit with the company for the enslaved persons they took with them when they left the marketplace. Allowed to make selections in a setting free of market controls, the small but ambitious group of Jamaican sugar planters were likely to do just as their counterparts in Barbados did. Taking for themselves the strongest, healthiest-looking men, together with a small proportion of women and children, the big planters would have left behind the dregs of a cargo, for which the agents would have been hard-pressed to find buyers. Had the company disposed of the slave cargoes sent to Jamaica in this fashion—selling its most profitable cargo to buyers unlikely to pay their debts when bills of exchange came due and incurring the expense of maintaining slaves slow to sell in the market—it would have suffered terrible losses in its business there.

This set of circumstances prompted the company to sell a large proportion of slaves in Jamaica in units of standard size and composition according to sex. After turning over whatever slaves were due to the captain in payment of commission and freight charges, the company agents usually sorted one-half to two-thirds of an African cargo into uniform "lots," which were sold to the planters at a standard price per head. The criterion for determining the composition of the lots is not entirely clear, for the agents rarely commented directly on the matter; however, their records clearly indicate that only adults were sold in this manner—children were never included in the lots.

The ratio of men to women generally reflected that of the cargo as a whole. As a result, the lots generally favored men only moderately, and groups composed of equal numbers of men and women were not uncommon. For buyers, the lot system employed in Jamaica meant that planters who came aboard the Royal African Company ships seeking the best-looking slaves in a cargo were compelled to take also some of those generally valued less—women and "ordinary" men. For the Africans, the system meant that a large proportion of the groups that left Port Royal harbor together en route to the plantations included at least some women among their number.

For example, when the *John Bonadventure* arrived in June 1686 with 431 Africans from the Gold Coast and the Bight of Benin, the agents went aboard and first delivered 107 slaves to the captain in partial payment of freight charges and commission. Of the 324 Africans who were to be sold for the company's account, the agents found 190 adults (59 percent of the remaining cargo) who appeared sound enough for sale by lot; these were sorted into thirty-eight groups of 5 slaves—3 men and 2 women—each to be sold for 110 pounds (or 22 pounds per head). Men made up 59 percent of the 274 adults available for sale, and there were one and a half times more men than women in the lots.[54]

Not all the cargoes delivered to Jamaica were divided into lots.[55] Occasionally, the company received a small proportion of slaves out of cargoes delivered on private contract, these usually being those rejected by the contractor as being too young or too old to comply with the contract stipulations. Such persons the agents usually sold at random. Other cargoes were too small, or too sickly, to warrant sale by lot; for example, the *Providence* arrived from the Bight of Biafra in 1680 with a "miserable parcell" of ninety-five persons, of whom sixty-four were delivered to the agents, after commission and freight charges had been settled with the captain. Selling the slaves at random, the agents managed to dispose of half the cargo on the first day of sale, but more than two weeks went by before the rest of the Africans were sold.[56]

Most of the cargoes that were not put into lots were sold to Spanish-American buyers who, much to English planters' dissatisfaction, frequently purchased slaves from the company, particularly in the 1680s. Upon reaching Jamaica after the long ocean crossing, these Africans left one slave ship for another and endured a second voyage to Spanish-American ports at Portobelo and Cartagena. From there the slaves were dispersed throughout South America.[57] The Spanish-American colonists were discriminating customers, and in some cases, the partial cargoes sold to them were choice slaves sought after by the island's planters. But generally the Spanish-American market served as an outlet for cargoes from African regions not favored by the Jamaicans, or occasionally for cargoes that had arrived in particularly bad condition, as was the case with the *Charles*. Having reached Jamaica early in 1681 with a cargo of 217 sickly Africans from the Bight of Benin, the agents found that the people were so ill from the spread of dysentery and smallpox, that "for makeing them into such Lotts as wee usually sell unto the Country wee could not find above fifty foure that would passe muster, the rest being Refuse and Boys & Girls soe very small that divers of them were under eight yeares old." Three days after their arrival, all but 3 of the 163 Africans to be disposed of by the company agents were sold to Capt. John Croaker, a Spaniard who regularly did business with the company.[58]

By comparison with Barbados and Jamaica, with their large demand for slaves, the less developed Leeward Islands remained a relatively peripheral market throughout the seventeenth century. On the whole, the Leeward planters were low on both cash and credit, having barely begun to convert their tobacco farms to sugar cultivation. As a result, the cargoes the Leewards attracted were not only fewer in number but also smaller in size.[59] Nevis was by far the most prosperous of the islands for most of the period and served as the Leeward entrepôt for the Royal African Company until the mid-1680s, much to the disgruntlement of planters in Antigua, Montserrat, and Saint Christopher. The company sent most of the Leeward cargoes to Nevis and expected the planters from the neighboring islands to make their purchases there. The company formally established independent factories at Antigua and Montserrat in 1686. "Wee have lately setled Factors at Antegua and Montserratt," the company's London officials wrote, "places to Leeward of Barbados, but not soe farr as Jamaica by much & they desire to have none but small vessells to come to them, none to bring to their Islands much above 200 Negroes at a time."[60] For their part, the planters complained that by the time they got to the sales held at Nevis, none but the "refuse" slaves were left.[61]

A 1678 Leewards census showed that in Nevis, the most developed of the four islands, eight planters owned more than sixty slaves. In addition, forty-five middling planters each held between twenty and fifty-nine slaves: these slaveholders owned almost half the slaves on the island. In Antigua, only six planters had large slaveholdings (of more than sixty slaves); while on Montserrat and Saint Christopher (for which figures on slaveholding are less readily available) only about three planters in each location owned at least sixty slaves.[62]

As in Barbados, in the Leeward Islands slave sales operated without market controls. The company agents there usually did set uniform prices for the most promising-looking men and women—potential workers whom they hoped to sell at profitable rates—but they did not sort the slaves into standard units. Like their counterparts sent to Barbados, Africans sold in the Leeward Islands left the slave ships in groups of widely varying size and composition. The strong presence of middling and small planters in the Leewards meant that Africans who landed there were more likely to be sold in small groups or alone. In a sample of 2,362 slaves delivered to the Leewards in the years 1674 to 1693, nearly 50 percent left the ships in groups of fewer than five slaves. Because 14 percent of the slaves delivered there sold singly, Africans who landed in the Leeward Islands were two and a half times more likely than those sent to Jamaica to leave the slave ship alone, without the company of shipmates.[63]

Would-be slaveholders in Virginia were considered to be the Royal African Company's least creditworthy customers in the seventeenth century. For this reason, the company was willing to send its ships to the Chesapeake Bay only if the sale of an entire cargo was guaranteed by prior contract. By this arrangement, a group of London merchants "agreed in advance with the company to buy

cargoes or fractions of cargoes at a fixed price payable in London."
A local representative of the London merchants took responsibility
for receiving and disposing of the slaves upon their arrival in Virginia. Thanks to this method, the company could count on "a guaranteed market and price, few or no agency costs, no debts, no law-
suits for the recovery of debts, and no problem of how to remit
effects from the West Indies to London."[64]

Though the sale of cargoes consigned to Virginia was handled by
prior contract, the company did appoint an agent there whose responsibilities included oversight of the cargoes' delivery. Cargoes
arranged by contract were no less subject to fraud than those sold
by the company's own agents, and so the company needed to hire
persons to represent its interests in Virginia, as it did in the West Indies. Thus, although no systematic record of their disposal was preserved, some details can be gleaned regarding the delivery and sale
of enslaved Africans sent to Virginia.

John Seayres was a newly appointed company agent when the
Katherine reached Virginia on 20 September 1678.[65] According to
Seayres's report, 399 slaves had boarded the ship on the African
coast—350 by the terms of the contract and an additional 49 above
that number.[66] "Before day the Night of his Arrivall," the ship's
captain (Thomas Bossenger) smuggled ashore "46 of the Choicest
and best Negroes of the Ships Loading," hoping to quietly sell them
to three persons well positioned to conceal the deceit: the collector
and deputy collector of His Majesty's Customs (Col. Warner and
Major Smith) and the comptroller general (Mr. Phillip Lightfoot).[67]

The captives having suffered terrible mortality on the Atlantic
crossing, only 30 percent of them remained alive, and their number
soon would decrease further. In addition to the forty-six, Seayres
reported, "there was only 74 left Alive After ye Expiration of 7
dayes"—this being the window of time following a ship's arrival
during which the death of African captives were counted toward
the Royal African Company's losses rather than toward the cargo

for which the contractor had agreed to pay. Of those seventy-four, thirteen appeared too old, too young, or too sick to be accepted by the contractor's Virginia representatives.

It was Seayres's responsibility to go aboard the ship to sell these thirteen "refused" slaves "by the Inch of Candle"—an auction at which prospective buyers offered competitive bids on each slave for as long as it took a candle to burn down by one inch. The method "was generally considered fair," writes economic historian David Galenson, "because it guaranteed a minimum time available for bidding, preventing an auctioneer from making quick sales to favored customers. The method was known to produce disputes, however, for disagreements could arise over who had been the final bidder before the flame flickered out."[68] But this surely was not a concern with regard to the thirteen persons Seayres was prepared to dispose of, for he reported that "five of that Number Dyed before I came aboard to sell them." Seayres auctioned only 6 of the remaining eight, because the other 2 "were dezesed [diseased] which no Body would bid for." One of these also died, while the other was sold by some other means.[69] The contractor's Virginia representatives sold the remaining 61 slaves and remitted bills of exchange to the company for them, which together with bills for the 46 the captain had tried to smuggle (minus 1 who died) made for a total of 106 people sold by contract.[70]

The "Refuse"

For the agents responsible for selling slave cargoes, the drama of the market consisted in the contest over terms and prices—how high the average price per head was, how much the arrival of another ship would affect the outcome of a sale already under way, and so on. But as agents fretted over such details and crafted explanations for disappointing outcomes, a fundamental truism presented itself to the captives themselves. Whatever the agreed-upon price or terms of payment, the bargaining unfailingly produced the same outcome: down to the weakest and the sickest, every single person in a newly arrived cargo was sold. Cargoes that suffered extraordinary incidence of disease or levels of mortality, endured exceedingly long ocean crossings, or whose demographic profile left much to be desired had the same fate as those which won buyers' admiration. All cargoes "found" a market somewhere in the Americas. No cargo found to be full of "superannuated" or poorly "sorted" or "meane" captives was rejected outright and returned to the African coast.[71]

Indeed, those who came to be called the refuse found their own specialized secondary market dominated by men whose enterprise was to purchase these unfortunates at low rates, in the hope that whichever among them recovered could be sold again for profit. Such transactions generally took place toward the end of the sale, when negotiations for all the other captives had been completed, and the "refuse" was all that remained. Out of the Africans who arrived in Barbados aboard the *Speedwell* in May 1681, this was the group of fifty-one slaves sold to Samuel Smart for the grossly reduced sum of two hundred pounds.[72]

Two Africans, a man and a woman, were "remaining under cure" and as yet unsold when the agents at Jamaica finished the sale of the cargo delivered in the *Sarah Bonadventure* in November 1677.[73] Following the conclusion of the sale held aboard the *John Bonadventure* in July 1680, there remained thirty-one Africans who were "brought on shoare to be sold," of whom one was dead when the agents balanced their accounts. The others were sold "to sundry persons for cash."[74] It is impossible to determine how many Africans reached the ports of the English colonies only to die there, but the number appears to have been substantial. Historian David Eltis has suggested that 95 percent of those delivered in English ships during the years from 1662 to 1713 were sold, the remainder being either dead or unmarketable.[75] This figure perhaps does not seem remarkable in the aggregate; however, when it is remembered that these losses to death and illness were measured within the small space of about one week between arrival and the tallying of sale proceeds, the continuing deadly impact of the Atlantic migration becomes readily apparent.

All this time the trauma of the ocean voyage continued to take its toll, particularly among those individuals who arrived in especially poor physical condition. Deaths at the port varied from ship to ship as can be seen from sale of the slaves brought in the *Sarah Bonadventure* and the *Vine,* which arrived in Jamaica in January 1680, the former ship with 470 slaves on board, the latter bringing 276 to harbor.[76] When the sale of the slaves began a week later, only two persons in the *Vine*'s cargo had died in the interim; the *Sarah Bonadventure* group, however, having arrived "meanly condition'd," had lost twenty of its number.[77] Having endured a "long Voyage" to Barbados, 130 "poore, miserable" and "very leane" people (mostly women, boys, and girls) arrived aboard the *Eglet* in August 1683. The condition of the survivors, together with news of the "greate mortality" that had occurred aboard the vessel, made "people unwilling to buy," the agents explained, "for which reason they goe off very heavily & at meane rates though all possible care hath bin used by Feeding & otherwise since they came hither to make them appeare & sell the best might be."[78] Those aboard the *Charles* had struggled against the common twin occurrence of smallpox and dysentery during their voyage from the Bight of Benin, and once they reached Jamaica on 20 January 1681, their suffering continued, "3 or 4 dying every day," although, as the agents noted in writing of the voyage, "wee observe that all possible care and cleanlinesse hath been used aboard & good order in accomidating the Sick."[79]

Sick, frightened, without orientation to time or place, and with bodies and minds bearing the weight of months of horror witnessed in the ocean crossing, most Africans proceeded through the processes of sale quietly. As buyers and sellers negotiated prices and terms of credit, the marketplace fiction that people were commodities remained, for the most part, intact. Some few, however, broke the silence. Through their loud, aggressive, and angry behavior, they placed themselves on the margins, though never fully outside the bounds, of the marketplace.

Africans who made known their refusal to play their prescribed role in the colonial economy from the moment of their arrival were deemed by the planter class to be too dangerous to bring into the heart of the plantation landscape. Among the Africans brought to Jamaica aboard the *Providence* in January 1681, one woman revealed herself to be "betweene mad & Foole, soe that noe body would give any thing for her or accept of her for nothing, being dangerous to be Kept in Port Royall or any Plantation where fyre may doe hurt." After some time, the woman was "sold" to a buyer from the remote north side of the island for 20 shillings. That amount being "about the Like sume" as what was expended to keep her all that time, the agents considered it unnecessary to include the transaction in their account book.[80] Similarly, at the conclusion of proceedings to disperse the cargo delivered aboard the *Diligence* in October 1676, after accounting for six slaves given to the captain toward his commission and one slave man who died during the sale, a "mad Woman" remained unsold; and when the sale of captives arriving aboard the *Marygold* came to a close in June 1677, "Two Mad Negroes Remained unsold."[81]

Finally, for some the transatlantic voyage ended in the violence that erupted among Africans themselves. When the *Eglet* came to anchor at Nevis on 24 February 1682, 119 Africans were on board, but when they were mustered onto the main deck by the company agents, one among them did not show up to be counted. Four days later, when the ship was sent to Saint Christopher for sale, the missing African was discovered hiding onboard. "Found among the Cask in the bottom of the Shipp," the man was forced to go ashore and submit to the workings of the marketplace. Before any of the island's planters could pretend to own his "very Lusty" body, though, he determined his own fate and that of another of the Africans around him. "That night for what reason noe body knowes," the agents reported, he "cut another Negroe mans Throate & Stabd him in the Brest & when he had soe done hanged himself in the Place."[82] Though we cannot know what provoked his act of murder and suicide, a few clues point to one possible interpretation. Upon further inquiry, the company agents learned that "the Negroe [who] . . . hanged himself . . . was much abused with blowes."[83]

Whether these "blows" took place in the middle passage or after arrival the agents did not say. But when the invoice of the cargo's sale was prepared, only the hanged man was listed as a loss; the other dead man was not counted as part of the cargo. Who was this man murdered by another African in the midst of the sale of a slave cargo? Perhaps he was one of the anonymous slave personnel employed in various capacities harborside, perhaps one of the linguists whose task was to board newly arrived ships and convince wary Africans that they would not be eaten once onshore, or perhaps a man whose dialect or facial markings betrayed him as an enemy to the man who took his life. Like the actions of "mad" slaves, events such as this one, whose causes were known only to those most directly involved, exposed the human complexity of the drama unfolding in the New World slave markets.

Amid all the activity and events that made up the slave marketplace, Africans looked on and struggled to make some sense of the scene in which they were the center of a sinister kind of attention. While the men (and occasionally women) who purchased slaves balanced such factors as the amount they could afford to spend, specific needs for their labor force, and the quality of the slave cargo on display before them, African migrants saw themselves sorted, separated, and regrouped into so many parcels of men, women, boys, and girls who would venture into unknown worlds together. Groups of newly purchased Africans climbed over the sides of the ship to be ferried ashore, and the pain of separation—for they might not see again the familiar faces of those with whom they had shared the ocean voyage—marked the end of one phase of their migration experience. The fear and anticipation all felt about what lay ahead marked the beginning of a new stage in the captives' lives.

7

Life and Death in Diaspora

To what extent, if at all, were Africans able to work free of the slave ship, the saltwater, and the agenda of the Atlantic slave market? The African as immigrant was not an inevitable by-product of the traffic in human commodities but rather a creation of his or her own arduous making. It is this that distinguishes African displacement in the Atlantic slave trade from all other emigration. Slaves' full personhood was the crux of the contest between Africans and those who commodified them. Traders and masters alike confronted the universal contradiction inherent in the idea of human beings as property; conceding that the slave had a will, in order to better devise means to control it, was not an acknowledgment of the slave's personhood.

The African slave, a victim of forced migration, cannot, then, be taken for granted as immigrant subject. This displaced being had to restore through her unassisted agency the pulse of social integration that saltwater slavery threatened to extinguish. That the Africans enslaved in America were immigrants was thus not an axiomatic truth, but rather one Africans had to fight for. Those who lived to walk away from the slave ship had to address the problem of their unique displacement and alienation. They did so in three ways that gave distinctive shape to their effort to build meaningful life in a new world. First, they engaged with the cognitive problem of orien-

182

tation: Where are we now that we have escaped the slave ship? Second, they created kinship and community out of the disaggregated units remaining after the market's dispersal of its human wares. Third, they came to terms with the saltwater journey's haunting imprint on their communities, regularly reinforced by the slave ships' return to deposit still more saltwater slaves on these unfamiliar shores.

"Thinking to Return to Their Own Country"

No less than their European counterparts or indeed than migrants in any place and time, Africans faced the problem of integration. Immigrants have to devise a means of connecting "the world they have left with the world they have entered."[1] The cultural tools people employ to make sense of displacement are the means by which migrants guard against that shattering or implosion of self and attachment. Without these tools, the disruption of migration leaves disintegration in its wake that neither the individual immigrant nor the community of immigrants can bear.

In the early modern Atlantic world, emigrants from Europe relied on letters and other media of transatlantic communication (pamphlets, newspapers, and the like) to restore integrity to lives fractured by overseas dispersal. Mariners in the age of sail crafted their own "culture at sea" to help them overcome the terror to which they subjected themselves. Their beliefs and rituals were cultural tools without which they could not survive the "confrontation between man and nature" aboard ship. "The sea's natural terror, its inescapable threat of apocalypse, imparted a special urgency to maritime social and cultural life," writes Marcus Rediker. "The chances for survival improved markedly as the ship's company became an effective, efficient collectivity, bound together in skill, purpose, courage, and community."[2] For Europeans before their age of discovery, the very impossibility of such cognitive reckoning made the Atlantic a "green sea of darkness"; until the end of the fifteenth century, notwithstanding the enormous technological strides that had been made by then, a man like Columbus was seen more as a fool than as a visionary in the community of his peers.[3]

Africans leaving the slave ship entered lives in which the imperative of cognitive integration was as great as it was for any other transatlantic immigrants. How did African captives guard against the disintegration of self in diaspora, following the implosion of the categories by which they had understood themselves and their world? If the active work of cognitive reorientation transformed Europe's "green sea of darkness" into a navigable and knowable bridge between the old and new worlds, how did Africans, who crossed the Atlantic not as mariners or willing migrants but rather as commodified people, reorient themselves? Landing on American soil put Africans into a new relationship to time-space, one that was at first a temporal and spatial disconnect. Through a variety of acts and gestures, Africans in the Americas responded to the instinct to heal the disruption that they experienced in time's circular path.

A recently arrived man makes "'three attempts, as he said, to get to his country'" from Virginia; a group of captives join forces near Petersburg, Virginia, "'being persuaded that they could find the Way back to their own Country'"; five captives found traveling in South Carolina are said to be following "'an East course as long as they could, thinking to return to their own country [Angola] that way'"; a woman is left stranded and alone on the banks of the Ogeechee River in South Carolina by four male companions who "'intended to go to look for their own country'": they had decided the canoe they had seized "'was not big enough to carry her with them.'"[4]

Through their actions, by pursuing the "forlorn attempt to find a return passage," Africans demonstrated their understanding that the transatlantic crossing could be brought to a definitive end only if they reversed their course by charting a route out of commodification.[5] Having finally escaped the restrictive existence of the slave ship, many found themselves turning to the same goal, setting about to retrace the ship's path, they hoped in the direction of home.

Though the urge to return was probably universal, the opportunity was rare. Most were stymied by the same obstacle: they could not find adequate means of transatlantic transport. Excluding a woman their canoe was "not big enough" to accommodate did not solve the dilemma faced by the four men on South Carolina's Ogeechee River. Having crossed the Atlantic once with the slave ship, they needed to retrace their path, but they were doubly trapped, inside the one-way route of saltwater slavery and also within a colonial regime of time-space imposed from without, whose contours they could not know and which they could not navigate on their own terms.

The stolen canoes and boats could not carry the desperate passengers far enough in any direction to put them beyond the reach of the American market. Only by returning to the Europeans' tall-masted ships and following the Cartesian coordinates of their geography could Africans find a means of transport out of American slavery. But any vessels that might carry Africans across the Atlantic traveled the same sea lanes as the slave ship and threatened the same horror. Thus, a man recently arrived from Senegambia explained the circumstances that put him on the run in Jamaica. When the "young Mandingo" was captured, he reported: "'He came to this Island in a Guineaman & belonged to a Captain who called him *Boatswain*. All the other negroes in the Cargo were sold but he & one other, who were going to go to England but their shipmates told them if they went again on Salt Water they would be eaten & so they escaped.'"[6] All courses that might lead home carried Africans back to the realm of the sea, its unbearable traumas, and in this case the renewed threat of cannibalism.

Some Africans made their way to seacoasts or riverbanks in

hopes of resolving the alienation of Atlantic captivity by another form of maritime travel. Dying by their own hand at a carefully chosen spot in or near the water might bring about their migration to the realm of the ancestors. According to the testimony of an ex-slave from Georgia, for example, Africans from the Bight of Biafra (Ibos) who were intending to take their lives "would 'mahch right down in duh ribbuh tuh mach back tuh Africa.'"[7]

As with any African death, however, this solution required pre-scribed ritual action. Cuban ex-slave Esteban Montejo explained that slaves who took their own lives did not just "throw themselves into rivers": first, "'they fastened a chain to their waists which was full of magic.'" It was also reported that for slaves in nineteenth-century Cuba, hanging was the preferred means of taking their own lives, because it "allowed for proper preparations for the expected return to Africa." A Cuban official explained, "'They put on all their clothes, put unconsumed food in them, the better to return well supplied to their native land where they believe they go body and soul.'" In Cape Cod, Massachusetts, the slave Congo Pomp prepared for death's journey by "placing at the foot of a tree a loaf of bread and a jug of water," before hanging himself from one of the tree limbs.[8]

The solution of a return journey by self-inflicted death was least available to those just released from the slave ship: their abject ma-terial poverty, weakness, and social isolation precluded such an un-dertaking. How could death achieve its desired end without the rit-ual objects and acts required to effect transmigration to the realm of one's ancestors and not to some unknown purgatory?

For most, no opportunity to attempt the return home material-ized. Instead, departure from the slave ship put captives, sorted, separated, and regrouped into the parcels buyers had claimed at the market, onto the roads and ferries that would carry them toward the farms and plantations, mines, and urban factories that would consume them as fuel in the engines of colonial production.

Inventing "Africa" in Diaspora

Unable to reverse the course of their commodification, Africans faced the realization that if there was to be life after the slave ship, it would be within the confines of American slavery. Just as the Atlantic market had pulled Africans to the Americas, the market set the ethnic and cultural boundaries of life after the slave ship, in determining how saltwater slaves fit into the great diaspora of captive people of which every cargo was but a small part. In fact, the signal feature of the Atlantic slave trade was its creation of not one diaspora, but many, each having its own distinct features, and each taking on a new configuration in the Americas.[9]

From our vantage point, several distinct patterns in the Gold Coast diaspora come into focus. Gold Coast captives reaching Barbados in the last quarter of the century found that their numbers (19 percent of newcomers) were overshadowed by a larger influx of immigrants from the Bight of Benin (43 percent). The picture shifted in the next quarter century, however, as those from the Gold Coast came to make up 48 percent of new arrivals in Barbados, as compared with 34 percent from the Bight of Benin. Moreover, whereas West-Central Africa, the Bight of Biafra, Senegambia, and southeast Africa each contributed between 7 and 13 percent of arrivals reaching Barbados in the last quarter of the seventeenth century, each of those four regions saw its proportions halved in the first quarter of the eighteenth century. Indeed, in this period, none but Gold Coast and Bight of Benin arrivals even exceeded the 5 percent mark.

The diaspora in Jamaica also reflects that colony's changing place in the Atlantic economy. Captives from the Gold Coast, 11 percent of newcomers reaching Jamaica in the late seventeenth century, were joined by larger streams (constituting 15–35 percent of the total) from the Bight of Biafra, Bight of Benin, and West-Central Africa. In the next quarter century, however, Gold Coast arrivals were the most numerous by far: together with those from the Bight of Benin, they accounted for nearly 80 percent of the island's incoming slave population. As for Nevis, captives from the Gold Coast alighting from slave ships there in the late seventeenth century made up 20 percent of new arrivals from Africa; they joined others coming in substantial numbers (12–25 percent) from Senegambia, the Bight of Benin, West-Central Africa, and the Bight of Biafra. As on Barbados and Jamaica, captives from the Gold Coast were the most numerous among new arrivals (45 percent), followed closely by those from the Bight of Benin (32 percent) in the following quarter century.[10]

Against this backdrop the Gold Coast migrations to English North America stand out in sharp contrast. These secondary streams, whose course diverged from the torrent of captives supplied as labor to the Caribbean cane fields, in the seventeenth century deposited in Virginia immigrants from the Gold Coast along with those from three other African regions, among whom natives of the Bight of Biafra and Senegambia predominated. The Gold Coast slaves diverted to Virginia in the following century worked alongside African migrants from still more diverse backgrounds, but more than half of these fellow newcomers had come from the Bight of Biafra. When rice cultivation began to draw cargoes directly from Africa to the Carolina lowcountry at the turn of the eighteenth century, the occasional shipment arrived from the Gold Coast too, contributing to an African immigrant population comprising almost exclusively Senegambians in the first quarter century of sustained African migration to that corner of the Anglo-Atlantic world.[11]

Whereas the slave cargoes gathered on the African coast reconfigured the normative boundaries of social life, the slave communities in the Americas exploded those boundaries beyond recognition. If an Akan-speaking migrant lived to complete a year on a West Indian sugar estate, he or she was likely by the end of that time to have come into close contact with unrelated Akan strangers as well as with Ga, Guan, or Adangbe speakers in the holding stations on the African littoral, with Ewe speakers on the slave ship, and with Angolans, Biafrans, and Senegambians on the plantation. This was the composite we can call diasporic Africa—an Africa that constituted not the continent on European maps, but rather the plurality of remembered places immigrant slaves carried with them.

Like any geographic entity, diasporic Africa varies according to the perspective from which it is surveyed. Viewed from a cartographic standpoint (in essence, the view of early modern Europeans), diasporic Africa is a constellation of discrete ethnic and language groups; if one adopts this perspective, the defining question becomes whether or not the various constituent groups in the slave community shared a culture.[12]

Only by approaching these questions from the vantage point of Africans as migrants, however, can we hope to understand how Africans themselves experienced and negotiated their American worlds. If in the regime of the market Africans' most socially relevant feature was their exchangeability, for Africans as immigrants the most socially relevant feature was their isolation, their desperate need to restore some measure of social life to counterbalance the alienation engendered by their social death. Without some means of achieving that vital equilibrium thanks to which even the socially dead could expect to occupy a viable place in society, slaves could foresee only further descent into an endless purgatory.[13]

Consider the scene ex-slave Charles Ball witnessed in South Carolina. Remembering an African-born slave's funerary ritual, Ball recalled that the man "decorated the grave of his departed son with 'a miniature canoe, about a foot long, and a little paddle, with which he said it would cross the ocean to his own country.'"[14] This man's ritual mortuary practice would not have held any meaning for his kin and community in Africa. None had been required to travel a distance so great and so perilous to reach the realm of the ancestors, and none had required the assistance of a canoe and paddle to achieve the soul's departure for another realm. It was a gesture that could be understood only by those who shared the memory of the slave ship. Through such public ritual acts the individual memory of the slave ship was shared with shipmates and other African-born immigrants. When others who had been part of his "country" in Africa encountered that slave in South Carolina, they found someone whose speech signaled their shared origin, and whose ritual practice was both novel and resonant at the same time: none had placed a canoe on a grave in this manner, but all shared the concern that had prompted this man to stake his hopes for his son's return migration on a carved wooden boat.

Africans began life in the Americas as subjects profoundly shaped by their Atlantic experience, and the communities they created in the Americas were organized around solutions to the specific problems they faced. The cultures they produced do not reflect the simple transfer and continuation of Africa in the Americas but rather reflect the elaboration of specific cultural content and its transformation to meet the particular needs of slave life in the Atlantic system: their need to reassert some kind of healthy relationship to ancestors; to manage death; to produce social networks, communities, and relations of kinship; to address the imbalance of power between black and white; to stake a claim to their bodies to counter the plantation economy's claim to ownership.

In this sense, the cultural practices of diasporic Africa could have meaning only outside Africa. Shared Atlantic experience and memory served as a touchstone for new cultural practices that emerged in the New World diaspora. Only through the capacity and willingness to invent and experiment—to grow and change the cultural tools carried in memory and create new ones to meet the demands of this new world—could Africans hope to remain recognizable to themselves as *human* beings in a system that held so much of their humanity in callous and calculated disregard. African immigrants retained that foothold in ways determined by the varied circumstances of their slavery: the immigrant slave might adapt a remembered ritual practice to new applications in American slavery or explore and perhaps ultimately adopt an entirely novel practice. The means were extraordinarily diverse because of the great variety of settings and conditions in which the colonial economies of the Americas enslaved human beings. The continuity Africans needed was not the static, ossifying connection of conformity of practice— doing things in the present as they had been done in the past, even when the content of past cultural forms no longer corresponded to the needs and circumstances of the present. Rather, the connection Africans needed was a narrative continuity between past and present—an epistemological means of connecting the dots between there and here, then and now, to craft a coherent story out of incoherent experience.

The Chains That Bound Saltwater Slaves

Every cargo that left a slave ship in the Americas was closely followed by a trail of others, and in this regard African migration to the Americas evolved along the same lines as all long-distance mass migrations. It formed a vast procession of people in motion, an infinite round of departures and arrivals. Notwithstanding the external "push-pull" factors generally understood to explain why and how migrations take place, the sheer scale of the displacement suggests that most long-distance migration systems call on some kind of generative energy from within to sustain themselves.

A new awareness of the integral role that social networks play in long-distance migration goes beyond traditional "rational-choice and decision-making models" drawn from classical economics that content themselves with explaining migration as the outcome of a "cost-benefit analysis of the most favorable destination."[15] According to recent theory, something more than the push and pull of differential labor markets, hunger, or the search for religious freedom sends people into long-distance emigration. Voluntary migrations do not depend merely on autonomous individuals weighing the costs and benefits of uprooting themselves. Rather, social networks and relationships bind uprooted people one to another like the links in a chain. "Chain migration" is sustained from within, and indeed "can become self-perpetuating," as "'each act of migration itself creates the social structure needed to sustain'" further migration.[16] News of another's good fortune in a distant place, information about unforeseen opportunities, invitations to follow in another's migratory footsteps, or a familial obligation to do so—the long reach of social relations such as these are the incentive that draws people into exile in other lands and accounts for the enormous scale of some systems of international migration.[17]

The Atlantic slave trade set in motion the largest international migration before the nineteenth century. This exodus, like later ones, derived its momentum from the generative energy of relationships between the individual emigrants. The mass displacement of slaves was a unique kind of "chain migration," however. The links in the chain of saltwater migration were formed not by networks of affiliation and communication between Africans as subjects but rather, as we know, by the market exchange of Africans as commodities. In place of the natural communication among emigrants exchanging news and information was only silence: African voices were muted by the unnatural deracination of commodification.

The Jamaican planter Cary Helyar, explaining how the fourteen Africans he purchased from a Dutch slave ship in January 1672 would compel more African migrants to follow in their wake, promised his brother that he would "make these negroes buy more."[18] The colony of Jamaica was still a frontier in the closing decades of the seventeenth century. Helyar's visits to slave ships in the Kingston harbor served to populate his plantation with its first generation of African settlers, and the same was true of many other pioneering plantations on the island.[19] But Helyar's happy vision of a slave community burgeoning in response to the workings of the market reflected his naivety as a novice buyer of slave labor. Wherever colonial American economies looked to African slaves to supply their labor needs, slave owners came to rely on the market not only to acquire an initial pool of African workers, but also to maintain the slave population.

Those who survived the slave ship were haunted by the rhythm of untimely fatality, for the death march continued on American soil. As many as half the slaves who disembarked in the Caribbean sugar colonies perished within the next three years. Philip Morgan has found that maybe a quarter of the slaves who came to eighteenth-century Virginia died within a year of their arrival, and in the Carolina lowcountry as many as a third were dead within the same space of time.[20]

The rapid demise of so many slave ship survivors was attributable to a combination of deadly forces. As we have seen, the ravages of the slave ship voyage itself loomed large: many of the captives were near death on their arrival. Moreover, we know now that extraction from one's native epidemiological environment leaves all long-distance migrants vulnerable to infectious diseases to which they have no natural or acquired immunity.[21] Though they possessed no scientific understanding of this phenomenon, European transatlantic migrants were well aware of the need to acclimate to their new communities; indeed, they coined the term "seasoning" to denote the one- to three-year period of adjustment necessary for all newcomers to the American colonies. The overriding challenge to Africans in America, though, derived from the regime of slavery itself. In the abject circumstances of foreign enslavement, it was a struggle for Africans to conceive children at all, let alone to raise them past infancy. The evidence of slave imports and population size indicates that Africans in the English Caribbean colonies in the seventeenth and early eighteenth centuries suffered a "demographic catastrophy," caused most directly by a tremendously high rate of infant mortality.[22]

The first of the English American colonies to turn to African slaves to meet its demand for labor, Barbados experienced a jump in its slave population from 1,000 to 20,000 in the first decade after sugar cultivation was introduced around 1640.[23] "Between 1640 and 1700," writes Richard S. Dunn, "the English sugar planters brought some 264,000 slaves from Africa into Barbados, Jamaica, and the Leeward Islands. In 1700, according to the census returns, the black population of these islands was barely 100,000—about 40,000 apiece in Barbados and Jamaica and 20,000 in the Leeward Islands."[24] A Barbados plantation manager, complaining about chronic dirt eating (a symptom of hookworm infestation) among the slaves and the "continual trouble in nursing and physicking" they occasioned, suggested that the estate owner ought to sell the sick slaves and buy new ones to replace them.[25] "The harsh demographic regime of the region furthermore meant that over the course of a typical decade planters would have to buy total numbers of new slaves equivalent to 30 percent of those present at the decade's beginning simply to prevent their slave populations from decreasing."[26] In Virginia, the slave population "experienced almost no natural increase" in the first decade of the eighteenth century, and conditions were no better in the Carolina lowcountry.[27]

The truth was that "West Indian slave masters soon gave up trying to keep their Negroes alive long enough to breed up a new generation and instead routinely bought replacement slaves year in and year out."[28] Survivors of the slave ship thus drew future migrants into saltwater slavery by the engine of their labor. Once converted into sugar (or tobacco or rice or any of the other staple commodities), the labor of those already in saltwater slavery cycled back to African shores to pull still more captives into circulation, thus "buying" more bodies to sustain the chain of captive migrants that bound Africa to the Americas.

The nature of the "demographic catastrophy" varied from place to place, however. For slaves whose sea voyage ended at Barbados—one out of three of those who departed from the Gold Coast in the period under consideration—the crisis of saltwater exile played out in a slave society that was already well established. The slave population there peaked at an estimated fifty thousand in 1690, before "level[ing] off at about forty-five thousand," where it remained through the 1730s.[29] By then New World–born slaves were "already approaching a majority."[30]

Nearly everywhere else, however, captives who departed from the Gold Coast in the late seventeenth and early eighteenth centuries joined immigrant communities that were themselves only just beginning to take shape—they comprised the pioneering generations of enslaved Africans in the colonial landscape: whether on the Caribbean islands where the sugar economy took off, at new mining sites on the Spanish-American mainland, on the plantations of South Carolina where rice cultivation had begun to flourish, or on the tobacco farms of Virginia. Dunn concludes that "all the evidence" regarding Africans in the English Caribbean colonies in the late seventeenth and early eighteenth centuries "points toward demographic catastrophy for the slaves"; and indeed that conclusion holds true of every place that the saltwater carried African slaves.[31] By working them to death, planters made them "buy more" slaves.

The demographic catastrophe, which sprang from the impossible conditions that framed African efforts, did not mitigate the need to build networks of kinship and community. Doomed to failure, Africans had no choice but to act with resolution. The web of social belonging that only kin could provide was a nonnegotiable element in the imperative to live again.

There was no more urgent task for slave ship survivors than to create a network of social relations adequate to their need for social belonging. Indeed, only by restoring kinship networks could the saltwater slaves hope to escape the purgatory of their unprecedented social death. That Africans throughout the Americas accorded the highest possible regard to those whom they designated as "shipmates"—and articulated the meaning of that relationship in the idiom of kinship—attests to the role the memory of the slave ship played in their pursuit of viable personhood in unfamiliar American worlds.[32] It was by naming those to whom they belonged socially that they could most powerfully affirm their own personhood.

Here too, though, the market left its imprint. It was the market, or more precisely Anglo-American behavior in the market, that determined how Africans were reconfigured into units of consumable labor. As a consequence, market considerations determined where Africans would plant the seeds of community and kinship in American soil, in response to a deeply felt need. Though the records detail demographic conditions rather than describe African responses to them, the invoices produced by the sale of slave cargoes in American markets are an important index of the variety of local plantation settings in which Africans lived out their lives in American slavery.[33]

At one end of the spectrum were those who left the slave ship alone and did not have the opportunity to transform shared survival of the ocean crossing into a kind of surrogate kinship. At the other end of the spectrum were those who left the slave ship in groups shaped by the presence of both men and women survivors— the lots of three men and two women that started into American slavery together in seventeenth-century Jamaica, for instance. In between, infinitely varied combinations emerged from the interplay of factors: the people of different sexes and ages that made up a cargo, the presence or absence of market controls, and the preferences buyers brought to the market. Most of the individual groups of shipmates that started life together in Jamaica and the Leeward Islands included at least a sizable minority of female immigrants and no doubt benefited immensely from their presence. When no women, or very few, were present among groups of shipmates, it must have been a particularly difficult task to negotiate the shoals of New World slavery without the benefit of the cultural knowledge and skills possessed by African women.

Indeed, it would be difficult to overestimate the difference made by women's presence in these embryonic groups. According to the labor regime of plantation slavery, men performed what had been regarded in the African societies from which they derived as "women's work"—the monotonous toil of labor-intensive agricultural production.[34] Indeed, it has been supposed that the difficult psychological adjustment to those rigors may have contributed to the higher rate of mortality among African men during their first three years off the ship.[35] Indeed, in many of their day-to-day struggles African immigrants in their first weeks and months in the Americas required skills and knowledge that in their homelands had resided largely with women.[36]

Perhaps no area of expertise was more important than the skills associated with acquiring and preparing food. Indeed, over time, the feeding of newly purchased slaves came to be recognized by New World planters as one of the most important determinants of their survival during the "seasoning period." By the eighteenth century, it was common in the English sugar islands to assign the care of newly purchased slaves to a trusted older slave who was responsible for overseeing their diet.[37] The pioneering generation of African immigrants who arrived in the English American colonies at the end of the seventeenth century, however, was thrown very much on its own resources everywhere save in Barbados.

To the extent that it was possible, some of the wealthier planters tried to maintain separate stores of provisions to sustain "new negroes" until such time as they were able to establish their own plots. Even so, the preparation of food and the development of culinary practices suited to the resources of the West Indies must have depended entirely on whatever solutions and strategies African women were able to devise.

In addition to this fundamental aspect of daily survival in the

Americas, areas of knowledge traditionally assigned to women very likely played a crucial role in other specific challenges African immigrant communities faced, from attending to medical needs to reestablishing rituals for mourning the dead and communicating with the ancestors. Without the presence and participation of African women in the project of New World settlement, there could be no return to some semblance of normal life. Women's roles as wives and mothers surely were among the most vital in this project; but beyond that, the contributions African women made to the communities of American slavery far exceeded the reproductive roles with which those women are generally associated.

"New Negroes"

Fictive kinship with others born out of the same "hollow place" into slavery provided the spark, as we have seen, for African efforts to ignite the eternal flame of kinship in America. Afterward, the conditions and structure of saltwater slavery made stability the essential element of immigrant community, the one that African slave ship survivors worked hardest to sustain.[38] Wherever the slave ship deposited its human cargo, Africans faced the same universal dilemma. The saltwater eroded the lives that African migrants strove to build in slavery precisely where strength and stability were most needed: at the very root.

As far as the planters' interest in maintaining the slave population was concerned, natural increase and purchase of slaves on the market were different means to the same arithmetic end—the replacement of lost workers with new ones—and purchase was by far the more efficient of the two, given the prodigious rate of population loss from high mortality among both African adults and American-born infants. Far more was at stake for the Africans themselves, however, than the slaveholder's tally. The standard against which they measured the viability of their fragile communities turned not on maintaining the body count with new arrivals or on the status quo, but rather on the accumulation of immigrant generations and the temporal and spatial extension of life that only ancestors and progeny could provide.

The difference in standards was greater than what any planter could record in his inventory of human property, for the population that maintained its size by supporting adults into old age and raising children past infancy grew beyond the purview of the slaveholders' accounts. When deceased slaves disappeared from the planter's inventory, they remained members of the slaves' community. Properly buried by a community of fellows and kin, they moved on to the realm of the ancestors. Whereas "natural" reproduction sustained the community of generations across time and space, restoring the rolls through slave purchases had the opposite effect. The extremely high rates of mortality carried countless Africans and their American-born children away from the earthly sphere without assurance of reaching the ancestral realm, without benefit of descendants, and thus without full restoration to the community.

The migrant chain that connected Africa to America was seemingly endless, however, and its length was due primarily to the market. Africans made to "buy more" Africans were thus compelled to be the agents of their own exploitation by an economic system that consumed the very lives of slaves. At stake for Africans was whether an American generation of African lineage would emerge and, more important still, also whether that generation could sustain itself by the fruit of its social networks, rather than by its labor, as bought and sold on the market.[39]

Only in the second decade of the eighteenth century and, more significantly, as yet only in tidewater Virginia, did a population of American-born descendants of saltwater slaves finally win the battle to put down stable roots of sufficient strength to anchor a sustainable web of community and kinship spanning the "big water" between Africa and America. In 1720s Virginia, American-born slave children finally began to survive to adulthood and raise children of their own.[40] This success signaled that a critical mass of African migrants had begun to claim an American life: their experiments among new peoples, unfamiliar surroundings, and unknown metaphysical powers had born fruit.

The women who bore these first surviving generations were the founding ancestresses of a wholly new people in diasporic Africa. They did not descend from the sky or emerge from holes in the ground, but like Ankyewa Nyame, they were the progenitors for a new historical time and place. Also like their counterparts in Asante tradition, Africans of the first generation in diaspora were memorialized as founding ancestors. In Suriname, for example, the Saramaka maroons remembered these as the "Old-Time People" and conferred on them a special place in Saramaka historical consciousness. This founding generation was composed of the saltwater slaves who survived seasoning to become "old" Africans and of the children born to African mothers who survived past infancy. Their era was the "First-Time."[41] In due course, every black slave population in the Americas outlived a "first-time" epoch that gave birth to a New World generation, marking the beginning of a new people and a new history. But the routes toward that achievement were strewn with the bodies of thousands of saltwater slaves who lost the battle to sink immigrant roots in American soil.

This circulation of people as commodities gave diasporic Africa its distinctive cast: slave communities came to embrace a heterogeneous assortment of "seasoned" Africans, American-born children, and the "new Negroes" who repeatedly arrived by ship. Ravaged by infant and adult mortality, their communities endured constant flux and reformation, as new groups of involuntary migrants arrived. The relentless stream of newcomers sustained the slave community's numerical strength. It also held the community suspended in the unsteady state of an immigrant community in the making, one forever being created afresh by the arrival of new saltwater slaves. Thoroughly American-born communities emerged only very slowly. In this important regard, the road followed from African immigrant beginnings to a thoroughly African-American end was not quite the linear generational progression depicted by the usual model, with its presentation of "African" and "creole" as "way stations of generational change" unfolding "along a single track with Africans inexorably becoming creoles."[42]

They were pioneering generations that all but disappeared from the genealogical histories of slave communities, their lives on the far side of the Atlantic truncated by mortality and all memory of them erased by the absence of descendants who could call them by name. Their only heirs were those who trailed after them on the returning slave ships, to take the place of dead and departed saltwater laborers in the cane fields, on the tobacco farms, and in the rice paddies.

In ways that saltwater slaves no doubt realized, their travails prepared the way for their children. Though the timetable varied from one colonial landscape to another, eventually the children of enslaved African migrants survived more often than they died. Their efforts to coax communities and cultural norms out of the oppressive conditions of their enslavement formed the bedrock on which succeeding diasporic generations built meaningful lives in the New World. While the societies of their homelands continued to fuel the ever-expanding bounties of Atlantic commerce, those who labored as slaves in the Americas looked on as thousands and eventually millions of others followed in their footsteps. Though the travelers were unable to carry their newfound knowledge of a wider world back to African shores, saltwater slavery made these immigrants the accidental architects of an Africa in diaspora.

Rather than reflecting the absence of connection, therefore, the African migration produced a unique kind of connection. The echo produced by the serial repetition of one-way departures, the voices of saltwater slaves, could not reverberate back to Africa. The individual stories of saltwater slavery form the antithesis of historical narrative, for they feature not an evolving plot of change over time but rather a tale of endless repetition that allows no temporal progression. Every protagonist was a pioneer, blazing a trail on the same ground traveled by predecessors in saltwater slavery, but without the benefit of historical memory. It is a narrative in which time *seems* to stand still.

In this sense, saltwater slavery formed a chain of migration that not only linked Africa and the Americas in space but also continually projected the "saltwater" into the American present of diasporic Africa. New groups of saltwater slaves, entering communities of immigrant settlers and their descendants, added further links in the chain of one-way movement from Africa to America. It was thus, for example, that derogatory meanings attached to being a newly arrived African. The stigma of being a saltwater slave was not Africanness per se but rather the ignorance and inexperience that African birth symbolized in a world increasingly dominated by American-born, or "creole," slaves—a world rooted more firmly in the African diaspora in America than in Africa itself.

"Old" Africans and the Slave Ship in Memory

'Sibell was an "Old African Female Slave" in Barbados when she shared her story in 1799 with a white man by the name of John Ford. The circumstances of their ethnographic encounter are unknown, but we can surmise that Ford was perhaps one of the many English travelers curious to see the slave labor that produced their sugar, to know something of the people whose sweat sweetened their tea. We can assume also that the woman who answered to the name 'Sibell had come to Barbados sometime in the second half of the eighteenth century, probably as an unmarried adolescent girl, though from which region of Atlantic Africa it is impossible to know.

As 'Sibell spoke, John Ford transcribed, doing his best to capture the rhythm and intonation of her speech. Transmitted via Ford's ear and hand, 'Sibell's spoken words became a written text that eventually made its way to Oxford University's Bodleian Library, where it now resides in a collection of "miscellaneous" English manuscripts.[43] To protect the integrity and coherence of her voice, the text is reproduced here in its entirety:

THE FOLLOWING ACCOUNT RELATED TO THE WRITER BY AN OLD AFRICAN FEMALE SLAVE NAMED 'SIBELL.

Massah,' my Dahdy was a great man in my Country and called Makcrundy, he have great many Slaves, and hire many Man.——— And one of my Budders was a great man in de fight in my Country.———my Dahdy nebber want.—he have ground two, tree Miles long and hire so many Man dat he put de vittles in large Tubs for dim.———When he cut honey, he fill tree, four Barrel he have so muchee.———When we want good drink in my Country we go and cut de Tree and de juice will run, and keep some time will make good strong drink.———————

I bin reddy fond of my Sister—and she went out of de House one Day and let me alone, and my Budder in law come in, and take me up and say he going to carry me to see his udder Wife, he take and carry, carry, carry, carry, carry me all night and day, all night and day way from my Country.———in de way me meet a Man, and de Man know my Dahdy and all my Family.———Ah! Budder (me beg pardon for calling you Budder, Massah,) you see me here now but dere has bin grandee fight in my Country for me, for he will tell my Family.———as my budder in law carry me 'long, me hear great noise, and me wonder, but he tell me no frighten———and he carry me to a long House full of new negurs talking and making sing——— but veddy few of dem bin of my Country and my Budder in Law sell me to de Back-erah people [White people]—me nebber see de White people before, me nebber see de great Ships pon de Water before, me nebber hear de Waves before which me frighten so much-ee dat me thought me would die.———My Budder in Law took up de Gun and de Powder which he sell me for and wanted to get 'way from me, but me hold he and cry—and he stop wid me 'till me hold Tongue and den he run way from me.———De Sailors keep me in dere long time and bring down two, tree ebbery day 'till de long House bin full.——— dere bin many Black people dere reddy bad man, dey talk all kind of Country and tell we all dat we going to a good Massah yonder yonder, where we would workee workee picka-nee-nee [little], and mesoy mesoy [eat eat] grandee and no fum-fum [no whipping]———————

Me no know nobody in de House, but ven me go in de Ship me find my Country woman Mimbo, my Country man Dublin [&c. so named by the English], My Country woman Sally, and some more, but dey sell dem all about and me no savvy where now.———here she burst into tears and could say no more.———————

'Sibell's story is a narrative account of captive migration, but the sequence and content of her narrative differ from the story I have told here in several regards. A measured narrative connecting Africa, the Atlantic, and the Americas in a linear arc of displacement contrasts with 'Sibell's account and the irregularity of its cadence. The themes in my historical narrative derive from an analysis of commodification, while 'Sibell's narrative is animated thematically by the relationships that shaped her migration. Whereas the linearity in my account assumes movement toward narrative closure, 'Sibell disappoints the listener or reader anticipating the same from her account. Her narrative draws instead to an abrupt end—she "pulls the audience forward through time" only to leave it in midstream, for this is where the experience of saltwater slavery has left her.[44] In one final sentence, 'Sibell's narrative moves from isolation in a coastal African holding station ("Me no know nobody in de House") to relationships formed aboard the slave ship ("but ven me go in de Ship me find my Country woman Mimbo, my Country man Dublin, My Country woman Sally, and some more") to renewed isolation in American slavery ("but dey sell dem all about and me no savvy where now"). Bringing her account forward in time from an African past to an American present leads not to narrative closure but rather to its dissolution: "Here she burst into tears and could say no more."

'Sibell's story reflects an important truth underlying the distinctive outlines of our respective narratives: hers is a window not onto the experience of the slave ship, but rather onto the memory of it. The effort to construct a history—tracing the movement of captives from Africa to America—stands quite apart from the effort to integrate a memory—looking from America to Africa through the experience of the slave ship. 'Sibell supplies a narrative that is less about enduring the crisis of the slave ship than about surviving it. Indeed, what is most striking about 'Sibell's story is its unambiguous message that the trauma of the slave ship survivor lay in the effort of integration—the challenge to integrate pieces of a narrative that do not fit neatly together, to suture the jagged edges and bleeding boundaries of lives fragmented by captive migration. In this regard, it is intriguing also to consider the ways her narrative differs from Equiano's *Narrative*. Because Equiano shaped his text in response to eighteenth-century British antislavery sentiments specifically, and Enlightenment humanism and moral reformism generally, he wove a tale of migration and progressive displacement that, like this book, moves along a trajectory that any reader familiar with the tropes of early modern travel literature would recognize.[45] In stark contrast, the fractured shape of 'Sibell's account reflects the nonlinear temporality of a nonwestern subject and the familiar rhythms of oral, as distinct from written, narrative expression.[46]

'Sibell's account reflects also the ways trauma disrupts normative narrative structures (whatever the cultural background of the subject) and the role that storytelling plays in the integration of traumatic memory. It is not just that "traumatic events" disrupt "attachments of family, friendship, love, and community" or "shatter the construction of the self that is formed and sustained in relation to others." More fundamentally, trauma specialist Judith Herman asserts, trauma directly disrupts the very "systems of attachment and meaning that link individual and community." Thus, another specialist has defined traumatic events as ones "that cannot be assimilated with the victim's 'inner schemata' of self in relation to the world." The "work of reconstruction," Herman writes, "actually transforms the traumatic memory, so that it can be integrated into the survivor's life story."[47]

Especially difficult to discipline was 'Sibell's recollection of the transaction that set her on the irreversible journey into saltwater slavery. The act of sale did more than transfer property rights to her person. In her reminiscence, it also propelled her, seemingly in an instant, into a new world—a world molded by the European Atlantic political economy—the world of white people, big ships, the expanse of the sea, and its ominous soundscape. In memory, the transaction also had a messy social dimension that belied the seeming simple exchange of economic values, for it drew 'Sibell, the brother-in-law, gun, and gunpowder together in a moment of collective embrace. This was the moment when social and mercantile values collided. By the rationalized logic of the market, this was a clean bartering of goods, one in which the girl, the gun, and the powder exchanged hands smoothly. But the transaction held the opposite meaning in 'Sibell's experience: it was not a smooth exchange but rather one marked by friction. She clung to her kinsman, and he could not let her go as long as her voice continued to resound in his ears. Only when she finally fell silent did he let her go.

'Sibell's remembered experience cannot fit into the neat temporal and spatial categories that frame my narration of the "middle passage," with its orderly narrative progression from African captivity through Atlantic commodification to American slavery. It is the meaning of remembered events rather than their temporal order that governs their place in 'Sibell's narrative. 'Sibell "finds" the people who she will remember in Barbados, already constructed as American subjects on the slave ship, already answering to what will be their plantation slave names, Sally, Dublin, and so on. The temporal and spatial categories of her remembered middle passage overlap, as past, present, and future comfortably commingle ("in de way me meet a Man, and de Man know my Dahdy and all my Family.——Ah! Budder . . . you see me here now but dere has bin grandee fight in my Country for me, for he will tell my Family"). 'Sibell's story conveys the very important truth that hers is a narrative that cannot come to closure, because the events that give it shape have not yet exhausted their dramatic content. Her original captivity is not a past event; rather, it remains unresolved: her father and family continue to look for her; she is here in American slavery now, but her return to the world that framed her remembered African self is imminent.

'Sibell's narrative suggests that the slave ship charted no course of narrative continuity between the African past and American present, but rather memorialized an indeterminate passage marked by the impossibility of full narrative closure. The saltwater in African memory, then, was perhaps the antithesis of a "middle" passage, with all that phrase implies about a smooth, linear progression leading to a known end. For many in the pioneering generations of slaves, there could be no such integration of the terror of Atlantic memory.

Notes

Introduction

1. Requests for such reports were among the instructions given, upon appointment, to all governors of English colonies that dealt in slaves. Initially the reports went to the Committee for Trade and Foreign Plantations; subsequent to the creation of the Board of Trade in 1696, reports went to that body. See Elizabeth Donnan, ed., *Documents Illustrative of the History of the Slave Trade to America*, 4 vols. (Washington, D.C.: Carnegie Institution, 1930; reprint, New York: Octagon Books, 1965), 4:183–185, for the report, "An Accot. of Negroes imported into the District of York River from the 25th of March 1718 to the 25th of March 1727 from the Coast of Africa"; quotation, p. 56. See also Edmund S. Morgan, *American Slavery, American Freedom: The Ordeal of Colonial Virginia* (New York: Norton, 1975), pp. 347–348; Peter Laslett, "John Locke, the Great Recoinage, and the Origins of the Board of Trade: 1695–1698," *William and Mary Quarterly*, 3rd ser., 14 no. 3 (1957): 370–402; Anna Lane Lingelbach, "The Inception of the British Board of Trade," *American Historical Review* 30, no. 4 (1925): 701–727.
2. A contemporary explanation of what economist William Petty had contributed to seventeenth-century English thought, cited in Mary Poovey, *A History of the Modern Fact: Problems of Knowledge in the Sciences of Wealth and Society* (Chicago: University of Chicago Press, 1998), p. 142; "Instructions to the Council of Trade, 1650," quoted in Joan Thirsk and J. P. Cooper, eds., *Seventeenth-Century Economic Documents* (Oxford: Clarendon Press, 1972), p. 501.
3. David Eltis, *The Rise of African Slavery in the Americas* (Cambridge: Cambridge University Press, 2000); David Richardson, "Slave Exports from West and West-Central Africa, 1700–1810: New Esti-

mates of Volume and Distribution," *Journal of African History* (hereafter *JAH*) 30 (1989): 1–22.

4. For a general history of the company, see K. G. Davies, *The Royal African Company* (London: Longmans, 1957); on the shift from monopoly to free trade, and for a thorough overview of the Atlantic slave trade, see James A. Rawley, *The Transatlantic Slave Trade: A History* (New York: Norton, 1981).

5. John Oldmixon, *The British Empire in America, Containing the History of the Discovery, Settlement, Progress and present State of all the British Colonies, on the Continent and Islands of America,* 2 vols. (London: n.p., 1708), 2:121–122; Edward Long, *The History of Jamaica,* 2 vols. (London, 1774; reprint, New York: Arno Press, 1972), 2:410. See also Frederic G. Cassidy, *Jamaica Talk: Three Hundred Years of The English Language in Jamaica* (London: 1961), pp. 18, 156; Orlando Patterson, *The Sociology of Slavery: An Analysis of the Origins, Development and Structure of Negro Slave Society in Jamaica* (Rutherford, N.J.: Fairleigh Dickinson University Press, 1967), p. 146; Gerald W. Mullin, *Flight and Rebellion: Slave Resistance in Eighteenth-Century Virginia* (Oxford: Oxford University Press, 1972), x; Philip D. Morgan, "British Encounters with Africans and African-Americans, circa 1600–1780," in *Strangers within the Realm: Cultural Margins of the First British Empire,* ed. Bernard Bailyn and Philip D. Morgan (Chapel Hill: University of North Carolina Press, for the Institute of Early American History and Culture, 1991), p. 199; see also Michael A. Gomez, *Exchanging Our Country Marks: The Transformation of African Identities in the Colonial and Antebellum South* (Chapel Hill: University of North Carolina Press, 1998), pp. 14, 168, 189, 191.

6. Stuart Hall, "Cultural Identity and Diaspora," in *Colonial Discourse and Post-Colonial Theory: A Reader,* ed. Patrick Williams and Laura Chrisman (New York: Columbia University Press, 1994), p. 394; David Cressy, *Coming Over: Migration and Communication between England and New England in the Seventeenth Century* (Cambridge: Cambridge University Press, 1987); Charles Tilly, "Transplanted Networks," in *Immigration Reconsidered: History, Sociology, and Politics,* ed. Virginia Yans-McLaughlin (New York: Oxford University Press, 1990), pp. 79–95.

1. The Gold Coast and the Atlantic Market in People

1. Cape Coast Castle (hereafter CCC) to Royal African Company (hereafter RAC), 23 February 1721, T70/7, f. 17. All T70 sources are found in Treasury Papers Collection, British Public Record Office, Kew, Eng.

2. See, among others, eighteenth-century slave ship captain William Snelgrave, speaking of slaves from the Gold Coast: "These People are the stoutest and most sensible Negroes on the Coast: Neither are they so weak as to imagine as others do, that we buy them to eat them; being satisfied we carry them to work in our Plantations, as they do in their own Country." Quoted in George Francis Dow, *Slave Ships and Slaving* (1927; reprint, Mineola, N.Y.: Dover, 2002), p. 123.

3. *The Trans-Atlantic Slave Trade: A Database on CD-ROM* (hereafter *TSTD*), query parameters: "1721–1725" (five-year time period) and "Gold Coast" (region where slaves embarked).

4. James Phipps, CCC, to RAC, 25 June 1721, T70/4, f. 12; Phipps, CCC to RAC, 23 February 1721, T70/7, f. 17; RAC to CCC, 14 December 1721, T70/53, f. 21v; RAC to CCC, 13 June 1721, T70/53, f. 38. Percentages are rounded to the nearest whole number throughout.

5. John Vogt, *Portuguese Rule on the Gold Coast, 1469–1682* (Athens: University of Georgia Press, 1979), p. 4. The "River of Gold" referred to by medieval geographers probably was either the Senegal or Niger, both being rivers that pass through the gold-rich areas of the western Sudan. See also Duarte Pacheco Pereira, *Esmeraldo de Situ Orbis*, trans. and ed. George H. T. Kimble (London: Hakluyt Society, 1937), p. 122; John W. Blake, *European Beginnings in West Africa, 1454–1578* (London: Longmans, Green, 1937); John Thornton, *Africa and Africans in the Making of the Atlantic World, 1400–1680* (Cambridge: Cambridge University Press, 1992), pp. 26–27.

6. Vogt, *Portuguese Rule*, p. 5.

7. Ibid., p. 8; Blake, *European Beginnings*, p. 10.

8. Pereira, *Esmeraldo de Situ Orbis*, 117–122; quotation p. 122. Cabo das Redes means, literally, "Cape of the fishing nets."

9. The Dutchman Pieter de Marees wrote one of the earliest published descriptions of the region in 1602. See De Marees, *Description and Historical Account of the Gold Kingdom of Guinea (1602)*, trans. and ed. Albert van Dantzig and Adam Jones (Oxford: Oxford University Press, 1987), p. 6.

10. Timothy F. Gerrard, *Akan Weights and the Gold Trade* (London: Longmans, 1980), pp. 9–10, 101; Philip Curtin, Steven Feierman, Leonard Thompson, and Jan Vansina *African History: From Earliest Times to Independence*, 2nd ed. (London: Longmans, 1995), pp. 73–76.

11. Peter Shinnie, "Early Asante: Is Wilks Right?" in *The Cloth of Many Colored Silks: Papers on History and Society, Ghanaian and Is-*

lamic, in honor of Ivor Wilks, ed. John Hunwick and Nancy Lawler (Evanston, Ill.: Northwestern University Press, 1996), pp. 198–201.

12. Ivor Wilks, "Slavery and Akan Origins? A Reply," *Ethnohistory,* 41, no. 4 (1994): 657–665.

13. Ivor Wilks, "Wangara, Akan, and Portuguese in the Fifteenth and Sixteenth Centuries," in Wilks, *Forests of Gold: Essays on the Akan and the Kingdom of Asante* (Athens: Ohio University Press, 1993), pp. 1–39. Ray A. Kea, Settlements, Trade, and Polities in the Seventeenth-Century Gold Coast (Balimore: Johns Hopkins University Press, 1982), pp. 187, 197–198; Gerrard, *Akan Weights,* p. 7.

14. On Begho and Bono Manso, see Graham Connah, *African Civilizations: An Archaeological Perspective,* 2nd ed. (1987; Cambridge: Cambridge University Press, 2001), pp. 152–155.

15. Pereira, *Esmeraldo de Situ Orbis,* pp. 118–122; De Marees, *Description and Historical Account,* pp. 78–87. On Chinka, see P. E. H. Hair, Adam Jones, and Robin Law, eds., *Barbot on Guinea: The Writings of Jean Barbot on West Africa, 1678–1712* (London: Hakluyt Society, 1992), 2:450n.

16. De Marees, *Description and Historical Account,* pp. 42, 79, 113–114, 163–164; quotation p. 113. See also Andreas Josua Ulsheimer (1603–1604) in Adam Jones, ed., *German Sources for West African History, 1680–1700* (Wiesbaden: Franz Steiner Verlag, 1985), p. 29; Kenneth F. Kiple, *The Caribbean Slave: A Biological History* (Cambridge: Cambridge University Press, 1984), p. 25.

17. Kea, *Settlements, Trade, and Polities,* pp. 12–13.

18. De Marees, *Description and Historical Account,* pp. 15, 33 (plate no. 2), 46–50, 58–59, 82–83, 96.

19. Kea, *Settlements, Trade, and Polities,* p. 197; Ivana Elbl, "The Volume of the Early Atlantic Slave Trade, 1450–1521," *JAH* 38 (1997): 31–75. Annual volume fluctuated widely, with Gold Coast slave imports ranging "between 150 and 700 slaves a year" in this period.

20. Quoted in John D. Fage, "Slaves and Society in Western Africa, c. 1445–c. 1700," *JAH* 21 (1980): 298.

21. Ibid. Eustache de la Fosse was a Flemish member of an interloping Spanish fleet trading at Elmina in violation of the 1479 treaty between Spain and Portugal. See Vogt, *Portuguese Rule,* 14–15. See also Vogt, "The Early São Tomé–Príncipe Slave Trade with Mina, 1500–1540," *International Journal of African Historical Studies* (hereafter *IJAHS*) 6, no. 3 (1973): 453–467; Blake, *European Beginnings,* p. 93; Kwame

Daaku, "Aspects of Precolonial Akan Economy," *IJAHS* 5, no. 2 (1972): 237.

22. Elbl, "Volume of the Early Atlantic Slave Trade," p. 72 and Table 7; A. C. de C. M. Saunders, *A Social History of Black Slaves and Freedmen in Portugal, 1441–1555* (Cambridge: Cambridge University Press, 1982); Robin Blackburn, *The Making of New World Slavery: From the Baroque to the Modern, 1492–1800* (London: Verso, 1997), pp. 102–119.

23. Philip D. Curtin, *The Atlantic Slave Trade: A Census* (Madison: University of Wisconsin Press, 1969); Colin A. Palmer, *Slaves of the White God: Blacks in Mexico, 1579–1650* (Cambridge: Harvard University Press, 1976); Frederick P. Bowser, *The African Slave in Colonial Peru, 1524–1650* (Palo Alto, Calif.: Stanford University Press, 1974); C. R. Boxer, *The Portuguese Seaborne Empire, 1415–1825* (New York: Knopf, 1969).

24. David Eltis, *The Rise of African Slavery in the Americas* (Cambridge: Cambridge University Press, 2000), Table 1–1, p. 9.

25. This was distinct from the inland market for slaves which continued to flourish. See Patrick Manning, *Slavery and African Life: Occidental, Oriental, and African Slave Trades* (Cambridge: Cambridge University Press, 1990); Paul E. Lovejoy, *Transformations in Slavery: A History of Slavery in Africa* (Cambridge: Cambridge University Press, 1983).

26. Curtin, *Atlantic Slave Trade,* Table 33.

27. Vogt, *Portuguese Rule,* p. 147.

28. Ibid.

29. *TSTD,* voyage ID #29496, *San Francisco,* Capt. Manuel Méndez; Enriqueta Vila Vilar, *Hispanoamérica y el comercio de esclavos* (Seville: Escuela de Estudios Hispano-Americanos, 1974), p. 174.

30. Vogt, *Portuguese Rule,* pp. 170–193; Johannes Menne Postma, *The Dutch in the Atlantic Slave Trade 1600–1815* (Cambridge: Cambridge University Press, 1990).

31. A. Teixeira da Mota and P. E. H. Hair, *East of Mina: Afro-European Relations on the Gold Coast in the 1550s and 1560s: An Essay with Supporting Documents* (Madison: African Studies Program, University of Wisconsin-Madison, 1988), p. 4.

32. Elizabeth Donnan, ed., *Documents Illustrative of the History of the Slave Trade to America,* 4 vols. (Washington, D.C.: Carnegie Institution, 1930; reprint, New York: Octagon Books, 1965), 1:193.

33. Vogt, "Early São Tomé–Príncipe Slave Trade," 464–467.

34. Ernst van den Boogaart and Pieter C. Emmer, "The Dutch Participation in the Atlantic Slave Trade, 1596–1650," in *The Uncommon Market: Essays in the Economic History of the Atlantic Slave Trade,* ed. Henry A. Gemery and Jan S. Hogendorn (New York: Harcourt Brace Jovanovich,1979), Table 14.1 (p. 360), Table 14.5 (p. 369), pp. 371, 373–374; Postma, *Dutch in the Atlantic Slave Trade,* pp. 19, 26–29.

35. Eltis, *Rise of African Slavery,* Table 7–1, p. 166; David Eltis, "The Volume and African Origins of the British Slave Trade before 1714," *Cahiers d'Etudes Africaines* 138, vol. 35, no. 2 (September, 1995): 617–627.

36. Samuel Brun, quoted in *German Sources for West African History,* pp. 67–68, 91, 93–95.

37. Ibid., p. 94.

38. Ibid., Michael Hemmersam, quoted pp. 116–117.

39. Ibid., Wilhelm Johann Müller, quoted p. 198.

40. Gold Coast correspondence of the Dutch directors-general (translated from Dutch), Furley MSS, Balme Library, University of Ghana (Legon), N8, 1658, p. 29. See also N7, 1656–1657.

41. The argument builds on Lovejoy's *Transformations in Slavery.*

42. The symbol of power under the *oman* was (and remains) the stool (*akonnwa,* pl. *nkonnwa*), the most important being the golden stool, *Sika Dwa,* possessed by the Asantehene (king of Asante). Wilks, "Founding the Political Kingdom," in *Forests of Gold,* pp. 91, 94; T. C. McCaskie, "State and Society, Marriage and Adultery: Some Considerations Towards a Social History of Pre-Colonial Asante," *JAH* 22, no. 4 (1981): 483.

43. Eltis, *Rise of African Slavery,* Tables 7–2 (p. 168) and C–1 (p. 300). Guns emerged as a major import commodity, along with textiles and metals, in the second half of the seventeenth century. Measured by their value in British pounds sterling, guns and gunpowder, accounting for 5 percent of English imports, ranked third after metals (6 percent) and textiles (77 percent). See also Ray A. Kea, "Firearms and Warfare on the Gold and Slave Coasts from the Sixteenth to the Nineteenth Centuries," *JAH* 12 (1971): 185–213.

44. Kea, *Settlements, Trade, and Polities,* pp. 95–168.

45. Ibid., p. 130.

46. De Marees, *Description and Historical Account,* p. 88.

47. Müller in *German Sources,* p. 198, and pp. 192–197; in war, Andreas

Josua Ulsheimer observed at the beginning of the century, "they make peace again as soon as two or three men have been killed on their side or their enemy's." Quoted ibid., p. 34.

48. Kwame Y. Daaku, *Trade and Politics on the Gold Coast, 1600–1720: A Study of the African Reaction to European Trade* (Oxford: Clarendon, 1970), pp. 144–181.

49. Daaku, "Aspects of Precolonial Akan Economy," 246–247.

50. Ivor Wilks, "The Rise of the Akwamu Empire, 1650–1710," *Transactions of the Historical Society of Ghana* 3 (1957): 99–136.

51. Kwame Arhin, "The Structure of Greater Ashanti (1700–1824), *JAH* 8, no. 1 (1967): 65–85; Ivor Wilks, *Asante in the Nineteenth Century: The Structure and Evolution of a Political Order* (Cambridge: Cambridge University Press, 1975).

52. Wilks, "The Mossi and Akan States, 1500–1800," in *History of West Africa*, ed. J. F. A. Ajayi and Michael Crowder, 2 vols. (London: Longmans, 1971), 1: 365–367.

53. Ibid., p. 367.

54. Daaku, "Aspects of Precolonial Akan Economy," p. 247. Also see correspondence of 9 July 1683, in Rawlinson MSS, Bodleian Library, Oxford, Eng. (hereafter Rawl.), C745, explaining that Ansa Sasraku did not allow upland Akan merchants to come to the coast, and charged a threefold markup on European goods they purchased from Akwamu.

55. Wilks, "Mossi and Akan States," pp. 367–368; Wilks, "Rise of the Akwamu Empire," pp. 106–112.

56. Ronald R. Atkinson, "Old Akyem and the Origins of Akyems Abuakwa and Kotoku," in *West African Culture Dynamics: Archaeological and Historical Perspectives,* ed. B. K. Swartz, Jr., and Raymond E. Dumett (The Hague: Mouton, 1980), pp. 355, 359n.

57. The state was not defeated until 1730. Wilks, "Rise of the Akwamu Empire," pp. 109, 112–132.

58. Kea, *Settlements, Trade, and Polities,* p. 37.

59. RAC to CCC, 18 May 1686, T70/50, f. 18.

60. Patrick Manning's estimation that "roughly one-third of all surviving captives were retained in Africa in the period up to 1850" provides a general picture of the scale of African and Atlantic markets for slaves. Manning, *Slavery and African Life,* p. 92.

61. Kea, *Settlements, Trade, and Polities,* pp. 11–50, passim; Daaku, *Trade and Politics;* Wilks, *Asante in the Nineteenth Century;* James

Sanders, "The Expansion of the Fante and the Emergence of Asante in the Eighteenth Century," *JAH* 20, no. 3 (1979): 349–364.

62. Arhin, "Structure of Greater Ashanti," 72–73; T. C. McCaskie, "Komfo Anokye of Asante: Meaning, History and Philosophy in an African Society," *JAH*, 27, no. 2 (1986): 315–339; Joseph K. Adjaye, "Asantehene Agyeman Prempe I, Asante History, and the Historian," *History in Africa* 17 (1990): 1–29.

63. See Marcia Wright, *Strategies of Slaves and Women: Life-Stories from East/Central Africa* (New York: Lilian Barber, 1993), p. 15, on the particular marginalization of women and its significance for understanding African social systems.

64. Martin Klein, discussing terminology of slavery among the Wolof and Sereer, in *Slavery in Africa: Historical and Anthropological Perspectives*, ed. Suzanne Miers and Igor Kopytoff (Madison: University of Wisconsin Press, 1977), p. 343; Fage, "Slaves and Society in Western Africa, c. 1445–c. 1700," p. 298, on the distinction between captives and slaves. For the term "bought" slave, see Gold Coast correspondence of the Dutch directors-general, Furley MSS, N7 (1656–1657) and N8 (1658). On the various categories of slavery in the Gold Coast, see Kea, *Settlements, Trade, and Polities,* abdub in196–201, and De Marees, *Description and Historical Account,* 176, n. 2. On African slavery generally, see Lovejoy, *Transformations in Slavery;* Manning, *Slavery and African Life,* p. 91; Joseph C. Miller, *Way of Death: Merchant Capitalism and the Angolan Slave Trade, 1730–1830* (Madison: University of Wisconsin Press, 1988), pp. 380–381; Claude Meillassoux, *The Anthropology of Slavery: The Womb of Iron and Gold,* trans. Alide Dasnois (1986; Chicago: University of Chicago Press, 1991).

65. Orlando Patterson, *Slavery and Social Death: A Comparative Study* (Cambridge, Harvard University Press, 1982), pp. 38–51.

66. De Marees, *Description and Historical Account,* p. 176.

67. James Phipps, CCC to RAC, 28 June 1721, T70/7, f. 20.

68. Ambrose Baldwyn, Whydah, to RAC, 9 August 1723, T70/7, f. 62.

69. Ernst van den Boogaart, "The Trade between Western Africa and the Atlantic World, 1600–90: Estimates of Trends in Composition and Value," *JAH* 33 (1992): 369–385; David Eltis, "The Relative Importance of Slaves and Commodities in the Atlantic Trade of Seven-

teenth-Century Africa," *JAH* 35 (1994), pp. 237–249, see esp. Table 1 and p. 246.

2. Turning African Captives into Atlantic Commodities

1. CCC to London, 30 September 1721, T70/7, ff. 30–31v; James Phipps et al., CCC, to London, 30 September 1721, T70/4, f. 22.
2. I draw here on Arjun Appadurai's situational definition of the commodity in Arjun Appadurai, ed. *The Social Life of Things: Commodities in Cultural Perspective* (Cambridge: Cambridge University Press, 1986), p. 13.
3. Jean-Christophe Agnew, *Worlds Apart: The Market and the Theater in Anglo-American Thought, 1550–1750* (Cambridge: Cambridge University Press, 1986).
4. The methods and practices of commodification can profitably be understood to have underwritten a "technology of power"—that is, tools that not only physically subdued African bodies but also produced and served an ideological regime that regarded control of African bodies as a natural, self-evident fact. See Steven Shapin and Simon Shaffer, *Leviathan and the Air-Pump: Hobbes, Boyle, and the Experimental Life* (Princeton, N.J.: Princeton University Press, 1985), p. 25 n. 4; Carl Mitcham, "Philosophy and the History of Technology," in *The History and Philosophy of Technology*, ed. G. Bugliarello and D. B. Doner (Urbana: University of Illinois Press, 1979), pp. 163–201, esp. pp. 172–175; Michel Foucault, *The History of Sexuality: An Introduction*, vol. 1, trans. Robert Hurley (1978; New York: Vintage Books, 1990), pp. 90, 109, 115–116, 123, 127; Kathleen M. Brown, *Good Wives, Nasty Wenches and Anxious Patriarchs: Gender, Race, and Power in Colonial Virginia* (Chapel Hill: University of North Carolina Press, for the Omohundro Institute of Early American History and Culture, 1996), pp. 14, 110.
5. Dalby Thomas, CCC, to London, 11 October 1708, T70/5, ff. 49–50.
6. Michel Foucault, *Discipline and Punish: The Birth of the Prison*, trans. Alan Sheridan (1975; New York: Vintage Books, 2nd ed.); Elaine Scarry, *The Body in Pain* (New York: Oxford University Press, 1985); Saidiya V. Hartman, *Scenes of Subjection: Terror, Slavery, and*

Self-Making in Nineteenth-Century America (New York: Oxford University Press, 1997); Jonathan Sawday, *The Body Emblazoned: Dissection and the Human Body in Renaissance Culture* (London: Routledge, 1995).

7. A. W. Lawrence, *Trade Castles and Forts of West Africa* (Stanford, Calif.: Stanford University Press, 1964), p. 132.

8. Arda (sometimes also spelled Ardra) was the English rendering of Allada, the kingdom in the nearby Bight of Benin region from which much of the castle's resident slave labor force derived.

9. P. E. H. Hair, Adam Jones, and Robin Law, eds., *Barbot on Guinea: The Writings of Jean Barbot on West Africa 1678–1712* (London: Hakluyt Society, 1992), 2:391.

10. Ibid., p. 392.

11. Ibid., p. 404, n. 11, editors quoting from Barbot's English translation of his manuscript about his second voyage, published in Awnsham Churchill and John Churchill, eds., *A Collection of Voyages and Travels,* 6 vols., (London: n.p., 1732), vol. 5.

12. Pieter de Marees, *Description and Historical Account of the Gold Kingdom of Guinea (1602),* trans. and ed. Albert van Dantzig and Adam Jones (Oxford: Oxford University Press, 1987), p. 82 and n. 18.

13. Lawrence, *Trade Castles,* p. 185; Hair, Jones, and Law, *Barbot on Guinea,* 2: p. 403, n. 5.

14. Lawrence, *Trade Castles,* p. 72.

15. John Bloom to CCC, 6 June and 2 November 1694, Rawl. C747, ff. 370v, 331.

16. John Bloom to CCC, 25 May, 6 June, 2 August, and 2 November 1694, Rawl. C747, ff. 368, 370v, 381v, 331.

17. Hair, Jones, and Law, *Barbot on Guinea,* 2:416–417, 422, n. 11.

18. See Lawrence, *Trade Castles:* on Fort Saint Sebastian at Shama, Fig. 27 and p. 278; on the English fort at Komenda, Fig. 31; on Dixcove Fort, Fig. 35 and p. 316; on Fort Patience at Apam, Fig. 38; on Fort Orange at Sekondi, Fig. 40; on Fort Good Hope at Beraku, Fig. 42 and p. 345; and on the second English fort at Anomabu, Fig. 43 and p. 352.

19. Howsley Freeman, Komenda, to CCC, 1 June 1695, Rawl. C746, f. 100.

20. Arthur Richards, Anishan, to CCC, 22 February 1681, Rawl. C745,

f. 5v; 2 March 1681, f. 6v. The new factory was occupied in January 1681. See T70/365, f. 60v.

21. Ralph Hassell, Accra, to CCC, 18 October 1681, Rawl. C745, f. 35v.

22. Peter Blake, "A Journall of my Intended Voyage for ye Gold Coast kept by mee Peter Blake Commander of ye Royall Companys ship *James* in ye searvis of ye Royall African Company of England," 1675–1676, T70/1211, f. 61. Extracts of Blake's journal are published in Elizabeth Donnan, ed., *Documents Illustrative of the History of the Slave Trade to America*, 4 vols. (Washington, D.C.: Carnegie Institution, 1930; reprint, New York: Octagon Books, 1965), 1:199–209.

23. Slave ships carried their own supply and presumably the castle received occasional shipments of slave irons from London, as well. They also were fabricated on site at the castle: on two occasions in April and June 1687, for example, "3 good iron barrs" were dispensed to the blacksmith "to make shackles and long irons for ye slaves." T70/372, ff. 104v, 113.

24. Edward Searle, Accra, to CCC, 29 July 1697, Rawl. C746, f. 246.

25. The captain received ten pairs of irons a week later. Charles Towgood, Allampo Road, to CCC, 17 March 1682, Rawl. C746, f. 147; 24 March 1682, Rawl. C746, f. 148.

26. Mark Bedford Whiting, Accra, to CCC, 10 October 1691, Rawl. C747, f. 249.

27. Ralph Hassell, Accra, to CCC, 5 August 1682, Rawl. C746, f. 170v.

28. Mark Bedford Whiting to CCC, 1 and 5 March 1687, Rawl. C747, ff. 3, 5.

29. Lawrence, *Trade Castles,* p. 90; Tarikhu Farrar, *Building Technology and Settlement Planning in a West African Civilization* (Lewiston, N.Y.: Edwin Mellen, 1996), pp. 137–138.

30. Mark Bedford Whiting, Accra, to CCC, 16 October 1687, Rawl. C747, f. 104v.

31. The term "bumboy" designated castle slaves whose responsibilities included management of captives held for export.

32. Mark Bedford Whiting, Accra, to CCC, 15 December 1687, Rawl. C747, f. 153v.

33. William Cooper, Winneba, to CCC, 30 November 1695, Rawl. C746, f. 134v.

34. Darold D. Wax, "Negro Resistance to the Early American Slave

Trade," *Journal of Negro History* 51, no. 1 (1966): 1–15; Adam Jones, ed., *Brandenburg Sources for West African History, 1680–1700* (Wiesbaden: Franz Steiner Verlag, 1985), p. 187.

35. Captain William Maple, CCC, to RAC, 15 January 1683, Rawl. C746, f. 26.

36. Mark Bedford Whiting, Accra, to CCC, 24 January 1686, Rawl. C745, f. 320v.

37. Edward Searle, Accra, to CCC, 12 September 1695, Rawl. C746, f. 122v.

38. RAC, London, to CCC, 5 December 1723, T70/53, f. 113v.

39. Dalby Thomas, CCC, to RAC, 31 March 1704, T70/28, f. 30v.

40. Wilhelm Johann Müller, quoted in Jones, *Brandenburg Sources,* p. 208.

41. Mark Bedford Whiting, Accra, to CCC, 2 March 1686, Rawl. C745, f. 333.

42. Ralph Hassell, Accra, to CCC, 25 June 1682, Rawl. C746, f. 165v; William Bosman, *A New and Accurate Description of the Coast of Guinea* (London, 1705; reprint, with notes by J. D. Fage and R. E. Bradbury, London: Frank Cass, 1967), p. 297; Ray A. Kea, *Settlements, Trade, and Polities in the Seventeenth-Century Gold Coast* (Baltimore: Johns Hopkins University Press, 1982), p. 46.

43. This figure is calculated for the eight slaves present in the prison for the entire month of January and does not include the three slaves purchased during that month. T70/367, CCC, Accounts-Journals, 1681–1682, ff. 30, 31v.

44. Ralph Hassell, Accra, to CCC, 12 June 1683, Rawl. C745, f. 205v.

45. See Mark Bedford Whiting, Accra, to CCC, 30 September 1686, Rawl. C745, f. 377: "Here is now in the castle 48 [slaves] which is enough for the great canoe passage up."

46. James Bayley, aboard the *Adventure,* near Allampo, to CCC, 29 June 1687, Rawl. C747, f. 55v.

47. Thomas Price, Accra, to CCC, 30 June 1687, Rawl. C747, f. 56; Mark Bedford Whiting, Accra, to CCC, 8 July 1687 Rawl. C747, f. 58. The number of slaves delivered to Accra from the sloop was fifty-nine; it appears that Bayley conveyed the slaves to Accra by canoe, since Whiting refers to Bayley as being at Accra, while his vessel was at "Labordee" (Labadi, due east of Accra).

48. Mark Bedford Whiting, Accra, to CCC, 17 July 1687, Rawl. C747,

f. 61v. The vessel left Accra on 16 July with ninety-one slaves taken out of the prisons there (forty-nine men, forty-two women).

49. On the rapid deterioration caused by dehydration, see Kenneth F. Kiple and Brian T. Higgins, "Mortality Caused by Dehydration during the Middle Passage," in *The Atlantic Slave Trade: Effects on Economies, Societies, and Peoples in Africa, the Americas, and Europe,* ed. Joseph E. Inikori and Stanley L. Engerman (Durham, N.C.: Duke University Press, 1992), pp. 321–337.

50. James Bayley, aboard the *Adventure,* Accra, to CCC, 27 July 1687, Rawl. C747, f. 64.

51. Mark Bedford Whiting, Accra, to CCC, 27 July 1687, Rawl. C747, f. 64v.

52. Mark Bedford Whiting, Accra, to CCC, 2 August 1687, Rawl. C747, f. 66.

53. Mark Bedford Whiting, Accra to CCC, 9 August 1687, Rawl. C747, f. 69v; James Bayley, aboard the *Adventure,* en route to CCC, 20 August 1687, Rawl. C747, f. 73v. The vessel was dispatched on the morning of the eighth, but as the winds were insufficient, his vessel "could not stir."

54. John Rootsey, Anomabu, to CCC, 24 April 1695, Rawl. C746, f. 90v; William Cooper, Winneba, to CCC, 3 May 1695, Rawl. C746, f. 94.

55. Shapin and Schaffer, *Leviathan and the Air-Pump,* pp. 42, 45.

56. John Bloom, Accra, to CCC, 25 February 1694, Rawl. C747, f. 493; 6 March 1694, f. 356v.

57. Lawrence, *Trade Castles,* p. 72.

58. Ibid., p. 90.

59. Edward Searle to CCC, 7 December 1695, Rawl. C746, f. 135.

60. Ibid.

61. De Marees reported that the bread "grits between your teeth a little, which results from the stones with which it is ground," a remark suggesting that it was not uncommon to find some amount of stone in cankey. De Marees, *Description and Historical Account,* p. 112. See Kea, *Settlements, Trade, and Polities,* pp. 301–302, on the typical daily diet.

62. Charles Towgood, Allampo, to CCC, 19 March 1682, Rawl. C746, f. 148; Kenneth F. Kiple, *The Caribbean Slave: A Biological History* (Cambridge: Cambridge University Press, 1984), p. 63. The woman's refusal to eat was characteristic of a cause of death commonly known

by slave traders and New World planters as "fixed melancholy" that was induced by a wide range of conditions including depression and dehydration, as well as "outright starvation."

63. Charles Towgood, Allampo, to CCC, 24 March 1682, Rawl. C746, f. 148.

64. CCC, Accounts-Ledgers, January–September 1712, T70/664, f. 53. "Cabosheer" was the English rendering of a term used generically to designate local African elites.

65. Ibid.

66. Mark Bedford Whiting, Accra, to CCC, 15 December 1687. The records are silent as to the final outcome and their fate.

67. Ralph Hassell, Anomabu, to CCC, 23 July 1687, Rawl. C747, f. 62.

68. See T70/365–384, CCC, Accounts-Journals, 1679–1718, passim.

69. Arthur Richards, Anishan, to CCC, 13 July 1681, Rawl. C745, f. 48v.

70. William Cooper, Winneba, to CCC, 16 May 1695, Rawl. C746, f. 97.

71. William Cooper, Winneba, to CCC, 24 May 1695, Rawl. C746, f. 98.

72. Patrick Manning, *Slavery and African Life: Occidental, Oriental, and African Slave Trades* (Cambridge: Cambridge University Press, 1990), pp. 92, 97–98.

73. Edward Searle, Accra, to CCC, 20 June 1695, Rawl. C746, f. 107v.

74. Edward Searle, Accra, to CCC, 21 April 1697, Rawl. C746, f. 219. In all likelihood, the man was put in chains rather than allowed to return to the retinue of castle slaves at the fort.

75. Snelgrave, in George Francis Dow, *Slave Ships and Slaving* (1927; reprint, Mineola, N.Y.: Dover Publications, 2000), p. 122.

76. T. C. McCaskie, "Kinship and Family in the History of the *Oyoko KɔKɔɔ* Dynasty of Kumase," *JAH* 36, no. 3 (1995): 361, describing the matrilineal structure of Akan systems of kinship and inheritance. Though none of the European sources on seventeenth-century Gold Coast societies demonstrated understanding of the matriclan, their descriptions of inheritance patterns reflect that matrilineal descent was well established by this time. See De Marees, *Description and Historical Account,* pp. 182–183; Wilhelm Johann Müller, in Adam Jones, ed., *German Sources for West African History, 1680–1700* (Wiesbaden: Franz Steiner Verlag, 1985), pp. 258–590.

77. *Some Memoirs of the Life of Job, the Son of Solomon the High Priest of Boonda in Africa; Who was a Slave about two Years in Maryland; and afterwards being brought to England, was set free, and sent to his*

native Land in the Year 1734 (London: n.p., 1734), excerpted in Philip D. Curtin, ed., *Africa Remembered: Narratives by West Africans from the Era of the Slave Trade* (Madison: University of Wisconsin Press, 1967), p. 57.

78. Orlando Patterson, *Slavery and Social Death: A Comparative Study* (Cambridge: Harvard University Press, 1982), pp. 38, 45.

79. Ibid., pp. 45–46, 51, 52.

80. Ibid., pp. 53–54.

81. Joseph C. Miller, *Way of Death: Merchant Capitalism and the Angolan Slave Trade, 1730–1830* (Madison: University of Wisconsin Press, 1988), pp. 4–5; Wyatt MacGaffey, "Dialogues of the Deaf: Europeans on the Atlantic Coast of Africa," in *Implicit Understanding: Observing, Reporting, and Reflecting on the Encounters between Europeans and Other Peoples in the Early Modern Era,* ed. Stuart B. Schwartz (Cambridge: Cambridge University Press, 1994), pp. 249–267; Thornton, "Cannibals, Witches, and Slave Traders in the Atlantic World," *William and Mary Quarterly,* 3rd series, 60, no. 2 (2003): 273.

82. Jane Guyer, "Wealth in People and Self-Realization in Equatorial Africa," *Man,* n.s. 28, 1 (March 1993): 256, glossing an observation by Joseph C. Miller, "Imbangala Lineage Slavery," in *Slavery in Africa: Historical and Anthropological Perspectives,* ed. Suzanne Miers and Igor Kopytoff (Madison: University of Wisconsin Press, 1977).

83. Ralph Hassell, Anomabu, to CCC, 25 May 1687, Rawl. C747, f. 39. For a general discussion of suicide in the slave trade and in American plantation societies, see William D. Piersen, "White Cannibals, Black Martyrs: Fear, Depression, and Religious Faith as Causes of Suicide among New Slaves," *Journal of Negro History* 62, no. 2 (1977): 147–159.

3. The Political Economy of the Slave Ship

1. RAC, Ships Books, *Sarah Bonadventure,* Capt. Henry Nurse, 1677, T70/1212, n.p.

2. Ray A. Kea, *Settlements, Trade, and Polities in the Seventeenth-Century Gold Coast* (Baltimore: Johns Hopkins University Press, 1982), p. 192; Marion Johnson, "The Ounce in Eighteenth-Century West African Trade," *JAH* 7 (1966): 197–214.

3. David Eltis, *The Rise of African Slavery in the Americas* (Cambridge: Cambridge University Press, 2000), p. 115.
4. Ibid., p. 114.
5. Ibid., pp. 135, 66, 14. In this regard, the African side of the Atlantic market for slaves is best understood as a wholesale operation, where Europeans buyers were "entrepreneurs rather than simple consumers." In their transactions, European and African sellers of people were engaged in the passing of merchandise "from one entrepreneur to another, intended for resale by the second." To put it differently, the African side of the Atlantic market initiated what Marx understood to be the conversion of money into capital—that is, "the transformation of money into commodities, and the re-conversion of commodities into money: buying in order to sell." James E. Vance, Jr., *The Merchant's World: The Geography of Wholesaling* (Englewood Cliffs, N.J.: Prentice Hall, 1970), p. 24; Karl Marx, *Capital: A Critique of Political Economy*, vol. 1, trans. Ben Fowkes (1867; New York: Vintage, 1976), p. 248.
6. Pieter de Marees, *Description and Historical Account of the Gold Kingdom of Guinea (1602)*, trans. and ed. Albert van Dantzig and Adam Jones (Oxford: Oxford University Press, 1987), p. 176; T70/50, f. 142, and passim for "quantitys of Blacks."
7. Eltis, *Rise of African Slavery*, p. 118.
8. K. G. Davies, *The Royal African Company* (London: Longmans, 1957), pp. 187–189, 194–195.
9. John Pery, secretary, RAC, to Joseph Bingham, 20 June 1706, T70/44, n.p.
10. Ships purpose built specifically for the slave trade did not appear in great number before the second half of the eighteenth century. James A. Rawley, *The Transatlantic Slave Trade: A History* (New York: Norton, 1981), pp. 252, 256–258.
11. John Pery to Joseph Bingham, 2 July 1706, T70/44, n.p.
12. Ibid.
13. Davies, *Royal African Company*, p. 197.
14. John Pery to Joseph Bingham, 15 August and 19 September 1706, T70/44, n.p.
15. John Pery to Joseph Bingham, 2 July 1706, T70/44, n.p.
16. RAC, London, to CCC, 13 May 1701, T70/51, f. 85v.

17. Eltis, *Rise of African Slavery,* pp. 118, 123, 127, and Table 5.1.
18. RAC, London, to Whydah, 12 August 1701, T70/51, f. 105.
19. RAC, London, to Whydah, 6 November 1701, T70/51, f. 107.
20. RAC, London, to CCC, 28 June 1709, T70/52, f. 119.
21. RAC, London, to CCC, 8 September 1702, T70/51, f. 148v.
22. RAC, London, to CCC, 10 September 1700, T70/51, f. 69v.
23. Abolitionists picked up on this supposed correlation between crowding and shipboard mortality and made it the leading edge of their late eighteenth-century campaign for reforms in the shipboard treatment of slaves. After much analysis and debate, modern investigators have come to agree that the evidence does not support the correlation. Shipboard mortality resulted from the interaction of African and Atlantic causal factors; by itself, neither ship size, crowding, nor voyage length caused greater levels of mortality in the Atlantic crossing. Joseph C. Miller, "Mortality in the Atlantic Slave Trade: Statistical Evidence on Causality," *Journal of Interdisciplinary History* 11 (1981): 385–423; Miller, "A Reply," *Journal of Interdisciplinary History* 13 (1982): 331–336; Raymond L. Cohn and Richard A. Jensen, "Mortality in the Atlantic Slave Trade," *Journal of Interdisciplinary History* 13 (1982): 317–329; Richard H. Steckel and Richard A. Jensen, "New Evidence on the Causes of Slave and Crew Mortality in the Atlantic Slave Trade," *Journal of Economic History* 16 (1986): 57–78; Herbert S. Klein and Stanley L. Engerman, "Long-Term Trends in African Mortality in the Transatlantic Slave Trade," *Slavery & Abolition* (Special Issue), *Routes to Slavery: Direction, Ethnicity and Mortality in the Transatlantic Slave Trade* 18, no. 1 (1997): 37–48; Herbert S. Klein, Stanley L. Engerman, Robin Haines, and Ralph Shlomowitz, "Transoceanic Mortality: The Slave Trade in Comparative Perspective," *William and Mary Quarterly,* 3rd ser., 58, no. 1 (2001): 93–117.
24. William Falconer, *Falconer's Marine Dictionary (1780)* (1769; reprint of London, 1780, ed., New York: Augustus M. Kelley, 1970), p. 142.
25. Peter Blake, "A Journall of my Intended Voyage for ye Gold Coast kept by mee Peter Blake Commander of ye Royall Companys ship *James* in ye searvis of ye Royall African Company of England," 28 November 1675, T70/1211, f. 54v. See Falconer, *Marine Dictionary* for explanation of nautical terms. See also Johannes Menne Postma,

The Dutch in the Atlantic Slave Trade 1600-1815 (Cambridge: Cambridge University Press, 1990), pp. 142–144.

26. See Marcus Rediker, *Between the Devil and the Deep Blue Sea: Merchant Seamen, Pirates, and the Anglo-American Maritime World, 1700–1750* (Cambridge: Cambridge University Press, 1987), pp. 77–115, passim, and especially p. 87, on shipboard social hierarchy in the seventeenth and eighteenth centuries.

27. On scuttles, see Falconer, *Marine Dictionary*, pp. 145 and 258; on carlings and ledges, pp. 78 and 172; see also Plate 3. See Elizabeth Donnan, ed., *Documents Illustrative of the History of the Slave Trade to America*, 4 vols. (Washington, D.C.: Carnegie Institution, 1930; reprint, New York: Octagon Books, 1965), 1:202n, for explanation of this adapted use of carlings (also "commings," "coamings," or "combings") aboard slave ships.

28. Blake, "A Journall of my Intended Voyage," 6 January 1676, f. 58v.

29. Ibid., f. 59, 8 January 1676. On "meerine," see Kea, *Settlements, Trade, and Polities*, p. 100.

30. Blake, "A Journall of my Intended Voyage," 9 January 1676, f. 59.

31. Ibid.

32. Ibid., 10 January 1676, f. 60.

33. Ibid., 11 and 12 January 1676, ff. 60–60v.

34. Ibid.

35. Ibid., 12, 13, and 14 January 1676, f. 60v.

36. Ibid., 21 January 1676, f. 62.

37. Ibid., 22 January 1676, f. 62. Blake sent his pinnace a few leagues east of the Castle to Agga for the stanchions on 22 January.

38. William Bosman, *A New and Accurate Description of the Coast of Guinea* (London, 1705; reprint, New York: Barnes & Noble, 1967), p. 365.

39. P. E. H. Hair, Adam Jones, and Robin Law, eds., *Barbot on Guinea: The Writings of Jean Barbot on West Africa 1678–1712* (London: Hakluyt Society, 1992), 2:774.

40. Thomas Phillips, *A Journal of a Voyage Made in the Hannibal of London, Ann. 1693, 1694 . . .* in *A Collection of Voyages and Travels*, 6 vols., ed. Awnsham Churchill and John Churchill (London, 1732) 6:218.

41. On this point see especially Manning's discussion of African slave exports in the Atlantic market: Patrick Manning, *Slavery and African*

Life: Occidental, Oriental, and African Slave Trades (Cambridge: Cambridge University Press, 1990).

42. Mark Bedford Whiting, Accra to CCC, 15 January 1686, Rawl. C745, f. 317. "Ahenesa is fighting against the Argins [Agona] who is an hindrance to our trade."

43. Mark Bedford Whiting, Accra, to CCC, 27 January and 2 and 16 March 1686, Rawl. C745, ff. 324, 333, 338v.

44. Mark Bedford Whiting, Accra, to CCC, 27 May and 5 June 1686, Rawl. C745, ff. 348v, 350.

45. Mark Bedford Whiting, Accra, to CCC, 18 July and 12 and 18 August 1686, Rawl. C745, ff. 358v, 369v, 365v.

46. Mark Bedford Whiting, Accra, to CCC, 31 August and 11, 19, and 30 September 1686, Rawl. C745, ff. 369v, 372, 375, 377. Figure calculated from Whiting's reports to officials at CCC, T70/371, CCC, Accounts-Journals, September 1686 accounts for slaves received at CCC from Accra.

47. E. A. Boateng, *A Geography of Ghana* (Cambridge: Cambridge University Press, 1970), pp. 16–18. Kea, *Settlements, Trade, and Polities,* p. 139.

48. Mark Bedford Whiting, Accra, to CCC, 30 September 1686, Rawl. C745, f. 377. On Akropong (Kyerepon) and other Akwapim polities, see Kea, *Settlements, Trade, and Polities,* pp. 69–72; see also Michelle Gilbert, "'No Condition Is Permanent': Ethnic Construction and the Use of History in Akuapem," *Africa: Journal of the International African Institute* 67, no. 4 (1997): 501–533; and Louis E. Wilson, *The Krobo People of Ghana to 1892: A Political and Social History* (Athens: Ohio University Center for International Studies, 1992).

49. Mark Bedford Whiting, Accra, to CCC, 21 and 31 October 1686, Rawl. C745, ff. 381, 383v.

50. Mark Bedford Whiting, Accra, to CCC, 8 November 1686, Rawl. C745, f. 389.

51. Mark Bedford Whiting, Accra, to CCC, 14 and 15 November 1686, Rawl. C745, ff. 392, 392v.

52. Mark Bedford Whiting, Accra, to CCC, 27 November and 1 and 5 December 1686, Rawl. C745, ff. 396, 397, 401v.

53. Mark Bedford Whiting, Accra, to CCC, 1 December 1686, ibid.

54. Thomas Price, Accra, to CCC, 24 December 1686, Rawl. C745, f. 422.

55. Mark Bedford Whiting, Accra, to CCC, 5 December 1686 and 1 February 1687, Rawl. C745, ff. 401v, 432; Whiting to CCC, 18 January 1687, Rawl. C745, f. 428.
56. CCC, Accounts-Journals, January 1680, T70/365, ff. 20, 24.
57. 2, 27, and 31 March 1680, T70/365, ff. 26v, 27.
58. 31 March 1680, T70/365, f. 28. His capacity to do so indicates that Attabarba was an *obirempon,* a member of the elite class of men who, thanks to their accumulated wealth or political or military status, controlled trade in the coastal port towns. Kea, *Settlements, Trade, and Polities,* p. 98.
59. 30 April 1680, T70/365, f. 30.
60. Nathaniel Bradley, Henry Spurway, Theobald Pysing, and John Mildmay, CCC, to RAC, 20 April 1680, T70/15, f. 38.
61. Edwyn Stede and Stephen Gascoigne, Barbados, to London, 12 July 1680, T70/15, ff. 36v–37.
62. RAC, London, to Thomas Corker, James Island, Gambia River, 3 October 1699, T70/51, f. 27v. See also Copies of Instructions from the Royal African Company of England to the Captains of Ships in Their Service, T70/61, passim; RAC, London, to Alexander Cleeve, James Island, Gambia River, 12 January 1686, T70/50, f. 4v; RAC, London, to John Freeman, Sherbrow River, 4 August 1702, T70/51, ff. 141–141v; RAC, London, to Spencer Broughton, CCC, 11 August 1702, T70/51, ff. 146v–147; RAC, London, to Dalby Thomas, CCC, 8 July 1703, T70/51, ff. 177–178v; RAC, London, to Thomas Weaver, James Island, Gambia River, 8 July 1703, T70/51, f. 180.
63. Nathaniel Bradley, Henry Spurway, Theobald Pysing, and John Mildmay, CCC, to RAC, 26 April 1680, T70/1, f. 54v; Bradley, Spurway, Pysing, and Mildmay to RAC, 3 May 1680, ff. 55–57.
64. Diary of William Baillie, 12 January 1716, T70/1464, f. 37v; John Atkins, *A Voyage to Guinea, Brasil, and the West-Indies* (1721) in Donnan, *Documents Illustrative of the History,* 2:267.
65. On "common mortality," see RAC, London, to Jamaica, 7 December 1704, T70/58, f. 78v.
66. John Groome, Anomabu, to CCC, 8 August 1683, Rawl. C745, f. 280.
67. Eltis, *Rise of African Slavery,* p. 175; David Eltis and Stanley L. Engerman, "Was the Slave Trade Dominated by Men?" *Journal of Interdisciplinary History* 23, no. 2 (1992): 237–257.

68. Phillips, *Journal of a Voyage,* p. 219.
69. Robert Young, Accra, to CCC, 22 July 1683, Rawl. C745, f. 227.
70. John Groome, Allampo, to CCC, 18 September 1683, Rawl. C745, f. 289v.
71. John Groome, Allampo, to CCC, 29 September 1683, Rawl. C745, f. 296.
72. Hugh Shears, aboard *Cape Coast Brigantine* at Teshi (near Accra), to CCC, 22 September 1683, Rawl. C745, f. 291.
73. Eltis, *Rise of African Slavery,* pp. 114–115.
74. Peter Holt, Anomabu, to RAC, 20 June 1715, T70/3, f. 141.
75. James Phipps, CCC, to RAC, 25 January 1721, T70/4, f. 12.
76. Robin Law, *The Slave Coast of West Africa, 1550–1750: The Impact of the Atlantic Slave Trade on an African Society* (Oxford: Oxford University Press, 1991), pp. 156–166.
77. It was also common to put contingents of Gold Coast captives designated as guardians and "cankey women" aboard ships en route to gather the major part of their cargoes at the Bight of Benin, and sometimes as afield as West-Central Africa. Eltis, *Rise of African Slavery,* pp. 228–229; Stephanie E. Smallwood, "The Mysterious Figure of the African Guardian: The Problematics of Power in the Atlantic Worlds of the Slave Ship," unpublished manuscript.
78. Henry Greenhill, Henry Spurway, and Daniell Bridge, CCC, to RAC, 6 April 1681, T70/10, f. 47v; Inventory of Goods in Cape Coast Castle, CCC, Accounts-Journals, 29 January 1691, T70/366, f. 2.
79. Inventories of goods remaining at Anomabu, Anishan, Agga, and Accra, CCC, Accounts-Journals, 29 January 1681, T70/366, ff. 2v–3.
80. Edwyn Stede, Barbados, to RAC, 12 May 1681, T70/10, f. 18; Nathaniel Bradley, CCC, to RAC, 7 December 1680, T70/10, f. 46v; CCC, Accounts-Journals, accounts for January 1681, T70/365, f. 63v.
81. Henry Greenhill, Henry Spurway, and Daniell Bridge, CCC, to RAC, 6 April 1681, T70/10, f. 47v.
82. CCC, Accounts-Journals, 16 February 1681, T70/366, f. 6v. Also aboard the *Edgar* were James Nightingale, the factor in charge of purchasing the vessel's captives, and his associate, Robert Hollings.
83. James Nightingale, aboard the *Edgar,* Allampo, to CCC, 25 March 1681, Rawl. C745, f. 11; Nightingale, Winneba, to CCC, 9 March 1681, Rawl. C745, f. 8.

84. James Nightingale, Winneba, to CCC, 9 March 1681; Nightingale, Allampo, to CCC, 25 March 1681.
85. James Nightingale, Allampo, to CCC, 25 March 1681.
86. *Barbot on Guinea,* 2:439.
87. Robert Hollings, Allampo, to CCC, 25 March 1681, Rawl. C745, f. 11v; James Nightingale, Allampo, to CCC, 6 April 1681, Rawl. C745, ff. 13–13v.
88. James Nightingale, Allampo, to CCC, 25 March 1681.
89. Charles Bowler, Allampo, to CCC, 25 March 1681, Rawl. C745, f. 11v. By insisting that the company pay "demurrage" charges when ships were forced to overstay the prescribed duration of their time at African ports, ship owners sought to protect their interest in the timely completion of a voyage. Davies, *Royal African Company,* p. 197.
90. James Nightingale, Allampo, to CCC, 6 April 1681, Rawl. C745, ff. 13–13v.
91. Ibid.
92. James Nightingale, Allampo, to CCC, 11 April 1681, Rawl. C745, f. 14.
93. Charles Bowler to James Nightingale, Allampo, 20 April 1681, Rawl. C745, f. 15; James Nightingale and Robert Hollings, aboard the *Edgar* between Accra and Winneba, to CCC, 25 April 1681, Rawl. C745, f. 16; Nightingale, Winneba, to CCC, 11 May 1681, Rawl. C745, f. 18v.
94. James Nightingale and Robert Hollings, aboard the *Edgar,* to CCC, 25 April 1681; Charles Bowler, aboard the *Edgar,* between Accra and Winneba, to CCC, 25 April 1681, Rawl. C745, f. 16v.
95. James Nightingale and Robert Hollings, Winneba, to CCC, 7 May 1681, Rawl. C745, f. 17v; Nightingale to CCC, 11 May 1681, Rawl. C745, f. 18v; CCC, Account-Journals, passim, T70/365–372.
96. Charles Bowler, Winneba, to CCC, 15 May 1681, Rawl. C745, f. 20.
97. James Nightingale, Winneba, to CCC, 15 May 1681, Rawl. C745, f. 20v; Nightingale, Winneba, to CCC, 20 May 1681, Rawl. C745, f. 21.
98. Kenneth F. Kiple and Brian T. Higgins, "Mortality Caused by Dehydration during the Middle Passage," in *The Atlantic Slave Trade: Effects on Economies, Societies, and Peoples in Africa, the Americas, and Europe,* ed. Joseph E. Inikori and Stanley L. Engerman (Durham, N.C.: Duke University Press, 1992), p. 325.

99. Charles Bowler, Winneba, to CCC, 11 and 15 May 1681, Rawl. C745, f. 19v.
100. Ibid., 11 May 1681.
101. James Nightingale and Robert Hollings, Winneba, to CCC, 7 May 1681.
102. T70/366, f. 40.
103. Arthur Wendover, Accra, to CCC, 25 April 1681, Rawl. C745, f. 15v.
104. Richard Thelwall, Anomabu, to CCC, 12 May 1681, Rawl. C745, f. 20; James Nightingale, Winneba, to CCC, 15 May 1681.
105. James Nightingale, Allampo, to CCC, 6 April 1681; James Nightingale and Robert Hollings, between Accra and Winneba, 25 April 1681; Nightingale, Winneba, to CCC, 11 May 1681.
106. Charles Bowler, Winneba, to CCC, 15 May 1681.
107. James Nightingale, Winneba, to CCC, 20 May 1681, Rawl. C745, f. 21.
108. Robert Hollings, Accra, to CCC, 23 May 1681, Rawl. C745, f. 22.
109. "Testimony of Robert Norris," 3 June 1788, *Minutes of the Evidence before the Committee of the Whole House,* House of Commons, Great Britain; Bosman, *A New and Accurate Description,* 104–105; Akin Mabogunje, "The Land and Peoples of West Africa," in *History of West Africa,* 2 vols., ed. J. F. A. Ajayi and Michael Crowder (London: Longmans, 1971), 1:1–3.
110. Robert Hollings, Accra, to CCC, 23 May 1681, Rawl. C745, f. 22.
111. There are no surviving letters from Bowler following his departure from Accra, but when Thomas Phillips was on the coast in 1694, he left Accra on 17 May and arrived at Whydah (about fifteen miles short of Offra) three days later, on the morning of the twentieth. Phillips, *Journal of a Voyage,* pp. 213–214.
112. William Cross, Offra in Arda [Allada], to CCC, 18 August 1681, Rawl. C745, f. 62v; Law, *Slave Coast of West Africa,* pp. 16, 17. Offra was adjacent to Jakin, the primary Atlantic port of the Allada kingdom.
113. John Thorne, Glehue in Whydah, to CCC, 24 May 1681, Rawl. C745, f. 62; William Cross, Offra, to CCC, 18 August 1681, Rawl. C745, ff. 62v–63v.
114. William Cross, Offra, to CCC, 18 August 1681; John Thorne, Glehue in Whydah, to CCC, 20 August 1681, Rawl. C745, f. 67.
115. Manning, *Slavery and African Life,* p. 66, estimates that the popula-

tion of the entire coastal plain and forest and savanna hinterland of the Gold Coast in 1700 (an area larger than modern Ghana) numbered around three million people.

116. Eltis, *Rise of African Slavery,* p. 173.
117. RAC, London, to CCC, 2 May 1699, T70/51, f. 15.
118. John Browne, CCC, to RAC, 28 February 1706, T70/5, f. 12.
119. Regarding the *Carlton,* see, for example, James Phipps, CCC, to RAC, 23 December 1721, T70/7, f. 34.
120. See Eltis, *Rise of African Slavery,* Table 7-I.
121. RAC, London, to CCC, 10 August 1704, T70/52, f. 22.
122. K. Y. Daaku, *Trade and Politics on the Gold Coast, 1600–1720: A Study of the African Reaction to European Trade* (Oxford: Oxford Clarendon Press, 1970); J. K. Fynn, *Asante and Its Neighbours, 1700–1807* (London: Longmans, 1971); Kwame Arhin, "The Structure of Greater Ashanti," *JAH* 8, no. 1 (1967): 72–73; James Sanders, "The Expansion of Fante and the Emergence of Asante in the Eighteenth Century," *JAH* 20, no. 3 (1979): 349–364; David Henige, "John Kabes of Komenda: An Early African Entrepreneur and State Builder," *JAH* 18, no. 1 (1977): 1–19.
123. CCC, Accounts—Ledgers, January–September 1712, T70/664, f. 53.
124. Ibid.
125. Alfred W. Crosby, *The Measure of Reality: Quantification and Western Society, 1250–1600* (Cambridge: Cambridge University Press, 1997), p. 200; see also Raymond de Roover, "The Development of Accounting Prior to Luca Pacioli, According to the Account Books of Medieval Merchants," in *Business, Banking, and Economic Thought in Late Medieval and Early Modern Europe: Selected Studies of Raymond de Roover,* ed. Julius Kirshner (Chicago: University of Chicago Press, 1974), pp. 119–180.
126. Mary Poovey, *A History of the Modern Fact: Problems of Knowledge in the Sciences of Wealth and Society* (Chicago: University of Chicago Press, 1998), p. 36.
127. T70/50 f. 113 ("conveniently stow"); RAC to Petley Weybourne, Whydah, 17 December 1689, T70/50, f. 103.

4. The Anomalous Intimacies of the Slave Cargo

1. Michael Mullin, *Africa in America: Slave Acculturation and Resistance in the American South and the British Caribbean, 1736–1831*

(Urbana: University of Illinois Press, 1992); Gwendolyn Midlo Hall, *Africans in Colonial Louisiana: The Development of Afro-Creole Culture in the Eighteenth Century* (Baton Rouge: Louisiana State University Press, 1992); John Thornton, *Africa and Africans in the Making of the Atlantic World, 1400–1800,* 2nd ed. (1992; Cambridge: Cambridge University Press, 1998); Philip D. Morgan, *Slave Counterpoint: Black Culture in the Eighteenth-Century Chesapeake & Lowcountry* (Chapel Hill: University of North Carolina Press for the Omohundro Institute of Early American History and Culture, 1998); Michael A. Gomez, *Exchanging Our Country Marks: The Transformation of African Identities in the Colonial and Antebellum South* (Chapel Hill: University of North Carolina Press, 1998).

2. RAC to John Booker, Gambia River, 27 September 1692, T70/50, ff. 135–135v, 137; "Invoice of Negroes & Provisions Laden on Board the *America,*" 23 April 1693, T70/946, f. 37v; William Harding, Barbados, to RAC, 30 May 1693, T70/12, f. 29, reporting that the *America* stopped there en route to Jamaica on 25 May with a cargo that included slaves "of the taking of Goree & Senegall." See Philip D. Curtin, *Economic Change in Precolonial Africa: Senegambia in the Era of the Slave Trade* (Madison: University of Wisconsin Press, 1975), p. 103, on English seizure of Gorée and Saint Louis in 1693.

3. John Booker, James Island, Gambia River, to RAC, 25 April 1693, T70/11, f. 76.

4. Curtin, *Economic Change,* pp. 68–75, 83–87, 178, 12–13, 182–185.

5. William Snelgrave, in George Francis Dow, *Slave Ships and Slaving* (1927; reprint, Mineola, N.Y.: Dover Publications, 2000), pp. 129–130. "Cetre-Crue" [Seltera Crue] was in the vicinity of the Sestos River on the Windward Coast (present-day Liberia).

6. Ibid., pp. 130–131.

7. Anthony D. Smith, *National Identity* (Reno: University of Nevada Press, 1991); *Nationalism: Theory, Ideology, History* (Cambridge, England: Polity, 2001).

8. Philip D. Morgan, "The Cultural Implications of the Atlantic Slave Trade: African Regional Origins, American Destinations and New World Developments," *Slavery & Abolition* 18 (1997): 128.

9. Before the end of the fifteenth century, Portuguese mariners had noted that the speech of the Africans with whom they dealt changed markedly at around Beraku. See Duarte Pacheco Pereira, *Esmeraldo de Situ*

Orbis, trans. and ed. George H. T. Kimble (London: Hakluyt Society, 1937), p. 122. And in the late sixteenth century, De Marees likewise noted a major linguistic shift around Beraku, observing, "These people speak another language: up to here [the people of] all the places mentioned above speak one and the same language." Pieter de Marees, *Description and Historical Account of the Gold Kingdom of Guinea (1602),* trans. and ed. Albert van Dantzig and Adam Jones (Oxford: Oxford University Press, 1987), p. 85.

10. Joseph H. Greenberg, *The Languages of Africa,* 3rd ed. (Bloomington: Indiana University Press, 1970), p. 8; P. E. H. Hair, "An Ethnolinguistic Inventory of the Lower Guinea Coast before 1700: Part II," *African Language Review* 8 (1969): 230; M. E. Kropp Dakubu, ed., *The Languages of Ghana* (London: KPI, for the International African Institute, 1988); Sandra E. Greene, "Land, Lineage and Clan in Early Anlo," *Africa: Journal of the International African Institute* 51, no. 1 (1981): 455; Robin Law, *The Slave Coast of West Africa, 1550–1750: The Impact of the Atlantic Slave Trade on an African Society* (Oxford: Clarendon, 1991), pp. 21–24; Hounkpatin C. Capo, "Le Gbe est une langue unique," *Africa: Journal of the International African Institute* 53, no. 2 (1983): 47–57.

11. John Bloom, Accra, to CCC, 5 April 1693, Rawl. C747, f. 363v.

12. Edwyn Stede to CCC, 12 May, 1686, Rawl. C745, ff. 367–367v.

13. William Freeman, Nevis, to RAC, 3 January 1678, T70/15, f. 5v; John Thornton, "The Coromantees: An African Cultural Group in Colonial North America and the Caribbean," *Journal of Caribbean History* 32, nos. 1–2 (1998): 161–178.

14. Diaries of William Baillie, at Komenda, 1714–1717, 4 August 1715, T70/1464, f. 27.

15. J. B. Harley, "Maps, Knowledge, and Power," in *The Iconography of Landscape: Essays on the Symbolic Representation, Design, and Use of Past Environments,* ed. Denis Cosgrove and Stephen Daniels (Cambridge: Cambridge University Press, 1988), pp. 277–312; Martin W. Lewis and Kären E. Wigen, *The Myth of the Continents: A Critique of Metageography* (Berkeley: University of California Press, 1997); Edward W. Soja, *Postmodern Geographies: The Reassertion of Space in Critical Social Theory* (London: Verso, 1989).

16. The map was drawn by Dutch cartographer Hans Propheet at the Dutch trade post at Mori. See Ray A. Kea, *Settlements, Trade, and*

Polities in the Seventeenth-Century Gold Coast (Baltimore: Johns Hopkins University Press, 1982), p. 26.

17. Ibid., pp. 28, 30, 32.

18. Among a growing literature on the history of sovereign states, nations, and national identity, see Benedict Anderson, *Imagined Communities: Reflections on the Origin and Spread of Nationalism* (London: Verso, 1983); Hendrik Spruyt, *The Sovereign State and Its Competitors: An Analysis of Systems Change* (Princeton, N.J.: Princeton University Press, 1994); Adrian Hastings, *The Construction of Nationhood: Ethnicity, Religion, and Nationalism* (Cambridge: Cambridge University Press, 1997); Eric Hobsbawm and Terence Ranger, *The Invention of Tradition* (Cambridge: Cambridge University Press, 1983); Leroy Vail, ed., *The Creation of Tribalism in Southern Africa* (London: James Curry, 1991).

19. Jean Barbot (1732), cited in Ivor Wilks, "Founding the Political Kingdom: The Nature of the Akan State," in *Forests of Gold: Essays on the Akan and the Kingdom of Asante* (Athens: Ohio University Press, 1993), p. 95.

20. Willem Bosman, *A New and Accurate Description of the Coast of Guinea* (London: n.p., 1705), p. 147.

21. This version of the tradition comes from a text produced in the early twentieth century by the Asante ruler Asantehene Agyeman Prempeh I, during the years he spent in exile in the Seychelles under British colonial rule. Entitled "The History of Ashanti Kings and the whole country itself" the account records the oral history of Asante as it was known to Prempeh I and his mother. The manuscript is now published under the title *"The History of Ashanti Kings and the whole country itself" and Other Writings by Otumfuo, Nana Agyeman Prempeh I* [hereafter *HAK*], ed. A. Adu Boahen, Emmanuel Akyeampong, Nancy Lawler, T. C. McCaskie, and Ivor Wilks (Oxford: Oxford University Press, for the British Academy, 2003); quotations p. 86. On the origins of the Akan states, see Wilks, "Founding the Political Kingdom," pp. 91–92.

22. On the corresponding archaeological record, see Merrick Posnansky and Roderick McIntosh, "New Radiocarbon Dates for Northern and Western Africa," *JAH* 17, no. 2 (1976), pp. 164–167; J. E. G. Sutton, "Archaeology in West Africa: A Review of Recent Work and a Further List of Radiocarbon Dates," *JAH* 23, no. 3 (1982), pp. 291–313;

Susan Keech McIntosh and Roderick J. McIntosh, "Recent Archaeological Research and Dates from West Africa," *JAH* 27, no. 3 (1986), pp. 413–442; Christopher R. DeCorse, ed., *West Africa during the Atlantic Slave Trade: Archaeological Perspectives* (London: Leicester University Press, 2001).

23. Ivor Wilks, *One Nation, Many Histories: Ghana Past and Present* (Accra: Ghana Universities Press, 1996), p. 16.

24. In addition to the recently published account of Asante tradition cited earlier, the following draws also from my reading of the collection of Asante stool histories held at the Institute of African Studies, University of Ghana, Legon. David Henige and others have noted their limited use as historical sources. I use them here not as empirical "evidence" to verify specific historical subjects or events, but rather as evidence of an Akan historical consciousness, dating at least to the seventeenth and eighteenth centuries, that illuminates broad patterns and processes of migration and settlement that have shaped the region's social and political history. See David Henige, "The Problem of Feedback in Oral Tradition: Four Examples from the Fante Coastlands," *JAH* 14, no. 2 (1973): 223–235; Henige, "Akan Stool Succession under Colonial Rule—Continuity or Change?" *JAH* 16, no. 2 (1975): 285–301. See also Joseph C. Miller, ed., *The African Past Speaks: Essays on Oral Tradition and History* (Hamden, Conn.: Archon, 1980); Jan Vansina, *Oral Tradition as History* (Madison: University of Wisconsin Press, 1985).

25. See Wilks, *One Nation, Many Histories*, p. 17, recounting a conversation with an elder explaining the origin stories of another Akan group.

26. T. C. McCaskie, "*Konnurokusεm*: Kinship and Family in the History of the Oyoko Kɔkɔɔ Dynasty of Kumase," *JAH* 36, no. 2 (1995): 358.

27. T. C. McCaskie, "State and Society, Marriage and Adultery: Some Considerations Towards a Social History of Pre-Colonial Asante," *JAH* 22, no. 4 (1981): 483; A. R. Radcliffe-Brown and Daryll Forde, eds., *African Systems of Kinship and Marriage* (1950; London: KPI, 1987).

28. On matrilineal descent among seventeenth-century Akan-speaking groups, see Wilks, "Founding the Political Kingdom"; De Marees,

Description and Historical Account, pp. 182–183; Wilhelm Johann Müller, in Adam Jones, ed., *German Sources for West African History, 1680–1700* (Wiesbaden: Franz Steiner Verlag, 1985), pp. 258–590.

29. *HAK,* p. 86.
30. Ibid., p. 87.
31. My interpretation of the historical dimension of ethnicity in precolonial Africa in general, and the Gold Coast specifically, draws from Hobsbawm and Ranger, *Invention of Tradition;* Vail, *The Creation of Tribalism in Southern Africa;* Fredrik Barth, ed., *Ethnic Groups and Boundaries: The Social Organization of Culture Difference* (1969; reissue, Prospect Heights, Ill.: Waveland, 1998); Sandra E. Greene, *Gender, Ethnicity, and Social Change on the Upper Slave Coast: A History of the Anlo-Ewe* (Portsmouth, N.H.: Heinemann, 1996); Greene, "The Past and Present of an Anlo-Ewe Oral Tradition," *History in Africa* 12 (1985): 73–87; Enid Schildkrout, "The Ideology of Regionalism in Ghana," in *Strangers in African Societies,* ed. William A. Shack and Elliott P. Skinner (Berkeley: University of California Press, 1979), pp. 183–207; Schildkrout, *People of the Zongo: The Transformation of Ethnic Identities in Ghana* (Cambridge: Cambridge University Press, 1978); Carola Lentz and Paul Nugent, eds., *Ethnicity in Ghana: The Limits of Invention* (New York: St. Martin's, 2000); Michelle Gilbert, "'No Condition is Permanent': Ethnic Construction and the Use of History in Akuapem," *Africa: Journal of the International African Institute* 67, no. 4 (1997): 501–533; D. Kiyaga-Mulindwa, "The Akan Problem," *Current Anthropology* 21, no. 4 (1980): 503–506.
32. Richard Thelwall, Anomabu, to CCC, 9 August 1682, Rawl. C746, f. 172v. See also Thelwall, Anomabu, to CCC, 10 October 1681, Rawl. C746, f. 57v.
33. Richard Thelwall, Anomabu, to CCC, 12 October 1682, Rawl. C746, f. 8v.
34. Ivor Wilks, *Asante in the Nineteenth Century: The Structure and Evolution of a Political Order* (Cambridge: Cambridge University Press, 1975); T. C. McCaskie, *State and Society in Precolonial Asante* (Cambridge: Cambridge University Press, 1995).
35. P. E. H. Hair, Adam Jones, and Robin Law, eds., *Barbot on Guinea:*

The Writings of Jean Barbot on West Africa, 1678–1712 (London: Hakluyt Society, 1992), 2:549.

36. Sidney Mintz and Richard Price, *The Birth of African-American Culture: An Anthropological Perspective* (1976; Boston: Beacon, 1992), p. 18.

5. The Living Dead aboard the Slave Ship at Sea

1. Olaudah Equiano, *The Interesting Narrative of the Life of Olaudah Equiano, Written by Himself* (London, 1789; reprint, ed. Robert J. Allison, Boston: Bedford, 1995), p. 55, emphasis mine.

2. Ibid.

3. On recent debate questioning whether Equiano was a native of Africa or born in slavery in the Americas, see Vincent Carretta, "Olaudah Equiano or Gustavus Vassa? New Light on an Eighteenth-Century Question of Identity," *Slavery & Abolition* 20, no. 3 (1999): 96–105; Carretta, "Questioning the Identity of Olaudah Equiano, or Gustavus Vassa, the African," in *The Global Eighteenth Century*, ed. Felicity Nussbaum (Baltimore: Johns Hopkins University Press, 2003), pp. 226–235; Alexander X. Byrd, "Eboe, Country, Nation, and Gustavus Vassa's *Interesting Narrative*," *William and Mary Quarterly*, 3rd series, 63, no. 1 (January 2006): 123–148.

4. Here I am speaking of the deep waters of the Atlantic, as distinct from the inland waters or the coastline, whose contours and patterns African fishermen knew intimately.

5. Little has been written on this dimension of African experience, beyond William D. Piersen's examination of suicide among Africans enslaved in the Atlantic system, "White Cannibals, Black Martyrs: Fear, Depression, and Religious Faith as Causes of Suicide among New Slaves," *Journal of Negro History* 62 (1977): 147–159. Especially important for this reason is John Thornton, "Cannibals, Witches, and Slave Traders in the Atlantic World," *William and Mary Quarterly*, 3rd series, 60, no. 2 (April 2003): 273–294.

6. Elaine Scarry, *The Body in Pain: The Making and Unmaking of the World* (New York: Oxford University Press, 1987), p. 49.

7. Marcus Rediker, *Between the Devil and the Deep Blue Sea: Merchant Seamen, Pirates, and the Anglo-American Maritime World, 1700–1750* (Cambridge: Cambridge University Press, 1987), p. 179.

8. David Cressy, *Coming Over: Migration and Communication between England and New England in the Seventeenth Century* (Cambridge: Cambridge University Press, 1987), pp. 146, 152.

9. John Wollcott and William Cutter, cited ibid., p. 147.

10. Ibid., pp. 146, 147.

11. Colonial promoter William Wood, as quoted ibid., p. 148.

12. See Wilhelm Johann Müller, cited in Adam Jones, ed., *German Sources for West African History, 1680–1700* (Wiesbaden: Franz Steiner Verlag, 1985), pp. 233–239, on the variety of fish harvested by Gold Coast fishermen, for example. See, on techniques employed to extract salt from seawater, ibid., p. 244, and Robin Law, *The Slave Coast of West Africa, 1570–1750: The Impact of the Atlantic Slave Trade on an African Society* (Oxford: Oxford University Press, 1985), p. 25.

13. See William Bosman, *A New and Accurate Description of the Coast of Guinea* (London, 1705; reprint, New York: Barnes & Noble, 1967), 368v, 383; Michael Hemmersam, cited in Jones, *German Sources*, pp. 118–119.

14. Pieter de Marees, *Description and Historical Account of the Gold Kingdom of Guinea (1602)*, trans. and ed. Albert van Dantzig and Adam Jones (Oxford: Oxford University Press), pp. 72–73.

15. James Gohier, Barbados, to RAC, 7 March 1719, T70/8, f. 215; see also Gohier to RAC, 25 May 1719, T70/8, f. 217.

16. James Gohier to RAC, 30 August 1719, T70/8, f. 218.

17. J. H. Parry, *The Age of Reconnaissance* (Berkeley: University of California Press, 1963), pp. 83–113.

18. Stephen Greenblatt, *Marvelous Possessions: The Wonder of the New World* (Chicago: University of Chicago Press, 1991); Mary W. Helms, *Ulysses' Sail: An Ethnographic Odyssey of Power, Knowledge and Geographical Distance* (Princeton, N.J.: Princeton University Press, 1988); Anthony Grafton and Ann Blair, eds., *The Transmission of Culture in Early Modern Europe* (Philadelphia: University of Pennsylvania Press, 1990); Hildegard Binder Johnson, "New Geographical Horizons: Concepts," in *First Images of America: The Impact of the New World on the Old*, ed. Fredi Chiappelli, 2 vols. (Berkeley: University of California Press, 1976); Peter Hulme, *Colonial Encounters: Europe and the Native Caribbean, 1492–1797* (London: Methuen, 1986).

19. There is a rich literature on the anthropology of time. I have benefited in particular from the essays collected in John Bender and David E. Wellbery, eds., *Chronotypes: The Construction of Time* (Stanford, Calif.: Stanford University Press, 1991); and Johannes Fabian, *Time and the Other: How Anthropology Makes Its Object* (New York: Columbia University Press, 1983).

20. See Philip F. W. Bartle, "Forty Days: The Akan Calendar," *Africa* 48, no. 1 (1978): 80–84; Joseph K. Adjaye, "Time, the Calendar, and History among the Akan of Ghana," *Journal of Ethnic Studies* 15, no. 3 (1987): 71–100; T. C. McCaskie, "Time and the Calendar in Nineteenth Century Asante: An Exploratory Essay," *History in Africa* 7 (1980): 179–200. See also Paul Bohannan, "Concepts of Time among the Tiv of Nigeria," *Southwestern Journal of Anthropology* 9 (1953): 251–262; K. K. Bunseki Fu-Kiau, "Ntangu-Tandu-Kolo: The Bantu-Kongo Concept of Time," in *Time in the Black Experience*, ed. Joseph K. Adjaye (Westport, Conn.: Greenwood Press, 1994), 17–34; Adjaye, "Time, Identity, and Historical Consciousness in Akan," ibid., 55–77; Mechal Sobel, *The World They Made Together: Black and White Values in Eighteenth-Century Virginia* (Princeton, N.J.: Princeton University Press, 1987), pp. 15–67.

21. Andreas Josua Ulsheimer in Jones, *German Sources*, pp. 30–31.

22. Samuel Brun in Jones, *German Sources*, p. 86.

23. Müller found that among the Fetu agriculturalists, however, Sunday was the appointed day of rest. Müller, ibid., p. 167.

24. Müller, ibid., Appendix A, items 39–66.

25. Bartle, "Forty Days," p. 81; Adjaye, "Time, the Calendar, and History," p. 79.

26. Bartle, "Forty Days," pp. 81–82. Bartle suggests that the six-day week was observed by Guan-speaking peoples, while the seven-day week "may have been brought south with itinerant traders from the savanna" (p. 81).

27. These days of ritual observance also were referred to as bad days *(da bone)*, on account of the limitations placed on extensive activity on such days and the expectation that violation of the prohibition would bring misfortune. The precise number of ceremonial, or "bad," days within the forty-day cycle remains a subject of debate: see Adjaye, "Time, the Calendar, and History," p. 83.

28. Bartle, "Forty Days," p. 83. There is debate also regarding the number of *adaduanan* within an annual cycle. Whereas Bartle maintains that the number varied, Adjaye has argued that the measure was more precise, the year being "composed of nine 'monthly' cycles of forty days each" (p. 79).
29. Bartle, "Forty Days," p. 83.
30. See Parry, *Age of Reconnaissance*, pp. 83–99, on the slow and painstaking process by which European systems of time-space reckoning were adapted for use in a maritime arena.
31. Ivor Wilks, "On Mentally Mapping Greater Asante: A Study of Time and Motion," *Forests of Gold: Essays on the Akan and the Kingdom of Asante* (Athens: Ohio University Press, 1993), pp. 189–214.
32. Ibid. See also McCaskie, "Time and the Calendar"; Walter J. Ong, *Orality and Literacy: The Technologizing of the Word* (London: Routledge, 1982). On Africans' lunar measurement of time in the Atlantic world, see Philip D. Morgan, *Slave Counterpoint: Black Culture in the Eighteenth-Century Chesapeake & Lowcountry* (Chapel Hill, N.C.: University of North Carolina Press, for the Omohundro Institute of Early American History and Culture, 1998), p. 201.
33. See Philip D. Curtin, "Epidemiology and the Slave Trade," *Political Science Quarterly* 83 (1968): 190–216.
34. See Stanley L. Engerman and Herbert S. Klein, "Experiences on Slave Ships Compared with those in Other Long-Distance Oceanic Migrations" (paper presented at conference, "Transatlantic Slaving and the African Diaspora," Omohundro Institute of Early American History and Culture, Williamsburg, Va., 11–13 September 1998), p. 11.
35. Alfred W. Crosby, "Smallpox," in *The Cambridge World History of Human Disease,* ed. Kenneth F. Kiple (Cambridge: Cambridge University Press, 1993), p. 1008; K. David Patterson, "Bacillary Dysentery" and "Amebic Dysentery," ibid., pp. 604–606, 568–571; William D. Johnston, "Tuberculosis," ibid., pp. 1059–1061; Don R. Brothwell, "Yaws," ibid., pp. 1096–1100.
36. On a related subject, examination of height data for slaves has shown that "slaves from the Gold Coast were about an inch taller than the average Africans entering the West Indies." Their stature reflected their superior nutritional profile; by contrast, "those regions such as the Bight of Biafra and Central Africa, where the diet centered on

yams or cassava, produced the shortest slaves introduced to the West Indies." Kenneth F. Kiple, *The Caribbean Slave: A Biological History* (Cambridge: Cambridge University Press, 1984), p. 58. For full presentation of the data, see B. W. Higman, "Growth in Afro-Caribbean Slave Populations," *American Journal of Physical Anthropology* 50 (1979): 373–386.

37. Joseph C. Miller, *Way of Death: Merchant Capitalism and the Angolan Slave Trade, 1730–1830* (Madison: University of Wisconsin Press, 1988), pp. 314, 314n, citing Robert Conrad's rendering of the term in Robert Conrad, ed., *World of Sorrow: The African Slave Trade to Brazil* (Baton Rouge: Louisiana State University Press, 1986).

38. Peter Blake, "A Journall of my Intended Voyage for ye Gold Coast kept by mee Peter Blake Commander of ye Royall Companys ship *James* in ye searvis of ye Royall African Company of England," 28 November 1695, T70/1211, f. 34.

39. My interpretation of ritual is influenced especially by Katherine Verdery, *The Political Lives of Dead Bodies: Reburial and Postsocialist Change* (New York: Columbia University Press, 1999); Jonathan Z. Smith, *To Take Place: Toward Theory in Ritual* (Chicago: University of Chicago Press, 1987); and Mary Douglas, *Natural Symbols: Explorations in Cosmology* (London: Routledge, 1970). My thinking on ritual in the context of migration is influenced by an emerging literature on religion and geography. See especially Chris C. Park, *Sacred Worlds: An Introduction to Geography and Religion* (London: Routledge, 1994).

40. See Park, *Sacred Worlds,* p. 213, on "necral space" and "landscapes of death." The fundamental grounding that a proper mortuary ritual accomplished was of course not unique to the Akan or other precolonial African societies, but rather was (and is) common to many cultures. My goal here is to take seriously the particular practices of Akan subjects. See also Achille Mbembe "Necropolitics," trans. Libby Meintjes, *Public Culture,* 15, no. 1 (2003): 11–40.

41. Verdery, *Political Lives of Dead Bodies,* p. 104, describing mortuary rituals of Ancient Greece and Rome. For a discussion of the rituals developed by seamen to adapt "burial" practices to the maritime setting, see also Rediker, *Between the Devil and the Deep Blue Sea,* pp. 194–198.

42. Blake, "Account of the Mortallity of Slaves aboard the Shipp *James*," in "A Journall of my Intended Voyage," ff. 100–101.
43. Blake, "A Journall of my Intended Voyage," f. 70v, 7, 8 March 1676.
44. Thomas Phillips, *Voyage Made in the* Hannibal *of London, Ann. 1693, 1694* . . . in *A Collection of Voyages and Travels*, 6 vols., ed. Awnsham Churchill and John Churchill (London, 1732), 6:229.
45. P. E. H. Hair, Adam Jones, and Robin Law, eds., *Barbot on Guinea: The Writings of Jean Barbot on West Africa, 1678–1712* (London: Hakluyt Society, 1992), 2:779.
46. Blake, "A Journall of my Intended Voyage," f. 71v. The majority of the slaves aboard the *James* having boarded in January, most had worn shackles for two months. Unlike the Africans aboard the *Hannibal,* commanded by Thomas Phillips, and Barbot's vessel, it appears that both male and female slaves aboard the *James* may have worn irons.
47. Blake, "A Journall of my Intended Voyage," ff. 76, 77, 78v.
48. Ibid., f. 79.
49. Richard S. Dunn, *Sugar and Slaves: The Rise of the Planter Class in the English West Indies, 1624–1713* (Chapel Hill: University of North Carolina Press, 1972; reprint, New York: Norton, 1973), p. 5.
50. Ibid.
51. Invoices of Goods sent home from the Factors abroad, Invoice Books Homewards of the Royal African Company of England [hereafter Invoice Books, Homeward], 25 May 1678, T70/937, f. 118.
52. Invoice Books, Homeward, 24 May 1677; 14 June 1677, T70/937, T70/937, f. 70v, ff. 79v–80. Scurvy is a disease associated with malnutrition, caused by a deficiency of vitamin C. The difficulty of maintaining a steady supply of fresh fruits and vegetables on long sea voyages made scurvy a chronic condition in the maritime arena, one whose cause was not formally understood until the publication of Dr. James Lind's "A Treatise of the Scurvy" in 1753. Nonetheless, the curative effect of citrus fruits was widely observed and noted throughout the Atlantic (and Mediterranean) maritime worlds from an earlier date. The requisite use of limes to provision RAC ships suggests that English slave traders may well have possessed incidental awareness (if not full understanding) of the causal relationship. See Miller, *Way of Death,* p. 435, who notes that in the eighteenth-century Portuguese

slave trade, at least, citrus and other forms of fresh produce were used more as a remedy after symptoms of scurvy had appeared than as a prophylactic or a strategy of prevention. See also Robert Harms, *The Diligent: A Voyage through the Worlds of the Slave Trade* (New York: Basic, 2002), p. 317, on theories that circulated, prior to Lind's work, about the cause of scurvy; and Kiple, *Caribbean Slave,* pp. 59–60, 90–91.

53. Invoice Books, Homeward, 7 May 1680, T70/938, f. 133. The Leeward Islands lay three hundred miles to the northwest of Barbados, the voyage there from Barbados took around three days. Dunn, *Sugar and Slaves,* pp. 6–7.

54. Edwyn Stede and Stephen Gascoigne to RAC, 10 June 1679, T70/15, ff. 17v–18; Invoice Books, Homeward, 14 June 1679, T70/938, f. 73v.

55. Ibid.

56. Dunn, *Sugar and Slaves,* p. 5, describing Colt's first view of the eastern shore of Barbados.

57. Ibid., p. 49.

58. Engerman and Klein, "Experiences on Slave Ships," p. 26, n. 8.

59. Orlando Patterson, *Slavery and Social Death: A Comparative Study* (Cambridge, Mass.: Harvard University Press, 1982), p. 18, on concealment as one of "two polar extremes" according to which the social (as distinct from the conceptual) "idiom of power" is articulated.

6. Turning Atlantic Commodities into American Slaves

1. "Account of Sales of Negroes by the *James,* Capt. Peter Blake, for Accompt of the Royal African Company of England," Barbados, Invoice Books, Homeward, 25 May 1676, T70/937, ff. 19v–20.

2. Ibid., f. 20.

3. See Walter Johnson's important study of the same process in a different time and place, *Soul by Soul: Life Inside the Antebellum Slave Market* (Cambridge: Harvard University Press, 1999).

4. Hender Molesworth to RAC, Jamaica, 10 June and 7 July 1682, T70/16, ff. 33v, 34v–35; Invoice Books, Homeward, 20 July 1682, T70/940, ff. 63v–66.

5. David Eltis, *The Rise of African Slavery in the Americas* (Cambridge: Cambridge University Press, 2000), p. 114.

6. Richard Ligon, *A True and Exact History of the Island of Barbadoes* (London, 1657; reprint, London: Frank Cass, 1970), p. 46.
7. Hender Molesworth and Charles Penhallow to RAC, 20 July 1682, T70/16, f. 35v.
8. On the nutritional costs of African migration to the Americas, see Kenneth F. Kiple, *The Caribbean Slave: A Biological History* (Cambridge: Cambridge University Press, 1984), pp. 57–75.
9. Invoice Books, Homeward, 20 January 1675, T70/936, f. 47v; 3 June 1681, T70/939, f. 85v.
10. Invoice Books, Homeward, 28 November 1677, T70/937, ff. 93v–94v.
11. Hender Molesworth and Rowland Powell to RAC, 15 February 1680, T70/1, ff. 46–7; Invoice Books, Homeward, 23 January 1680, T70/938, f. 109v.
12. Blake, "A Journall of my Intended Voyage for ye Gold Coast kept by mee Peter Blake Commander of ye Royall Companys ship *James* in ye searvis of ye Royall African Company of England," T70/1211, ff. 79–79v; Invoice Books, Homeward, 20 August 1693, T70/946, f. 34v.
13. Invoice Books, Homeward, 28 August 1688, T70/943, ff. 58–58v.
14. William Frye Montserrat, to RAC, 18 June 1714, T70/8, f. 159.
15. Invoice Books, Homeward, 1 May 1677, T70/937, f. 63v.
16. Invoice Books, Homeward, 5 August 1680, T70/939, f. 17v. The policy changed in Barbados in the 1690s, when the agents began to hold the sales on shore. A temporary solution employed during an epidemic in 1691 thereafter became the new standard practice. When the *Supply* reached Barbados in August 1691, the charges listed by the agents included one pound, ten shillings, "to cash paid ye watermen for bring[ing] negroes ashor" and seven pounds, ten shillings for cash paid "for ye accomodation of a house a little remott from ye towne for ye Negroes where they were till sold noe planters comeing to ye towne or aboard a ship to buy by reason of much sickness there." Invoice Books, Homeward, 24 November 1691, T70/945, ff. 59v–60. The same provision was made for the sale of the cargo delivered aboard the *Coaster* that month. Invoice Books, Homeward, 11 August 1691, T70/945, ff. 28v–29. By 1693, the practice of bringing African arrivals onshore for sale appears to have become standard. In addition to the usual charges for boat hire to muster the slaves, and food for the slaves and for the buyers when the *Katherine* ar-

rived in January 1694, there also was a charge of ten pounds "for accomadateing of the negroes ashore at sale." Invoice Books, Homeward, 29 January 1694, T70/946, ff. 61–62.

17. Invoice Books, Homeward, 23 November 1674, T70/936, f. 45v. The *William* was the first slave ship sent to Jamaica by the Royal African Company.
18. Invoice Books, Homeward, 2 February 1680, T70/938, f. 112v.
19. Invoice Books, Homeward, 24 May 1699, T70/948, f. 108v.
20. Edwyn Stede and Stephen Gascoigne to RAC, 28 July 1680, T70/15, f. 40v; Invoice Books, Homeward, 5 August 1680, T70/939, f. 17v; 22 June 1680, T70/939, f. 18.
21. Henry Carpenter and Robert Helmes to RAC, 21 October 1681, T70/16, ff. 15–15v.
22. Edwyn Stede to RAC, 29 December 1684, T70/12, f. 7.
23. Edwyn Stede and Stephen Gascoigne to RAC, 12 May 1681, T70/15, f. 60v; Invoice Books, Homeward, 13 May 1681, T70/939, ff. 66v–67. For other "ordinary" cargoes, see Stede and Gascoigne to RAC, 12 July 1680, T70/15, ff. 36v–37; Hender Molesworth and Charles Penhallow, Jamaica, to RAC, 10 July 1682, T70/16, f. 35; Stede and Gascoigne to RAC, 21 April 1684, T70/16, ff. 80–80v; Edward Parsons, Montserrat, to RAC, 23 April 1690, T70/17, ff. 7v–8.
24. Edwyn Stede to RAC, 26 October 1680, T70/15, f. 43.
25. The cargo of 416 slaves included 209 males (50 percent): 172 men and 37 boys. RAC to Petley Weybourne, Whydah, 7 August 1688, T70/50, f. 69v; Invoice Books, Homeward, 22 June 1688, T70/943, ff. 42v–43.
26. Edwyn Stede to RAC, 21 June 1688, T70/12, f. 17v; Stede to RAC, 29 June 1688, T70/12, f. 17v.
27. There were 165 males (124 men, 41 boys), constituting 48 percent of the cargo for sale. In all, there were 423 slaves aboard the vessel when it arrived, but only 345 of these were sorted for sale: the remaining 78 persons either died in port (10), or were turned over as payment to the doctor hired to treat the cargo's sickliest members (68). Invoice Books, Homeward, 28 August 1688, T70/943, ff. 58–58v.
28. RAC to Petley Weybourne, Whydah, 3 January 1689, T70/50, f. 88v; Edwyn Stede to RAC, 31 August 1688, T70/12, f. 18v.
29. Invoice Books, Homeward, 25 February 1682, T70/940, ff. 27v–29; Hender Molesworth, Rowland Powell, and William Wathing to RAC, 20 September 1681, T70/16, f. 12v.

30. Hender Molesworth to RAC, 28 September 1681, T70/1, f. 125; Molesworth, Rowland Powell, and William Wathing to RAC, 20 September 1681, T70/16, ff. 12v–13.

31. RAC to Petley Weybourne, Whydah, 3 January 1689, T70/50, f. 88v.

32. David W. Galenson, *Traders, Planters, and Slaves: Market Behavior in Early English America* (Cambridge: Cambridge University Press, 1986), p. 110 and Table 5.1. Galenson found that the proportion of children in the English trade rose over time in the late seventeenth and early eighteenth centuries, see pp. 101–105.

33. Henry Carpenter and Robert Helmes to RAC, 24 December 1681, T70/16, f. 16v. See also T70/10, f. 36v.

34. Invoice Books, Homeward, 8 April 1682 (dated on receipt in London), T70/940, ff. 17v–19; Henry Carpenter et al., to RAC, 24 December 1681, T70/10, f. 37.

35. Henry Carpenter and Robert Helmes to RAC, 24 December 1681, T70/16, f. 16v; Invoice Books, Homeward, 8 April 1682 (dated on receipt in London), T70/940, ff. 19v–20.

36. Invoice Books, Homeward, 27 September 1681, T70/940, ff. 4v–5v. The *Prosperous,* when it arrived, carried 476 slaves purchased in Angola: 145 men (30 percent), 189 women (40 percent), 91 boys (19 percent), and 51 girls (11 percent).

37. Edwyn Stede and Stephen Gascoigne to RAC, 19 March 1683, T70/16, f. 48v.

38. Edwyn Stede and Stephen Gascoigne to RAC, 17 December 1683, T70/16, f. 66v.

39. Numerous references to "old" or "superannuated" slaves appear in the agents' correspondence. See, for example, Edwyn Stede and Stephen Gascoigne to RAC, 2 December 1678, T70/1, f. 6; Hender Molesworth et al. to RAC, 28 September 1681, T70/1, f. 125; Edwyn Stede and Stephen Gascoigne to RAC, 3 February 1682, T70/16, f. 19v; Samuel Bernard to RAC, 16 December 1692, T70/12, f. 48v.

40. RAC, London, to CCC, 15 September 1720, T70/53, f. 10.

41. "Also" meaning this ship together with the *Cape Coast,* likewise consigned to Barbados. RAC, London, to CCC, 14 December 1720, T70/53, f. 21.

42. CCC to London, 28 June 1721, T70/7, f. 19.

43. Also referred to as Coromantis. Richard S. Dunn, *Sugar and Slaves: The Rise of the Planter Class in the English West Indies, 1624–1713* (Chapel Hill: University of North Carolina Press, 1972; reprint, New

York: Norton, 1973), p. 236; Orlando Patterson, *The Sociology of Slavery: An Analysis of the Origins, Development and Structure of Negro Slave Society in Jamaica* (Rutheford, N.J.: Fairleigh Dickinson University Press, 1967), pp. 137–138; Darold D. Wax, "Preferences for Slaves in Colonial America," *Journal of Negro History* 58 (1973): 371–401; Daniel C. Littlefield, "Price and Perception," in *Rice and Slaves: Ethnicity and the Slave Trade in South Carolina* (Baton Rouge: Louisiana State University Press, 1981), pp. 8–32; Philip D. Morgan, *Slave Counterpoint: Black Culture in the Eighteenth-Century Chesapeake and Lowcountry* (Chapel Hill: University of North Carolina Press, for the Omohundro Institute of Early American History and Culture, 1998), pp. 65–73.

44. The figure comes from the 1680 census of the island. See Dunn, *Sugar and Slaves*, Table 7, p. 96.
45. Galenson, *Traders, Planters, and Slaves*, p. 72.
46. Invoice Books, Homeward, 28 May 1678, T70/937, ff. 121v–122. On the voyage aboard the *Arthur*, see George Kingston, "Journal of the Arthur," 1677, T70/1213.
47. Ibid.
48. Blake, "A Journall of my Intended Voyage," 27 May 1676, T70/1211, f. 79v.
49. Galenson, *Traders, Planters, and Slaves*, p. 62.
50. Invoice Books, Homeward, 28 May 1678, T70/937, ff. 121v–122.
51. Dunn, *Sugar and Slaves*, p. 177.
52. Ibid., p. 170.
53. Stephanie Smallwood, "After the Atlantic Crossing: The Arrival and Sale of African Migrants in the British Americas, 1672–1693," Paper presented at International Seminar on the History of the Atlantic World, 1500–1800, Working Paper No. 96–13, Charles Warren Center, Harvard University, September 1996, p. 7.
54. Invoice Books, Homeward, 5 July 1686, T70/942, ff. 77v–79; Hender Molesworth to RAC, 16 June 1686, T70/12, f. 39.
55. Of the seventy-four cargoes delivered to Jamaica in Royal African Company ships in the period between 1674 and 1693, fifty-three, or 71 percent, were divided into lots for sale to the planters. Smallwood, "After the Atlantic Crossing," p. 10.
56. Invoice Books, Homeward, 7 May 1680, T70/938, ff. 141v–142.
57. On the company's trade between Barbados and Jamaica and the Span-

ish-American colonies in the seventeenth century, see K. G. Davies, *The Royal African Company* (London: Longmans, 1957), pp. 326–335, and Colin A. Palmer, *Human Cargoes: The British Slave Trade to Spanish America, 1700–1739* (Urbana: University of Illinois Press, 1981), pp. 6–7, 97.

58. Invoice Books, Homeward, 27 January 1681, T70/939, ff. 48v–49; Hender Molesworth to RAC, 24 January 1681, T70/15, ff. 49–49v.

59. Dunn, *Sugar and Slaves*, p. 117; Galenson, *Traders, Planters, and Slaves*, pp. 29–30.

60. RAC to Alexander Cleeve, Gambia River, 18 March 1686, T70/50, f. 7.

61. See David Barry Gaspar, *Bondmen and Rebels: A Study of Master-Slave Relations in Antigua* (Baltimore: Johns Hopkins University Press, 1985), pp. 68–70; C. S. S. Higham, *The Development of the Leeward Islands under the Restoration, 1660–1688* (Cambridge: Cambridge University Press, 1921), pp. 150–153.

62. Dunn, *Sugar and Slaves*, pp. 126–129.

63. Smallwood, "After the Atlantic Crossing," p. 7.

64. Davies, *Royal African Company*, p. 294. The sale of slaves by contract appears to have been the method commonly used when the market for slaves was limited in the English colonies, before 1672. Even with the dramatic growth of the English slave trade in the second half of the seventeenth century, contract sales continued to account for a small segment of the trade to Barbados and Jamaica.

65. John Seayres to RAC, 17 February 1679, T70/15, ff. 5v–6.

66. The Africans had boarded the *Katherine* in August 1678 at the company's factory at Offra in the Bight of Benin. CCC, Accounts-Ledgers, April–December 1678, T70/657, f. 51.

67. John Seayres to RAC, 17 February 1679.

68. Galenson, *Traders, Planters, and Slaves*, p. 82.

69. John Seayres to RAC, 17 February 1679.

70. Ibid. Seayres does not indicate where these transactions took place, but in all likelihood these Africans also were sold aboard the ship.

71. William Freeman to RAC, Nevis, 25 July 1681, T70/10, f. 36v.

72. Invoice Books, Homeward, 13 May 1681, T70/939, ff. 65v–66. Prime adult males sold for twenty pounds in Barbados at the time.

73. Invoice Books, Homeward, 28 November 1677, T70/937, ff. 93v–94v.

74. Invoice Books, Homeward, 20 July 1680, T70/939, ff. 18v–19v.

75. David Eltis, "The British Transatlantic Slave Trade before 1714: Annual Estimates of Volume and Direction," in *The Lesser Antilles in the Age of European Expansion,* Robert L. Paquette and Stanley L. Engerman, eds. (Gainesville: University Press of Florida, 1996), p. 184. On abolitionists' attempts to account for the New World side of slave trade mortality, see Stanley L. Engerman and Herbert S. Klein, "Experiences on Slave Ships Compared with those in Other Long-Distance Oceanic Migrations" (paper presented at conference, "Transatlantic Slaving and the African Diaspora," Omohundro Institute of Early American History and Culture, Williamsburg, Va., 11–13 September 1998), pp. 4–5.

76. Invoice Books, Homeward, 23 January 1680, T70/938, ff. 109v–112; 2 February 1680, T70/938, ff. 112v–114.

77. Hender Molesworth et al., to RAC, 15 February 1680, T70/1, ff. 46–47.

78. Edwyn Stede and Stephen Gascoigne to RAC, 30 August 1683, T70/16, ff. 60v–61. Of 230 persons aboard on the vessel's departure from Africa, 100, or 43 percent, died during the crossing.

79. Hender Molesworth and Rowland Powell to RAC, 24 January 1681, T70/15, f. 49. The slaves arrived "in a very bad condition the Flux and small Pox having made a great destruction amongst them."

80. Hender Molesworth and Rowland Powell to RAC, 24 January 1681, T70/15, f. 49v.

81. On the *Diligence,* see T70/937, 23 October 1676, f. 43; on the *Marygold,* see T70/937, 14 June 1677, f. 80.

82. Henry Carpenter to RAC, 15 March 1682, T70/16, f. 30v.

83. Henry Carpenter to RAC, 28 March 1682, T70/16, f. 31.

7. Life and Death in Diaspora

1. Caroline B. Brettell, "Theorizing Migration in Anthropology: The Social Construction of Networks, Identities, Communities, and Globalscapes," in *Migration Theory: Talking across Disciplines,* ed. Caroline B. Brettell and James F. Hollifield (London: Routledge, 2000), p. 106.

2. Marcus Rediker, *Between the Devil and the Deep Blue Sea: Merchant Seamen, Pirates, and the Anglo-American Maritime World, 1700–1750* (Cambridge: Cambridge University Press, 1987), pp. 153, 154.

3. J. H. Parry, *The Age of Reconnaissance: Discovery, Exploration and Settlement, 1450–1650* (Berkeley: University of California Press, 1963), p. 5.

4. Philip D. Morgan, *Slave Counterpoint: Black Culture in the Eighteenth-Century Chesapeake & Lowcountry* (Chapel Hill: University of North Carolina Press for the Omohundro Institute of Early American History and Culture, 1998), p. 446. For additional examples, see Michael Mullin, *Africa in America: Slave Acculturation and Resistance in the American South and the British Caribbean, 1736–1831* (Urbana: University of Illinois Press, 1992), pp. 34–40. See also documents regarding the storied efforts of the captives aboard the *Amistad*, in John W. Blassingame, ed., *Slave Testimony: Two Centuries of Letters, Speeches, Interviews, and Autobiographies* (Baton Rouge: Louisiana State University Press, 1977), pp. 200–208; Howard Jones, *Mutiny on the Amistad: The Saga of a Slave Revolt and its Impact on American Abolition, Law, and Diplomacy* (New York: Oxford University Press, 1987).

5. Morgan, *Slave Counterpoint*, p. 446.

6. Mullin, *Africa in America*, p. 35.

7. William D. Piersen, "White Cannibals, Black Martyrs: Fear, Depression, and Religious Faith as Causes of Suicide among New Slaves," *Journal of Negro History* 62, no. 2 (1977): 153.

8. Ibid.

9. Historians of slavery have learned a great deal in the last half century regarding the difference that place made in the lives of New World slaves with respect to such factors as labor regimes, the demographics of race, and diverse European approaches to colonial social control. In addition to the works already cited, see Frank Tannenbaum, *Slave and Citizen: The Negro in the Americas* (New York, 1947); Herbert S. Klein, *Slavery in the Americas: A Comparative Study of Cuba and Virginia* (Chicago: University of Chicago Press, 1967); Richard S. Dunn, *Sugar and Slaves: The Rise of the Planter Class in the English West Indies, 1674–1713* (Chapel Hill: University of North Carolina Press, 1972; reprint, New York: Norton, 1973); Philip D. Morgan, "Whither the Comparative History of New World Slavery," *Journal of Ethnic Studies* 8 (1980): 96–110; Mullin, *Africa in America;* Vera Rubin and Arthur Tuden, eds., *Comparative Perspectives on Slavery in New World Plantation Societies* (New York: New York Academy of Sciences, 1977); Ira Berlin and Philip D. Morgan, eds., *Cultivation*

and Culture: Labor and the Shaping of Slave Life in the Americas (Charlottesville: University of Virginia Press, 1993).

10. On the growth of the sugar industry and slave imports to Nevis and the other Leeward Islands, see Dunn, *Sugar and Slaves,* pp. 122–123, 126–127, 131, 140–141. All figures here and below are estimates taken from *TSTD* and are meant to show broad patterns rather than to chart precise population figures. These figures do not account for cargoes that combined captives from the Gold Coast and Bight of Benin on the same ship. It should be noted also that these estimates do not reflect the out-migration of captives reexported from Barbados and Jamaica. For preliminary assessment of this important inter-colonial slave trade, see Greg O'Malley, "The Intra-American Slave Trade: Forced African Migrations within the Caribbean and from Islands to the Mainland," unpublished paper presented at the 120th annual meeting of the American Historical Association, Philadelphia, Penna., 6 January 2006.

11. Slave imports to Virginia and South Carolina also included African- and American-born from the Caribbean islands. Susan Westbury, "Slaves of Colonial Virginia: Where They Came From," *William and Mary Quarterly,* 3rd ser., 42, no. 3 (1985): 228–237; Westbury, "Analysing a Regional Slave Trade: The West Indies and Virginia, 1698–1775," *Slavery & Abolition,* 7 (1986): 241–256; Donald M. Sweig, "The Importation of African Slaves to the Potomac River, 1732–1772," *William and Mary Quarterly,* 3rd ser., 42, no. 4 (1985): 507–524; David Richardson, "The British Slave Trade to Colonial South Carolina," *Slavery & Abolition,* 12 (1991): 125–172.

12. Interested less in *how* immigrant slaves navigated the varied social circumstances of diaspora in the Americas, scholars have put themselves to some trouble to explain whether and how different groups *could* create functional community out of so much cultural diversity. The central terms of the debate can be found in Sidney W. Mintz and Richard Price, *The Birth of African-American Culture: An Anthropological Perspective* (1976; reprint, Boston: Beacon, 1992); John Thornton, *Africa and Africans in the Making of the Atlantic World, 1400–1800,* 2nd ed. (Cambridge: Cambridge University Press, 1998); Philip D. Morgan, "The Cultural Implications of the Atlantic Slave Trade: African Regional Origins, American Destinations and New World Developments," *Slavery & Abolition* 18 (1997): 122–145. A growing body of work has begun to approach the problem

with greater sophistication. See especially Paul E. Lovejoy, ed., *Identity in the Shadow of Slavery* (London: Continuum, 2000); Linda M. Heywood, ed., *Central Africans and Cultural Transformations in the American Diaspora* (Cambridge: Cambridge University Press, 2002); James H. Sweet, *Recreating Africa: Culture, Kinship, and Religion in the African-Portuguese World, 1441-1770* (Chapel Hill: University of North Carolina Press, 2003); Paul E. Lovejoy and David V. Trotman, eds., *Trans-Atlantic Dimensions of Ethnicity in the African Diaspora* (London: Continuum, 2003); Michael A. Gomez, *Reversing Sail: A History of the African Diaspora* (Cambridge: Cambridge University Press, 2005); Gwendolyn Midlo Hall, *Slavery and African Ethnicities in the Americas: Restoring the Links* (Chapel Hill: University of North Carolina Press, 2005); José C. Curto and Renée Soulodre-LaFrance, eds., *Africa and the Americas: Interconnections during the Slave Trade* (Trenton, N.J.: Africa World Press, 2005).

13. Orlando Patterson, *Slavery and Social Death: A Comparative Study* (Cambridge: Harvard University Press, 1982), p. 45.

14. Charles Ball, cited in W. Jeffrey Bolster, *Black Jacks: African American Seamen in the Age of Sail* (Cambridge: Harvard University Press, 1997), p. 49.

15. Brettell, "Theorizing Migration in Anthropology," pp. 106–107.

16. Ibid., p. 107; she cites Douglas S. Massey, Joaquin Arango, Graeme Hugo, Ali Kouaouci, Adela Pellegrino, and J. Edward Taylor, "Theories of International Migration: A Review and Appraisal," *Population and Development Review* 19 (1993): 431–466, quotation on p. 449; Douglas S. Massey, "Why Does Immigration Occur? A Theoretical Synthesis," in Charles Hirschman, Philip Kasinitz, and Josh DeWind, eds., *The Handbook of International Migration: The American Experience* (New York: Russell Sage Foundation, 1999), p. 44.

17. On the function of social networks in international migration, see especially Charles Tilly and Charles H. Brown, "On Uprooting, Kinship, and the Auspices of Migration," *International Journal of Comparative Sociology* 8 (1967): 139–164; Charles Tilly, "Transplanted Networks," in Virginia Yans-McLaughlin, ed., *Immigration Reconsidered: History, Sociology, and Politics* (New York: Oxford University Press, 1990), pp. 79–95; John S. MacDonald and Leatrice D. MacDonald, "Chain Migration, Ethnic Neighborhood Formation, and Social Networks," in Charles Tilly, ed., *An Urban World* (Boston: Little, Brown, 1974), pp. 226–236; and Simone A. Wegge, "Chain

Migration and Information Networks: Evidence from Nineteenth-Century Hesse-Cassel," *Journal of Economic History* 58, no. 4 (1998): 957–986.

18. Helyar MSS, Somerset Record Office, Taunton, England, Bybrook Account, 1669–1672, entries for 10 November 1671, 10 January 1672, 4 February 1672; Cary Helyar to William Helyar, 27 November 1671, box 1089, part 3, #21; Cary Helyar to William Helyar, 12 January 1672.

19. Dunn, *Sugar and Slaves*, pp. 149–187.

20. Morgan, *Slave Counterpoint*, pp. 444, 445.

21. For the pioneering interpretive work on this point, see Philip D. Curtin, "Epidemiology and the Slave Trade," *Political Science Quarterly* 83, no. 2 (1968): 190–216.

22. Dunn, *Sugar and Slaves*, pp. 313, 315–316.

23. K. G. Davies, *The Royal African Company* (London: Longmans, 1957), p. 300.

24. Dunn, *Sugar and Slaves*, p. 314.

25. Cited ibid., p. 305n.

26. David W. Galenson, *Traders, Planters, and Slaves: Market Behavior in Early English America* (Cambridge: Cambridge University Press, 1986), p. 64.

27. Morgan, *Slave Counterpoint*, p. 80.

28. Dunn, *Sugar and Slaves*, p. 301.

29. Ibid., pp. 74–76, 87–89, 311–313; quotation on p. 313; Philip D. Curtin, *The Atlantic Slave Trade: A Census* (Madison: University of Wisconsin Press, 1969), p. 59, Table 14 gives an estimate of 40,000 slaves in 1668.

30. Michael Craton, *Testing the Chains: Resistance to Slavery in the British West Indies* (Ithaca, N.Y.: Cornell University Press, 1982), p. 114.

31. Dunn, *Sugar and Slaves*, p. 313.

32. For a general discussion of the relationship among shipmates, see Mintz and Price, *The Birth of African-American Culture*, pp. 43–44, 48. See also p. 66, on "the sheer importance of kinship in structuring interpersonal relations and in defining an individual's place in his society; the emphasis on unilineal descent, and the importance to each individual of the resulting lines of kinsmen, living and dead, stretching backward and forward through time."

33. For analyses of the invoices centered on the market behavior of Amer-

ican planters, see Galenson, *Traders, Planters, and Slaves*; Trevor Burnard, "Who Bought Slaves in Early America? Purchasers of Slaves from the Royal African Company in Jamaica, 1674–1708," *Slavery & Abolition* 17, no. 2 (1996): 68–92; Trevor Burnard and Kenneth Morgan, "The Dynamics of the Slave Market and Slave Purchasing Patterns in Jamaica, 1655–1788," *William and Mary Quarterly*, 3rd ser., 58, no. 1 (2001): 205–228.

34. Claire C. Robertson and Martin A. Klein, "Women's Importance in African Slave Systems," in *Women and Slavery in Africa*, ed. Robertson and Klein (Madison: University of Wisconsin Press, 1983), pp. 3–25.

35. Dunn, *Sugar and Slaves*, p. 317.

36. Jennifer L. Morgan, *Laboring Women: Reproduction and Gender in New World Slavery* (Philadelphia: University of Pennsylvania Press, 2004).

37. Frank W. Pitman, "The Breeding and Vitality of Eighteenth-Century Slaves in the British West Indies," *Journal of Negro History*, 11, no. 4 (1926): 632.

38. Mintz and Price, *The Birth of African-American Culture*, pp. 66–67.

39. Herbert S. Gutman, *The Black Family in Slavery and Freedom, 1750–1925* (New York: Vintage, 1976); Ira Berlin, *Many Thousands Gone: The First Two Centuries of Slavery in North America* (Cambridge: Harvard University Press, 1998).

40. Morgan, *Slave Counterpoint*, p. 81. For the pioneering work on this development, see Russell R. Menard, "The Maryland Slave Population, 1658 to 1730: A Demographic Profile of Blacks in Four Counties," *William and Mary Quarterly*, 3rd ser., 32, no. 1 (1975): 29–54; "From Servants to Slaves: The Transformation of the Chesapeake Labor System," *Southern Studies* 16, no. 4 (1977): 355–390; Allan Kulikoff, "A 'Prolifick' People: Black Population Growth in the Chesapeake Colonies, 1700–1790," *Southern Studies* 16, no. 4 (1977): 391–428.

41. Richard Price, *First-Time: The Historical Vision of an Afro-American People* (Baltimore: Johns Hopkins University Press, 1983).

42. Ira Berlin, "From Creole to African: Atlantic Creoles and the Origins of African-American Society in Mainland North America," *William and Mary Quarterly*, 3rd ser., 53, no. 2 (April 1996): 253–254.

43. "Two narratives of slave women, 1799, written down by John Ford,

Barbados," MS. Eng. misc. b. 4, ff. 50–50v, Bodleian Library, Oxford, England. For discussion of the narratives, see Jerome S. Handler, "Life Histories of Enslaved Africans in Barbados," *Slavery & Abolition* 19, no. 1 (April 1998): 129–141.

44. Alun Munslow, *Deconstructing History* (London: Routledge, 1997), p. 10.

45. On travel literature, see especially Mary Louise Pratt, *Imperial Eyes: Travel Writing and Transculturation* (London: Routledge, 1992).

46. Walter J. Ong, *Orality & Literacy: The Technologizing of the Word* (London: Routledge, 1982).

47. Judith Lewis Herman, *Trauma and Recovery: The Aftermath of Violence, from Domestic Abuse to Political Terror* (New York: Basic, 1992), pp. 51, 175. See also Kim Lacy Rogers, Selma Leydesdorff, and Graham Dawson, eds., *Trauma and Life Stories: International Perspectives* (London: Routledge, 1999); Françoise Davoine and Jean-Max Guadillière, eds., *History beyond Trauma: Whereof One Cannot Speak, Thereof One Cannot Stay Silent,* trans. Susan Fairfield (New York: Other Press, 2004); Leonard Shengold, *Soul Murder: The Effects of Childhood Abuse and Deprivation* (New Haven: Yale University Press, 1989), esp. chap. 3, "Did It Really Happen? An Assault on Truth, Historical and Narrative," pp. 32–40.

Acknowledgments

One of the great pleasures of finishing this book is the opportunity to remember all the people and institutions that helped me along my way. The list is long, and it begins with fellow students who spearheaded the anti-apartheid movement and South African divestment campaign at Columbia University. The divestment campaign got me interested in a history I had never encountered in thirteen years of prep-school education; Elliot P. Skinner and Marcia Wright, my first mentors at Columbia, provided a classroom setting in which to focus my interests. I am grateful to them for the guidance that helped turn that spark of intellectual energy into the foundation for a professional life of the mind.

My undergraduate mentor at Columbia University, Marcellus Blount, told me I could not expect to be a competent historian of African America without a solid foundation in the broader interdisciplinary field of African American studies. The truth of that wise counsel continues to manifest itself in my intellectual journey, and I am grateful for his advice. The book's dedication to John W. Blassingame reflects both my intellectual debt to the African and African American Studies Program he helped build at Yale University and my deep gratitude for his mentoring and friendship.

It was Blassingame who introduced me to early America as an important and as yet insufficiently developed arena of inquiry in African American history. Seemingly endless summer days spent in the frigid air of the Sterling Library microfilm room, scrolling through the shipping lists of colonial newspapers as Blassingame's research assistant sparked my fascination with the slave ship and its social history. His generosity of mind and heart, shared almost daily in long meetings and over more than a few cups of coffee in his favorite booth at Naples Pizza, did more than words can say to help me believe in the intellectual journey that has shaped my work. I only regret that he did not live to see it come to fruition in this book.

At Duke University Jan Ewald, Barry Gaspar, Ray Gavins, Julius Scott, and John TePaske were wonderful teachers. Peter H. Wood was everything one could want from a mentor—always an asker of tough questions, a firm yet gentle critic who didn't hesitate to check on my progress when research productivity waned, and close reader of countless drafts. Peter's friendship continues to be a gift I value tremendously.

My work came to life as a book during my assistant professorship in the History Department at the University of California, San Diego (UCSD). I benefited from the support of colleagues from all corners of the department; and I am especially grateful for the friendship and encouragement of department colleagues Frank Biess, David Gutiérrez, Rachel Klein, Michael Meranze, Becky Nicolaides, Naomi Oreskes, Michael Parrish, Pamela Radcliff, Stefan Tanaka, Emily Thompson, and Robert Westman. As a colleague and as a department chair, Danny Vickers has been a steadfast friend and committed advocate of my work. I am grateful for Alex Ruiz's support over the years and also for that of the wonderful staff who support the work of faculty in the History Department.

The research for this book would not have been possible without the generous assistance of staff at the British Public Record Office in London, the Bodleian Library at Oxford University, and the

Balme Library and Institute of African Studies at the University of Ghana. Research travel to the United Kingdom and Ghana was supported by awards from the Faculty Career Development Program, Center for the Humanities, and Faculty Senate Committee on Research at UCSD. With the "tenure clock" already ticking away, generous chunks of time to think and write without the pressures of teaching also proved invaluable to the development of this project. I am enormously grateful for the support of a postdoctoral fellowship at Princeton University's Shelby Cullom Davis Center for Historical Studies and a Chancellor's Postdoctoral Fellowship from the University of California, Berkeley. Lauren Cole's work as a summer research assistant was also a great help.

As the book took shape, numerous colleagues generously took the time to read and comment on all or parts of the manuscript, both in formal conference proceedings and in the informal exchanges that fuel so much of what we do as researchers and writers. Their critical insights and challenges did much to guide and correct my thinking and have helped make this a much better book. For that and more, I thank Edward Baptist, Mia Bay, Herman Bennett, Daphne Brooks, Christopher Brown, Vince Brown, Stephanie M. H. Camp, Sharla Fett, Anthony Grafton, Sandra Greene, Sarah Jansen, Walter Johnson, Nicole King, Joseph C. Miller, Jennifer Morgan, Philip Morgan, Marcy Norton, Nell Painter, Colin Palmer, Dylan Penningroth, Adam Rothman, and Valerie Smith. I offer thanks also for the support and feedback received from participants in the first Harvard University Seminar in Atlantic History; the New Studies in American Slavery symposia at the University of Washington and Rutgers University; and several sessions at the annual meetings of the Organization of American Historians.

I owe an enormous debt of gratitude to Joyce Seltzer, my editor at Harvard University Press, for her belief in this project from a very early stage and her commitment through to the end. Also at Harvard University Press, Susan Abel's copyediting pen has miraculously worked the kinks out of awkward passages and unraveled unruly turns of phrase, to give this book's prose more clarity than it ever would have possessed otherwise. I am happy to have benefited from Susan's mastery of her craft. I also thank Philip Schwartzberg of Meridian Mapping for the book's beautifully drawn maps.

Though moving to the far southwestern corner of the nation seemed counterintuitive for someone writing a book about the Atlantic slave trade, the rich interdisciplinary community of colleagues working on the broad themes of race and empire at (or otherwise connected to) UCSD has made this a wonderful place to begin my academic career. Jody Blanco, Yen Espiritu, Tak Fujitani, Gayatri Gopinath, Judith Halberstam, Sara Johnson, Curtis Marez, Shelley Streeby, Danny Widener, and Lisa Yoneyama provided a wonderful collective of interlocutors and friends with whom to share work, exchange ideas, and commune over much good food and drink.

I am happy to acknowledge an especially large intellectual and personal debt to Mia Bay, Alexander Byrd, Rod Ferguson, Walter Johnson, Lisa Lowe, Chandan Reddy, and Nayan Shah for sharing so much of their brilliant minds and big hearts. I thank also the many friends who, oftentimes without knowing it, helped me write this book. For providing so much love and laughter, thank you to Eileen Flanagan and Tom, Meagan, and Luke Volkert; Jeanne Tift and Will; Chee-Ai Wu and Liam Fitzpatrick; Marta Hanson; Val Hardie, and Joye and Tierra Ward; Juliana and Jocquin Scales; Rich Heitz; Susie Hernandez; K. R. Ridge; Mary Wilkinson; and Dr. Leslie Tam.

Finally, I am grateful to my families for their unstinting love and support. My partner, Sean Graham, has been the best friend I always wanted; as only a child can do, Sean's son, Gregory, has been the source of fun and distraction I needed to keep it all in perspective. The extended Graham clan—Mama Doris, Carolyn, Mike,

Libby, Brandon, and Habib—have made San Diego feel like a real home, and for that I thank them. The Smallwood clan—my ninety-seven year-old grandmother, Edwina, my uncle Howard, my aunt Shirley, my cousin Wesley, and my big brother, Chuck—have supported me without ever really understanding why writing a book had to take so long. Above all, I thank my mother and father, Marilyn and Charles Smallwood, for investing so generously in me and all my dreams. For all of their love, there are not enough words. I hope they know how much I love them.

Index

Nevis. *See* Leeward Islands: Nevis

New Calabar. *See* Bight of Biafra: New Calabar

Ocean crossing: African contrasted with European understanding of, 122–123, 124–125, 126; and European use of navigational instruments, 126–127, 131, 185; European mariners' understanding of, 127, 128, 183; English emigrants' fears of, 127–129; and African understanding of sea as supernatural realm, 129–130; and news of African return migrations, 130–131; psychological impact of, 157; food shortages during, 160; African memory of, 190, 205–207; narrative representation of, 204–206; modern Western contrasted with precolonial African understanding of, 206. *See also* Migration; "Saltwater" (derogatory term); Transatlantic shipping

Offra, 94, 106. *See also* Bight of Benin

Old Calabar. *See* Bight of Biafra: Old Calabar

Oldmixon, John, 6

Pereira, Duarte Pacheco, 11, 14

Portobelo, Panama. *See* Spanish American mainland: Portobelo, Panama

Portuguese, the: mariners' first contact with Gold Coast, 10–11, 13, 14, 23, 31, 32; gold trade in Africa, 12; introduction of New World cultigen (maize) on African coast, 13, 14; and slave imports to Gold Coast, 15–16; colonization of Brazil, 16, 29; slave exports from

Gold Coast, 17, 19, 31, 89, 95; competition with other European nations on African coast, 17–18, 89, 95; gold mining in Brazil (Minas Gerais), 32, 95

Potatoes: included in "refreshments" for slaves on arrival in American ports, 149, 159, 160; in American slave diets, 159

Rice: in Atlantic commodity circuits, 6, 159, 194; cultivation in South Carolina, 29, 95, 188, 195, 201; as staple in diet of slaves from Windward Coast, 104

Richards, Arthur, 40, 54

Royal African Company: founding of, 3, 18; transatlantic network of employees, 4–5; monopoly on English trade in Africa, 19, 95; and English interlopers, 19, 88, 89, 91, 95

Rum: in Atlantic commodity circuits, 6; exchanged for slaves, 86, 96–97; included in "refreshments" for slaves on arrival in American ports, 149

Saint Christopher. *See* Leeward Islands: Saint Christopher

"Saltwater" (derogatory term), 6–7, 202

São Jorge da Mina Castle, 15, 17, 18

Seayres, John, 175, 176

Senegambia, 2, 16, 58, 104, 185, 188; Gambia River, 102–103, 105, 162; Gorée Island, 102–103; Saint Louis, 102–103; the "Bambara," 103; Jolof kingdom, 103; Malinke language and people, 103; Senegal River, 103; Soninke language and people, 103; Wolof language and